Philosophy

AF652757

An Inquiry into the Cases of Pain and Suffering

About the Author

Debashis Guha teaches Ethics, Phenomenology and Existentialism in the Post-Graduate Department of Philosophy, Ranchi University, Ranchi. He earned his Master degree in Philosophy from Delhi University in 1980 and Ph.D. from Jadavpur University in 1988. He taught at the undergraduate level in a constituent college of Ranchi University from 1981 to 1989 and then joined the Post-Graduate Department. He was awarded the Visiting Associateship of the UGC during 1994-96 in Jadavpur University, Calcutta, where he worked out *An Inquiry into the Cases of Pain and Suffering,* which is an analytic work dealing with the clarification of nature and meaning of important concepts such as pain, suffering and evil. He was also awarded UGC's Major Research Project (1997-2000) on *Applied Ethics in Indian Context,* which has been now shaped in six volumes, under the series: **Practical and Professional Ethics.** Dr. Guha has fifteen papers to his credit, two of them were presented in International Congress.

An Inquiry into the Cases of Pain and Suffering

DEBASHIS GUHA

CONCEPT PUBLISHING COMPANY, NEW DELHI-110059

Cataloging in Publication Data—DK
Courtesy: D.K. Agencies (P) Ltd. <docinfo@dkagencies.com>

Guha, Debashis.
An inquiry into the cases of pain and suffering/ Debashis Guha.
p. cm.
Includes bibliographical references (p.)
Includes index.
ISBN-13: 9788180694561
ISBN-10: 8180694569

1. Pain—Philosophy. 2. Suffering—Philosophy. 3. Good and evil—Philosophy. 4. Pain—Religious aspects. 5. Suffering—Religious aspects. 6. Good and evil—Religious aspects. I. Title.

DDC 128.4 22

All rights reserved. No part of this work may be reproduced, stored in a retrieval system, or transmitted in any form or by any means electronic, mechanical, photocopying, micro-filming, recording or otherwise, without the prior written permission of the copyright owner and the publisher.

ISBN-13: 978-81-8069-456-1
ISBN-10: 81-8069-456-9

First Published 2007

© Concept Publishing Company, New Delhi

Published and Printed by
Ashok Kumar Mittal
Concept Publishing Company
A/15-16, Commercial Block, Mohan Garden
New Delhi-110059 (INDIA)

Phones : 25351460, 25351794
Fax : 091-11-25357103
Email : publishing@conceptpub.com

Sri Sri Kalikananda Vairab

&

Sri Sri Guru Mata

Foreword

I feel honoured when I was approached by Dr. Debasish Guha of the Department of Philosophy, Ranchi University, to write a foreword for his in-depth study on "An Inquiry into the cases of pain and suffering." It was my privilege to talk to him extensively when he first began to conceive the theme of his subject. I was at that time acting as the Head of the Department of Philosophy, Jadavpur University when Dr. Guha joined our department as a Visiting Associate. I found to my utter surprise that Dr. Guha was not interested in the day-to-day use or even philosophical twist to the fact of pain, sorrows, sufferings, misery and the like. These expressions are more often than not used interchangeably without clarifying the concepts. Philosophical enquiry rather began in accepting and recognizing the presence of these states in our every day life as a matter of fact. The philosophers simply wanted to know whether we could get rid of this unwanted situation and if so, how. But they seldom made any attempt at analysing what these nearly-synonymous concepts like 'pain', 'suffering', 'evil' actually mean. What should be the criteria for distinguishing one concept from another and also how the ambiguity and vagueness centring round these concepts can be ultimately resolved, if at all? The evaluation of these concepts in a purely disinterested and analytic manner formed the basis of Dr. Guha's enquiry. Though I did not see eye to eye with him on all that what he feels and believes, I could not but be impressed by the originality of his thinking and analytic approach to the subject. It goes to the credit of Dr. Guha that he refuses to tread the beaten track. I firmly believe that Dr. Guha's work on "An Inquiry into the cases of pain and suffering" will go a long way in filling the long-standing gap and will be generously received by all alike—philosophers, scientists and laymen.

Tapan Kumar Chakrabarti
Retired Professor of Philosophy
Jadavpur University

Preface

In the year 1992 I planned to inquire into the cases of "pain", "suffering" and "evil". A proposal was later on sent to the University Grants Commission, New Delhi, to grant Visiting Associateship to me to complete this project in Jadavpur University, Calcutta. The U.G.C subsequently granted Visiting Associateship to me for two years (1994-96), during which enough study materials were collected from the Jadavpur University and The National Library, Calcutta. During Associateship, I was greatly helped by many people at Jadavpur, particularly by Dr. Tapan Kumar Chakraborty, Professor and Head of Philosophy in the Philosophy department. Later on in 1997, I requested the Indian Council of Philosophical Research (ICPR) to sanction Contingency Grant towards preparing the manuscript of the work done. The ICPR generously funded for the same and the manuscript was ready by June 2000.

The inquiry has been intriguing and interesting for the simple reason that not much has been said about the concepts "pain", "suffering" and "evil" but fortunately a lot a has been explained about pain, suffering and evil as matter of fact . Although I was not interested in further advancing wise conjectures about pain-feelings, the state of suffering and evils present in nature and beyond, I found from a rich body of conjectures and explanations about these things, something of my interest. Many questions came to my mind. How do we use these concepts and how should we use these concepts? What interesting meanings do these concepts acquire when they are in function and what after all do they refer to? Most interesting is how differently we have defined "pain", "suffering" and "evil" and what purpose do they serve? If definitions do not serve any purpose in making a clear difference between these vaguely, ambiguously and even synonymously used words, what should be the criteria for making distinction between these words in force? This last question is crucial for me because we should not nourish vagueness and ambiguity any further. It is due to this that the work aims at *evaluating* these concepts on the basis of criteria to be discovered from the vast body of the uses of these concepts in the sciences and in philosophy. An inquiry into the cases of "pain", "suffering" and "evil" is thus a philosophical analysis of the concepts called "pain", "suffering" and "evil" for their nature and meaning. The work has been completed in five chapters.

It may take pages to express my heartfelt gratitude to a number of people who helped me directly and indirectly in finishing this work. I must thank the UGC, the ICPR, the Vice-chancellor of Ranchi University and Jadavpur University, teachers of philosophy and other member of Philosophy department of Jadavpur University, all the workers of the National Library, Calcutta and Dr. T.K.Chakraborty of Jadavpur University.

I am grateful to my guru, my mother, my brother, my wife and my children. I am thankful to Mr. D.N. Sinha, Mr. R.N. Sahu and Ms. Mili Sarkar to prepare the manuscript carefully. A special word is reserved for the publisher of the book, who took all pains to get the work published.

Ranchi,
3.7.2000

DEBASHIS GUHA

Contents

1

"Pain", "Suffering" and the Sciences

"PAIN", "SUFFERING" AND PHYSIOLOGY

Both science and philosophy takes great interest in pain and suffering. But their approaches are different. Let us first speak about a striking similarity in their approach. Sciences like medical science, psychology and sociology aim at explaining the nature, genesis and effects of pain-sensations and the states of suffering in clear objective terms. Descriptive philosophy takes such interest as well. It has been a long cherished pass time of descriptive philosophers to inquire into matters like what is pain and suffering? What causes them? What are their effects on animals and human beings (and in some cases on the nature as a whole)? And 'How these evils ought to be effectively managed'? The concern for management is unique to the sciences as well. But their approaches are different in so far as a descriptive philosophical inquiry is mostly subjective in nature and transgresses limits of human rationality and given facts to enter into wide ranging conjectures and presuppositions. We need not question the efforts and aims of these branches of knowledge but we may add that both scientists and philosophers may look at the matter from yet another angle. There is no doubt that both scientists and philosophers are said 'to have' the conception of—"pain" and "suffering" i.e. they know perfectly well that "pain" and "suffering" are *concepts* and not 'things out there in the world' and they know how to *use* these concepts in their scheme of language and know what they *mean*. But hardly are they careful about making an inquiry about these concepts or about these words in force.

To care about this is different from an inquiry about pain and suffering as sensations and as state of affairs.

Once we show interest in *inquiring about these concepts vis-a-vis*, inquiries about these phenomena, we are moving closer to the proper task of philosophy. To undertake this task is to take interest in the language of science and philosophy and in this context, analyze the uses, meanings and references of "pain" and "suffering". It is due to this, that I shall henceforth use *inverted commas* with pain and suffering to demarcate them as being used in the sense of concepts but not things or states. This is thus an inquiry about the concepts "pain" and "suffering" but not about pain and suffering as facts. To be precise, this is a *linguistic analysis* about the concept "pain" and "suffering".

Nevertheless, an inquiry like this is possible if we care to go through the rich body of technical language of the sciences and philosophy, where these concepts have been used profusely in different ways, i.e. having different forces as well as meanings. It is natural to encounter the descriptions of science and philosophy about pain and suffering. Thus, we cannot and perhaps need not neglect it lest our eyes are open to the language itself and not extra-linguistic matters. It is due to this that we should first start with the physiological view of pain and suffering to transcend further to "pain" and "suffering" in philosophy. In due course we shall try to see what are the definitions of "pain" and "suffering" in physiology. Later on we shall also provide a critique of these definitions.

Let us come to the medical man dealing with "pain" and "suffering" as reflected in the physiology and pathology of pain and suffering. Really speaking, it is not that the medical man is not aware of using these concepts but in the common parlance, the medical man deals with *experiences* of the *phenomena* of pain and suffering. However, not mainly to explain what happens in our minds when we experience such things, rather, how we come to experience them and when we experience them, what distinct physical processes are involved. Moreover, when we are in pain, what steps should be taken? The first part of medical man's query, that is, the way we experience pain and the way the quality of experience is related to the physical process and the stimulus of pain, and the way we experience suffering is what we may call the *physiology of pain.* Whereas the latter inquiry leads the medical man to the physical concerns related to pain and suffering, that is, to the patients in pain and their management. This, we may call, *pathology of pain.* This is however not to be confused with 'physiological pain' and 'pathological pain', which are again medical man's interest in kinds of pain for analysis and management. The first relates to the *healthy man*, who, however, suffers from physical pain owing to some injury, whereas the second relates to the *sick man*, whose persistent and profound pain itself has become a disease. We call it *algopathic disease* or 'disease of pain as such'.

Medical science considers that the concept of "pain" is *definable* in terms of stimuli, sensation, experience and responses. However, any one definition may not be fully satisfactory. But there is no doubt that in medical science, the word "pain" is an *abstraction* through complex experiences. Such an abstraction is used to refer to a great variety of different feelings, which have little in common except for the quality of *physical hurt* (headache etc.). Similarly, *physical sensations,* which are *unpleasant*, vary so much in quality, intensity, location and time course that only a special *attribute* is abstracted from all these conditions and termed "pain". Therefore, "pain" is to be ultimately defined by the *experiences,* is the basic presupposition of medical science.

However, in this science, not only is "pain" defined in terms of 'subjective experience', but in terms of stimulus for such experience, for example, "pain is what is produced when boiling water has been poured on your hand". Further, in this science, "pain" is defined as a 'class of *behaviours, which* operate to protect the organism from harm or to 'enlist aid in effecting relief'. For example, "pull your hand from a hot pot". These are known as *operational* definitions of "pain" to enable experiments or objective clinical evaluation etc.

It is clear that the word "pain" may be defined differently in medical science in terms of stimulus, experiences and responses. Hence, it is *not* possible to provide a definition of "pain" which is satisfactory for all purposes. Nevertheless, many biologists and physicians have defined "pain" in one way or the other and it will be interesting to consider these definitions.

Let us first consider a typical passage extracted from a prominent book of *physiology*, which expectedly prospective doctors read during their first year. It focuses pain in terms of *stimulus* and almost reduces the explanation to "human pain" (it may be extended in case of animals as well but we argue whether or not we are well informed about 'animal pain'). Any way, the passage is as follows: "Pain *is produced* when a *nociceptive* (injurious) *stimulus* is received (the nociceptive stimulus either causes actual damage or is a potentially damaging agent of the tissues). The injurious agent may be (i) *mechanical* (cuts, blows etc.), (ii) *chemicals* (acids etc.), (iii) *thermal* (burns) or (iv) disease".[1] The author continues to maintain however that "pain" is often understood as identical with *tenderness* (e.g. abdominal) and thus explained, but this is *not* the case, as 'tenderness' means pain elicited by *pressing* a part. The first question is, whether or not this is a definition at all? It is difficult to assume a physiological definition following the Aristotelian rule and those classical rules, which we ought to follow. Even if we overlook such ignorance, we may still ask, is it a definition in the form of 'X is by definition' or 'X = df = ...' or 'X is ....' or 'X may be defined as ....' or 'X means' etc.? It is very difficult to ascertain it because the author has proceeded as 'Pain is produced when ....'. It is straightaway a clarification - statement arrived at telling us the etiology of physical pain. This is thus a genetic account of 'pain phenomena' and traces the multiple factor or stimulus producing pain as either mechanical or chemical or thermal or a disease. An interesting expression in this clarification is 'nociceptive' or 'injurious', distinguishing the non-nociceptive ones, which is hardly pain producing in so far as tissue damage is concerned. Hence, we get an idea that a physical state of affairs may be identified as or called "pain" if and only if an 'injurious stimulus' damages the tissue. What we get is thus not how "pain" is defined, rather what causes pain. This is nothing odd because we can still *explain how* pain is produced instead of how it may be defined. The question is one of purpose, it may not be too purposeful to go for any strict definition of the concept "pain", rather elaborate in clear cut manner how it may be produced in *us*. But at least we come to know that the word "pain" in this context is considered as something *noxious*, which is elicited by physical stimulus. It is thus difficult to ascertain that here we have a physiological definition of "pain" in terms of "stimulus". Even the explanation is not about 'pain etiology', and neither about 'pain' nor about 'pain-stimulus'. There is no doubt howevers that "pain" stand out as an *abstraction* in physiological science about which our natural tendency is that it is *something noxious* to the human beings and which has a definite physical cause or a definite origin. The physiological explanation of pain is thus neither merely defining the term "pain" nor clarifying the concept but refers to a *method* of unfolding pain in physical line. Broadly speaking, the word "pain" stands for *sensory phenomena essentially noxious.* The use and meaning of 'pain' in physiology is clear. The abstraction has been extremely efficiently used in physiological literature, and the entire science has been so serious about the genesis that vast information and theory concerning pain and related phenomena have been accumulated. Even the non-scientists have been grossly influenced by such information and both the scientists and the non-scientists are caught in 'scientific prejudice' that 'the scientific' (the medical) account of pain is what is of worth considering because it gives us a measurable, public and quantitatively expressible account of 'pain phenomena'. The prejudice is deep rooted, it tells us that which is measurable, public and quantitatively expressible is what science is.

Quite akin to this account of 'physical pain' and its causes is another medical account that treats pain in terms of 'mental pain' as well. This is as we may call it 'psycho-physical explanation' of which, the 'aspect theories' are supporters. This theory treats pain on the model of *sensations* and tries to define likewise. There is no doubt, however, that the supporters of this theory tend to shift away from an explanation of mental pain to the physical pain, but the main line of thinking is that pain is a sensation. Charles Richet *defines* pain and I take it from Sauerbach and Wenke's book, *Pain its meaning and its significance*. He writes, "*Pain is a sensation* which makes us anxious to avoid subjecting ourselves to any further suffering".[2]

There is no doubt in Richet's case that he is providing a definition of the term "pain" in terms of an abstraction representing 'sensation'. Hence, even if he does not use the words 'pain means', 'pain may be defined as...' 'the definition of pain is.......' etc., it is not difficult to ascertain that the statement above is a *kind* of definition and it would not be very absurd to think that *not* necessarily should definition be given so ceremoniously as mentioned by me. But the definition given above is the one, which certainly *limits* the *use* of the term 'pain' and acquires a restricted meaning peculiar to psycho-physics. The main purpose is to make clear how the abstraction has to be understood and used in this field of knowledge. This purpose of clarification of the notion is the purpose of the definition that may be useful to clarify what pain *really is*, and the way we should understand it for all practical purposes. What the definition reveals is an unflinching claim that pain is 'a sensation' which is 'noxious' enough for one to try to avoid it, for it may end up in 'suffering'. We have here an idea of 'pain-sensation', as was the case with 'pain-stimulus'. Only a thin line divides the two, the 'pain stimulus' intends to present us with a set of physical factors which are noxious, for they harm or are capable of damaging tissues, whereas 'pain-sensation' presents us with the influence of stimulus on *us*. In this sense, we call it an influence on us owing to such and such noxious physical stimulus acting on our tissues. It now takes us to the considerations beyond pain etiology to how we are influenced by noxious stimulus and to trace its maturity and increasing complexity in the form of feeling, which is connecting 'pain-phenomena' to the 'feeling of pain' through nervous system and the mental apparatus. It also refers to an increasing loss of ego control or the capacity to organize the stimulus acting upon the receptor organs. The hopelessness of such control ends up in unbearable suffering. The anatomical and physiological considerations have important bearings on the concepts of "pain" as a sensation. In the common parlance, the concept of 'sensation' is closely tied to the so-called special sense organs. The sensation of light is through the retina and not any part of our body. This specificity does not apply to pain because it can be felt in almost any part of the body. In neurology however, we do identify certain structures as the specific receptors and conductors of pain but this is done for clinical usefulness rather than for explaining any genuine specificity of a sensory modality associated with a particular structure.

Richet's definition is particularly helpful in knowing that while defining pain, it is difficult to avoid the *behavioural* aspect. It is obvious that if pain is a sensation, which may end up intolerable suffering, most likely, we adopt defense against pain or that we *do* something, which is essentially evasive. This becomes clear in Richet's further assertion that "the whole intellectual, moral and social development of mankind is induced by this painful sensation to be avoided"[3]. Pain as something extremely unwanted (generally speaking) by man demanding *management*. Therefore, many people think that the pain-sensation is what has to be managed primarily and for that reason, the stimulus eliciting pain has to be avoided. This is the basis of medical management and other management of pain, which is thought of as the main spring of life and the fundamental element of human progress. In so far as the medical management is concerned, 'pain' has been looked upon as a *useful* abstraction referring to the special psycho-physical condition of a person, which demands immediate care. Pain is thus *purposeful*. We are thus on the brink of knowing the *teleos* of pain sensation. There is thus a pragmatic, designating 'biological purposefulness' of pain phenomenon. Pain has been looked upon as a 'warning noise' demanding preservation of life. Medical practitioners take this as extremely important. Sauerbach and Wenke have quoted some reactions in their book.[4] And I would like to refer to the one provided by Goldscheider. He writes, 'the pain sensation is related to the danger involved, and thus it appears as a warning and thus a guardian of the organism.... The symptomatic organic pain, which arises in the affected part of the body urgently, demands that the sufferer should spare the organ in question any overstrain. Pain is the most powerful ally a physician can have; the patient blindly rely on everything pain tells him to do".[5] The teleology of pain thus connects it to 'pain patients', concrete referent of pain needing management. This is crucial in medical science—the person who is in pain or precisely, the 'pain-patient'. "Pain-patient" refers to those who present themselves to doctors with a complaint of pain, seeking relief from it. It is not that 'pain' stands out as a signal for defense action for human beings. Pain in animals produces subsequent *defense reaction,* whereas in human beings it exercises the function of *protection* or *prevention* which Richet calls, 'preventive finality'. In case of animals, pain at best is a useful abstraction meaning sensation towards which subsequent defense reaction, which is almost instinctive, is expected but may hardly have any wider significance and use for animals because they are not so organized as to prevent future pain, nor can they retain pain experience in memory so as to face future pain and help others to take preventive measures. Moreover, the natural instincts of animals may not be enough to protect the animals against wide range of dangers lurking around them. The gesture and vocal expressions may be too confusing to know about animal pains and to suggest effective measures to prevent all such pains. But in case of human beings, pain can perform preventive function because human beings retain memory of pain experienced, inducing the capacity to avoid further pain sensation. It provides human beings to face wide range of dangers and they may be more expressive 'pain patients' so that diagnosis and treatment are possible. Pain is thus a signal having a purpose—a purpose to defend and to prevent all noxious sensation. Hence, the abstraction called 'pain' in this sense is extremely useful in so far as it functions as a *warning signal* to something noxious to animals and human beings which needs immediate management. 'Pain expression' is of great pragmatic value in the bio-medical science as it is to those who are in pain.

But many interesting questions arise as we face the implication of the operative definition. Is it proper to think that 'pain sensations' do really serve as warning signals in all cases of in-pain patients? One may be sceptical about the universal value of pain in the preservation of human life and for human progress. The reason is that there are many factors operating in cases of diagnosis and management of pain. There are cases where the warning signal of pain is *not* given, or is given late or is carefully and cunningly suppressed. The suggestion is that a warning was awaited and might have been extremely useful but this was not to be. Moreover, in many cases pain is so acute, intense and abrupt that it hardly has any pragmatic function as a warning. Hence the teleological value of pain in bio-medical science is there only with some obvious limits. We can now see that the purpose of using this concept in the specific sense of 'a warning signal' should be limited as well.

This is strengthened by cases drawn from animal life as well. Biologists speak of the *negative* effect of 'pain signal' indicating a disease etc. on animal life as a whole. In this sense, it is a 'disvalue' rather than a value. The reason is that an animal sending a warning signal in their world is prone to all dangers from one who predates on them. Hence, the only purpose of a rat squeaking owing to a damaged leg is that a cat ends it all too easily enough. This theory about pain-disvalue may be traced to the theory of natural selection. What is interesting is that this abstraction may *not* universally stand for positive value for pain-patients. One who has common sense of boxing knows that if you have identified a pain in any part of the face of opponent, 'hit there', obviously, not to help.

We have thus noticed that the bio-medical distinctions of "pain" as 'pain stimulus', 'pain sensations', 'pain experience' and 'pain management' reveal the different meanings of the abstraction "pain" in this vast literature. Let us now take a look at these definitions. Attempts at defining "pain" in terms of 'stimulus' may be easily referred to the one that speaks of the cause of pain, a cause which is easily traced in nature out there, and, therefore, can be produced. But producing a physical agent causing pain is far-away from clarifying any sense of the term "pain" because the agents are many and not one and it will be extremely difficult to produce one which may be called "pain". The *ostension* of pain in terms of *a thing* which was erstwhile unknown or whose existence was inferred is rather impossible. Hence, definition like, 'pain is X', where 'X' is some such thing existing out there in nature and which is believed to be the *cause* of a phenomenon called pain is not the synonym or even the meaning of the term "pain". Hence, defining "pain" in terms of 'stimulus' is neither synonymous nor ostensive definition of "pain", rather it is an explanation of "pain". If we delve into the purpose of such explanation, we could easily see that it is to find out a physical cause for an abstraction called "pain", an abstraction that covers widely those experiences which are noxious to human beings and animals. It will be then very difficult for me to accept either the fact that producing a stimulus is producing pain or the fact that "pain" may be defined by mentioning along with it a physical agent that causes pain. It is also difficult to accept that 'pain phenomenon' may be reduced to *a* cause of that phenomenon. If "pain" is considered to be a notion referring to noxious experiences in bio-medical use, hardly anything is there to be objected to but the objection is about reducing it to 'physical causes' and defining like that. In fact, "pain is x" (where x is the physical cause of pain) is *not* ostensive definition of "pain", nor is the statement expressive of the ostensive proof of pain. The former definition demands producing a noxious *experience* like 'burn' to mention, "well, you know, this is what is pain", and then, what we show is *not* that only "burn" is "pain" rather, there is but one way to make you *feel* for what experience is the abstraction "pain" meaningfully used (this may not be the only use however). Moreover, it is extremely difficult to ostensively prove pain. One may say that as we have never seen pain *per se* (because that is not a thing) and yet we know about it only through inference from 'in-pain' cases or from information we have from books or persons, we can really produce a case of pain, for example, "burn". Interestingly, one has never seen a burn case or has just inferred burn from a newspaper photograph, may be doubting "burn" seriously and can be ostensively proved that we may sensibly believe in "burn" cases. But by showing this, one cannot prove that pain exists, for the ostensive proof of pain, we have to produce a thing called pain, which is *ex-hypothesi* ruled out. We may object saying that one who does not know pain or doubts it seriously may be caused pain by inserting a pin or pouring hot water on him. But what we have produced are extremely noxious experiences subsumed under an abstraction "pain" and not pain in this sense. One may prefer to say that "pain is X" is expressive of the ostensive proof of pain in the sense that the meaning of "pain" in the statement may be analyzed to show that it is difficult to speak about "pain" without *relating* it to 'x', which can be physically produced. It is difficult to accept it because "pain is X" does *not* rule out 'pain is y', where 'y' is non-physical cause of pain. If the analysis concludes that we can speak about pain if and only if we relate it to a physically presentable object or objects (X etc.), we have reasons to object, for pain is *not* necessarily related to physically producible causes understood only in terms of it. A notoriously simple example is to show that in the statement '*pain is produced* by betrayal'; we cannot physically prove that this is 'betrayal'. Hence, 'pain' as such *cannot* be always ostensively proved. However, among many uses of this term, such a use is testimony to the fact that pain is quite often used as an abstraction to cover noxious experience caused by something or other.

Let us turn to the other definitions, which bear the character of being called a definition. What about "pain" being defined as either sensation or behaviour or experience? For the sake of discussion let us consider these definitions:

(i) "*Pain is* an *unpleasant experience* which we primarily associate with tissue damage or describe in terms of tissue damage or both;[6]

(ii) *Pain is* a *sensation* which makes us anxious to avoid subjecting ourselves to any further suffering;[7] and

(iii) "Pain is unpleasant sensation no doubt but it is usually beneficial to man (or animal)...However, in some cases, the presence of pain may be counter productive to the interest of the patient".[8]

For reasons given above in the foregoing discussion, it will be extremely difficult to consider that here we have examples of how "pain" can be either defined ostensively or be ostensively proved. There are reasons however to call the aforesaid assertions kinds of definitions and not explanations. One strong reason is that the *purpose* of these assertions is clear, they tend to *clarify* the *meaning* of "pain" as used in biological literature, thus telling us about its peculiar *use* as well. The other is that these assertions, when analyzed, can be easily classified under the headings of one *kind* of definition or the other about which logic has taught us something. Definitions (ii) and (iii) taken together are those that aim at clarifying two important bases of understanding what the abstraction is capable of expressing. "Pain" is capable of expressing the senses of "an unpleasant sensation", which one naturally aims at "avoiding" yet which is "beneficial" as well as "counter productive". Clearly, these definitions are *not* synonymous. I have already said that they are not ostensive either. The reason is that the definitions (ii) and (iii) which is about "pain" in the form of "pain = d.x" are nevertheless *not* the equivalent expressions of "pain" because the meaning of "pain" is not just reduced to these expressions, it rather makes clear the intension of the term on the one hand (viz. 'unpleasant sensation') and the semantic relation of this term to other terms on the other hand (avoidable, beneficial, counter productive etc.). The extension of the term is hardly expressed here but we must know on the basis of earlier discussion that (a) pain-sensation does *not* denote nor does it show sensations like, warmth, cold etc., it rather denotes noxious stimulation (physical and others) and (b) pain-sensation gives information about states of the in-pain body, but does *not* tell us about the *nature* of the noxious stimulation which elicited such sensation. Hence, the extension of "pain" is not the same as the revelation of its nature or characteristics. In so far as the intension is concerned, it is not universally accepted that "pain" loses its meaning if it is not taken as 'unpleasant sensation' in which case 'being unpleasant' is the distinguishing property among several sensations that we may have. The intention is debatable for two reasons. Many people argue that there may be deep pain *without* any sensation elicited by stimulus; for example, the pain felt at a distance by a person who has left his country. The other reason is that pain is not agreed to be always an unpleasant sensation, we speak of 'pleasant pain sensation' as well. We even speak of 'enjoyment of pain' and 'non-painful pain'.

The semantic relationship of "pain" and other terms expressed in the afore-mentioned definition (ii) and (iii) raises questions. First, one gets an idea that in the definitions (ii) and (iii) "pain" has been differently related to the term 'beneficial' as well as to the expression, 'counter productive'. Moreover, it may not be well accepted that 'pain' is related to 'noxious', 'to avoid' and not to 'caring to nourish'. The afore-mentioned definitions of "pain" however project a typical *pragmatic* aspect, because it is clear that the concept has been *used* to denote those stimulus which are noxious and towards which we show great displeasure. Moreover, the concept "pain" has been *used* to project feelings like pleasure and displeasure, and it has been *used* in a manner in medical literature so that a range of its semantic relation in the different statements becomes clear.

All this takes us to interesting conclusions. One is that defining "pain" by equivalent words is extremely difficult because it is often neither logically nor psychologically satisfactory. A lexical definition of "pain" is often unsatisfactory if it provides an equivalent definition of "pain". It is natural that in English we have many words, which do not often have a single word that is equivalent in meaning to the word being defined. Exact synonyms are thus rare. We may not even have a group of words in the language that is equivalent in meaning to the word "pain". Hence, the meaning of the lengthy expressions in (ii) and (iii) may not be interchanged with the word we are trying to define. Hence, verbal inadequacy of defining "pain" becomes prominent. The problem is that I have argued the near impossibility of ostensively defining this term as well. This does not rule out other verbal possibilities of defining "pain".

One possibility, particularly left open to the biological science, is to state what we are going to mean by a term; for example, "pain". This is to stipulate a meaning for "pain" and, therefore, we may have "stipulative definitions" of "pain". It is not too odd to give a stipulative definition, particularly in the context of the scientific definitions. But the stipulation has to be widely accepted and effectively used. Often this is not the case. Stipulations in biological science may vary largely due to the growth and change in biological information, so is the case with pain. Moreover, such stipulations work within a technically meaningful framework leaving out the broader perspective of people using this differently. Many people use it emotively or persuasively and so on. We have seen that the *denotative* definition of "pain" may not be satisfactory owing to our inability to denote pain *per se*. What we may try to denote is the stimulus, which induce pain and not the *nature* of the stimulus. Moreover, the denotation is particularly variable, as stimulus is many and not one. In so far as *connotative* definitions are concerned, we have seen that they are not satisfactory either, for disagreement about connotation of "pain" may continue not only with changing scientific information but also with people adducing one quality or the other to "pain" as it may satisfy their poetic, emotive and persuasive intentions. We cannot overlook the fact that avoiding the pragmatic aspect of the use of word in a literature is nearly impossible, and the way and the purpose for which "pain" may be pictorially, poetically, emotively and even persuasively used has to be seriously considered. Thus, connotative definitions may be too cumbersome and can never be exhaustive.

A definition of "pain" may be possible by giving a *real* definition of "pain". But real definitions are possible of not words but of things. How can we define the thing "pain"? We have seen that in medical literature, the irresistible impulse to give the definition of the thing called "pain" could be easily seen. Knowing fully well that "pain" is an abstraction, the tendency to search for a definition of a thing called pain is, as we have already seen, no definition at all. If it is a search for *essence* of "pain", we have seen that a search for defining characteristics of "pain" within a language-group is almost impossible. If it aims at an analysis of pain, then hardly any such analysis is possible, for a thing called pain cannot be analyzed in that way.

But we cannot reject the truth that in medical literature the tendency to provide *causal* definition of pain is prominent. This is rather most prominent we can say. To define "pain" in terms of "caused by X" or "produced by X" is quite common. But the trouble is that the list of "caused by ...." is infinite and it changes and grows with the great progress of biological science and with it the synoptic definition of "pain" in terms of one cause or the other is far from useful. John Hospers speaks elegantly about it. He says, "pain cannot be defined as 'stimulation of nerve endings'. One could talk doomsday about stimulation of nerve-endings and yet have no idea what pain is—and million people know very well what pain is without knowing anything about nerve–endings. The scientific discovery is that when pain is experienced, there is also (immediately, prior thereto) a stimulation of nerve–endings - usually, not always. But there is a discovery about pain, not a definition of the word "pain". You would already have to know what "pain" means to know what kind of experience the stimulation of nerve—ending leads to."[9] In Hospers' assessment of the possibility of causal definition, the final remarks are the most debatable issue, i.e. whether or not "pain" can be ostensively defined. He says "some words are used to label sensory experience—"red", "pain"... of which we cannot convey to others the specific experienced quality meant by the word unless we confront him with one or another of the experience which the word labels. We have to produce a pain in him, for example, by sticking him with a pin, to make him understand what the word "pain" means. No word or combination of words, nothing but direct confrontation with the experience itself, will suffice. Such words have to be ostensively defined"[10]. And he clarifies, "the process of making clear the meaning of word by non-verbal means, such as pointing, is called ostensive definition."[11] I have already justified my unwillingness to accept the possibility of the ostensive definition of "pain". Taking 'definition' more broadly, let us assume that it is a precise attempt at clarifying the meaning and significance of the term "pain". We have to further consider that for ostensive definition of "pain" to be possible, it has to be accepted as sensory experience of a special kind. But to distinguish it from other experiences, we have to call it generally speaking, "a noxious sensory experience" (because Hosper's example of pinprick reminds us of that). He now believed that to know what the meaning of the term "pain" is by definition, we have to go through one such experience like pin-prick. But really 'pin-prick' may be insufficient enough, we have to go through many such experiences. How did it start in our life? What Hospers says is that *learning* the meaning of "pain" with *only* ostension or pointing is only possible. Is it like that? I do not remember a crook mother or teacher who in his or her life has inserted a pin and smiled a bit and said. "Well, you see, this is pain". Do we teach our children, for instance, showing a limping or a bleeding man saying, "look: that is pain"? In fact, we do not show or point pain, for there is none, what we point is a phenomenon and teach in a language how to subsume it under a noise called "pain"—we teach the use of an abstraction in different contexts and do not show pain *per se*. I have argued that ostensively producing and proving pain is equally pointless. We must remember that pointing a thing, a phenomena involving 'in-pain' man, is not pointing out pain. Hence, that cannot be the basis of knowing the meaning of "pain".

What about "sensory experience called "pain"? We come to the definition no.(i). What does this definition reveal? It reveals what we have just said, the possibility of an ostensive definition of "pain". C.A. Keele, who says, "pain cannot be defined in words, which would mean anything to a person who had not experienced it"[12], has ably supported by Hospers. But the problem is whether what people who experienced 'pin-prick' has experienced pain or has experienced 'unpleasant experience', which is *called* "pain"? Clearly the latter assertion seems to be more adequate.

But in this definition (no. i) unlike definition no. ii, we are not simply trying to inform about the sensation or the stimulus that has elicited such sensation, rather about an *affective* accompaniment by calling it *unpleasant* experience. It is a *subjective* affair though it may be accompanied by measurable physiological responses. This draws attention to its value to the organism as a *whole*. It is thought that knowledge of the anatomical and physiological basis of the pain process alone is not sufficient to provide us with an understanding of the pain sensation. The reason is that in pain experience itself, the physiological bodily conditions are absent. It becomes very clear that physiological investigations are capable of recording pain *stimulus* and for its transmission, but the moment we speak of its experience, we start considering "pain" from psychological angle and when we so define (as in iii) we accommodate another angle. But the terminological use of the word "pain" gains more complexity and its ostensive definition does not cure it, rather aggravates it. There is no doubt that it is extremely difficult to accurately define "pain" or even describe it to one who in his life time has met a situation that is subsumable under this concept. But that does not mean that meeting with unpleasant situation called "pain" is meeting a thing called pain which may be shown to us. It is equally hopeless to imagine that verbal expression of subjective experiences like "pain experience" is satisfactory at all. We may soon get lost in the maze of such expressions. In clinical diagnosis, it at times creates a lot of trouble rather than help it. The *figurative description* of "pain" is thus inadequate representation of pain-experience: stabbing, burning, itching are all technical activities outside ourselves and inadequate to clarify the pain-experience.

From this we come to the point of deciding which definition of "pain" is most suited for Biology. Biological science no doubt has to go along with the causal and stipulative definitions and to a great extent with the ostensive definition as well. But the problems are (a) do we believe, like Locke, that "pain", like other simple ideas, cannot be defined or described? Or (b) do we believe that it should be defined ostensively only? Another question that eludes us is (c) should we at all define "pain"? We shall have an answer to this last question only in the last chapter. Question (a) is related to it. We have, however already answered question (b). Let us give it up now. What interests me most is that we have entered into the lively discussion of 'pain experience' and with it 'unpleasant experience *called* "pain"'. To delve into this issue, one has to consider the physiological and the psychological explanations for reasons already cited by me. But for the moment we shall first consider the qualifier, viz. 'unpleasant' in this regard. The qualifier has been extremely crucial in the understanding of pain-experience because we have been relating such experience to unpleasant sensation caused by stimulus capable of doing so.

First of all, I would like to go back to the problem of learning to use "pain" or learning the meaning of "pain". There is no doubt that we may try to teach the meaning of "pain" by showing or pointing out unpleasant sensations, 'in-pain' people etc. Nevertheless, to know the meanings and the uses of this concept in different contexts, we have to consider the fact that a person in his life time goes through such feelings and sensations as is also influenced by stimulus damaging his or her tissues and so on. Thus learning the meaning of "pain" is related to not only *seeing* cases of 'in-pain' people etc. but also to *identifying* such cases with one's own experience. Hence, having unpleasant experience of pain is of great importance, otherwise a comic situation awaits those who do not have such experience. He has to be kicked, pricked, smashed and so on to teach how to use this word or what its meaning is. Perhaps we will still not be able to show him this dreaded thing. But why should we always speak of this unpleasant sensation for having pain experience and learning its meaning? The obvious reply is that we have to ensure that one *differentiates* between these and unpleasant sensations of pressure and purutitis (itch) etc. which were *not* pains. This is to learn when *not* to use the term "pain". However, if we suppose that one has neither seen a case nor himself faced the situation of electric shock and yet knows the physical and psychological accompaniment of some pain cases, he may still utter, after getting first electric shock in life, that "I feel pain". How did he use this term at that moment? How did he learn to extend this concept to cover this new experience, which, however, was unpleasant to him? This takes us to the 'pain experience' which, when analyzed, reveals 'distress at a sensation' is basic to pains. Hence, distressful sensation or unpleasant sensation, generally speaking, is the basis of knowing about "pain", that is of knowing about the meaning of "pain" and the ability to clarify what are pains. This enables us to distinguish certain types of sensations, which are extremely unpleasant and yet not called 'pains'. From this we come to know that wherever we speak of "pain", we have to consider the 'sensory quality' of pain and that the 'feeling-tone' of distress or displeasure is associated with a sensation, which we generally call "pain". C.D. Broad says, "what we *call* 'a pain' is an *unpleasant experience* which owes to its *unpleasantness* to the fact that in it one of these *qualities* is *sensibly manifested*"[13]. Following this, one could say that some qualities are strongly unpleasant and have to be distinguished from others and for this, we have, for instance, expressions such as throbbing, burning, stabbing etc. I am reminded here of a book on homoeopathy that deals with such expressions under the heading: *Pain as if.*

How we are faced with the problem of subjectivity of pain-experience and the degree of displeasure shown, gesture and speech reactions when one is confronted with such experience and inhibitory mechanism that tends to appear like 'no pain'. The question is 'how is it possible to accept an universal formulation for pain-experience in terms of 'unpleasant sensation'? What Broad and others say is not that 'unpleasant sensation' is the sufficient condition for pain experience; rather it is the *necessary* condition no doubt. Greater problem lies elsewhere; i.e. with the pain-qualities, which are believed to be referents of unpleasantness of the sensations received which, precedes pain classifications. It will be extremely difficult to mention any one or a few adjectives as sufficient in this regard. To most people, these qualities refer to strongly unpleasant feelings and to many such is not the case. Hence, 'pricking' sensation may not be the one that is necessarily 'unpleasant'. All 'pricking' cases are not such that they may be regarded as pain-quality resulting into pain experience. Extending this to other qualities throbbing, gnawing etc. we find that they are not necessary referents of unpleasant sensations. Otherwise, why should a heart *throb* without pain? It is thus important in medical parlance to use "pain" in a more sensible manner. The same is true for 'stabbing sensation' as well, which is more or less believed to be referent of unpleasant pain sensation resulting in obvious pain experience. But we forget the subjective element again as the emotive aspects and even the pain inhibiting aspects are grossly overlooked. Do we say that once we classify a sensation as 'stabbing' no doubt we classify it further as 'pain' or 'pain sensation' resulting in a specific pain experience? It seems not. We shall come to it later on. At present let us concentrate on the emotive aspect and the imagery involved in pain qualities and in the expressions of such qualities. Is it not true that when one classifies a pain quality as 'stabbing', one is definitely showing an emotional reaction towards a state-of-affairs that involves his body and a stimulus that might have incited something utterly unpleasant? Further, is it not the case that the person is using imagery while classifying the pain quality? The answer must be in the affirmative but that does *not* mean that therefore, the person has been stabbed at least once in his lifetime. But this assertion goes right against what I have said early on. We may conceive of a person who has never been stabbed in his lifetime has never seen one being stabbed and yet the imagery is what he surely uses to describe his pain. Using pain imageries in life using analogies, which need not presuppose the person's having undergone through particular pain experiences. It is for this reason that for 'shooting pain' one need not have been shot or 'stabbing pain', one need not have been stabbed and so on. What I want to say is that learning to use the concept "pain" and learning the meaning of it depends on experiences of unpleasant sensation but learning the use of pain *imageries* does *not* depend on such experiences; but rather on learning how in a language situation people *use* imageries to express pain experience, imageries which are drawn from the external world. Thus, 'shooting pain' is imagery drawn from 'shooting star' referring to rapidly spreading pain and 'stabbing pain' referring to many objects that press us beyond our liking. The imageries are thus *analogies* from natural setting. Hence, 'pain expressions' involving imageries do not presuppose 'pain experiences'. Learning about the conceptual meaning and use of "pain" and expressing pain in English language are different. Emotive expressions such as those "while we are 'in-pain'," do not demand that we ought to be 'in pain' in just the same manner that we express our emotions in pain.

Returning to Broad's view, we find that beyond doubt *not* all experiences which are highly unpleasant are pains but these are not so for reasons Broad has mentioned, i.e. owing to the absence of pain qualities like stabbing etc. The precedence of classification of 'pain-qualities' before pain sensation and pain-experience is difficult to understand. Unpleasant sensations of smell and taste, for instance, which are not pains are not so because we do not have preceding pain qualities like 'burning smell' rather 'pungent smell', 'filthy smell' and so on. Broad's opinion commits *hysteron proteon* because the classification of sensations in terms of qualities has been done before we have classified them as 'pain'. Even when I was speaking of the learning the meaning and use of the concept "pain", we were learning about what unpleasant experiences are generally speaking subsumable under this concept and, therefore, it is not important that we learn qualities first to learn about pain. We must remember that for the genus 'pain' an analogy of 'shooting star' may be appropriate for a type of 'pain' within that genus. What is important is to learn what "pain" is rather in what ways pain is expressed through imageries. Similarly, it is more important to classify a sensation as pain and not to classify pain qualities at the outset. But the importance of 'pain quality' lies elsewhere.

As we have come to understand that 'pain' need *not* be defined as merely 'unpleasant sensation', we can now understand more clearly that the concept of 'pain-quality' becomes necessary for the establishment of this fact. Nevertheless, we ought to remember that classification of sensation as 'pain sensation' does not beg a name called "pain" that we have at our disposal, rather there is something special in 'pain-sensation' that makes it what it is or which enables us to subsume it under the broad name "pain". Hence, having sensations and looking at the specific characteristics help classify them as "pain". But what is this 'something' special in 'pain-sensation'? The most common point of agreement is that even if the defining characteristic of "pain-sensation" is not 'what is unpleasant', yet it does *refer* to some types of sensation which are *generally* unpleasant, and not to others. 'Pain-quality' may be responsible for distinguishing different kinds of bodily sensation. Without the notion of pain-quality we would be able to make nothing of the distinction that people often want to make between the sensation of the needle-prick and the 'pricking pain'. That the prick of a needle (which in itself is not a noxious stimuli yet has the inherent capacity to elicit a sensation of a kind on human body or elsewhere) has elicited the sensation of a needle-prick and that we classify it as not only 'pricking sensation' but 'pricking pain', because the concept of 'pain quality' help us to do this. Subsuming 'pricking sensation' under the class of "pain" is due to the *unpleasantness* of the 'pricking sensation' and *not* due to the quality called 'pricking' but this pain-quality called 'pricking' is the concept that further enables us to classify it as merely "pain" but "pricking pain". Hence, 'pain quality' helps us in the classification of pains as well. It enables us to understand and to tell people that we *experience pain* as we are incited with a specific unpleasant sensation. The word "pain" therefore, in medical literature is used so as to refer to a special class of sensation as different from other sensations viz. trickles, throb, itching etc. which are not pains. This does not rule out the possibility of different shades or kinds of pain (as are shades of a colour) which are related in an important way with the way they are felt. We can also conceive shades or kinds of 'pain-quality' that not only distinguishes pain experience from a specific unpleasant sensation, helps us to classify kinds of pain experiences that we have. It is due to this that 'pricking pain' is different from 'burning pain' and 'stabbing pain' and yet they are all related because all are experienced owing to a specific unpleasant feeling. But we need not suppose that the classification of pains helped by pain-qualities has anything to do with either duration or location of pain. R. Trigg in his book *Pain and Emotion* says, "A 'twinge' conceptually must only last for a brief period of time, whereas pains last for a moment or a very long time. A 'headache' could not be anywhere but in our head. Pain, on the other hand, can clearly be felt anywhere and still be pain. Intensity is also irrelevant to the concept of pain. Pain can be either mild or intense in a way that 'agony' cannot".[14] We can thus speak of different kinds of pain because pain-qualities help us in doing so. Once 'headache' has been classified as an unpleasant sensation and subsumed under "pain", the use of "bursting" with it makes it a 'bursting headache' and distinguishes it from other pains such as 'burning skin' and from sensations such as the 'sensation of burst in the head' or the 'sensation of burn in the skin'. Yet both remain under the class of "pain", as the sensations have been unpleasant so as to classify them like that. Thus, sensations cannot be "pains" in so far as the feeling of unpleasantness is not there and in so far as one element of 'pain quality' is not there. But I still maintain that to *define* "pain" in these terms will be fallacious most probably it will be *too narrow* as it disregards those sensations which are not unpleasant and yet called "pain". Psychological definitions of "pain" in terms of pain experience and pain-sensation may remain unsatisfactory. For all practical purpose, however, in day to day life in medicine, we shall continue to accept "pain" as 'unpleasant sensations' *qualified* further according to pain-qualities.

In medical science, we face many interesting situations as we delve deeper into the subjectivity of pain or pain experience. I have said just now that it may be a kind of prejudice in our mind that makes us thinks that 'unpleasant sensations' *only* are pains and these *must* be pains. That these are prejudices, we come to know from serious disagreement in opinion about whether or not some unpleasant sensations are *not* pains and that unpleasant sensations must not be pains at all for some of us. This may occur in border cases like 'electric shock', which we often hesitate to call pain and yet some classify it as a pain. Some think it is an unpleasant sensation whereas others do not think so. Not to speak of this, a person may even laugh while boiling water is being poured on him or a soldier may not feel pain while getting his legs amputated. Such disagreements take us to the question of the extent or the boundary of "pain" and to the problem of 'pain inhibition', which are important questions in medical science and have important philosophical implications as well.

Those who disagree about whether or not only unpleasant sensations are pains, they are really indecisive about the range of sensations to be subsumed within "pain". This, in fact, shows the learning of the meanings and uses of the concept of "pain", which enable us to understand the extent of the use of this concept as well. Such learning, however, depends on many factors. It will be absurd to think about an absolute directory, which clarifies the boundary of "pain". This is, of course, a subjective effort to learn about the adequate uses and meanings of "pain". But it may take us much deeper into the level of subjective experiences of sensations and classifying them as "pain". It also takes us to the level of subjective levels of inhibition, courage, bluff etc. when we ask whether or not unpleasant sensations must be called "pain". The linguistic use of "pain" and its learning, the *physio-psychological* factors involved in the experience and inhibition of pain and the *pragmatic* factors of the *avowal* of pain in different situations, all have to be taken into consideration to resolve these tricky questions. Several socio-cultural and anthropological explanations of using the concept of "pain" are thus extremely important for knowing the uses and meanings of "pain". Nevertheless, physiological and psychological explanations are no doubt central. The persistent disagreement, however, enables us to find an excuse for not having any one definition of "pain" in terms of unpleasantness of sensations.

What is crucial is to notice that in so far as expressions and avowals of pain and disagreements emerge, we cannot neglect the 'pain quality' that is the basis of classification of pains. We may sound like Wittgenstein in so far as we maintain that 'pain quality' is one of our normal presuppositions about pain. Any neglect shown towards this is to find no way to explain why we call some unpleasant sensations 'pains' and not others. Hence, 'pain-qualities' are the basis for avowal of 'pains' as either pleasant or unpleasant. Trigg says, "without the concept of 'pain-quality' we can make no distinction between the reporting of pain in abnormal circumstances (when, for instance, it is not disliked) and the misreporting of pain".[15] Learning the extent of "pain", the finer elements involved in "pain avowal" in terms of pleasantness or unpleasantness and the misreporting, bluffs and abnormalities of expression are extremely important for a medical practitioner because pains have medical significance. Doctor's problem is really the problem of distinguishing between the normal and abnormal reporting of pains. For, normal reporting takes care of the 'pain qualities' uttered by the patients and in that sense the 'unpleasantness of pain' is a key factor. Nevertheless, the doctor may not take care of the exact locations and intensity of pains as have been expressed by the patient. For, the physiological understanding of doctor may be better, his psychological sensations may be more adequate and measurements of intensity and duration more accurate. To face abnormal reporting, however, a doctor has to learn the extent to which "pain" may be used or may not be used under varying practical circumstances. This is, however, a problem with 'public avowal' of private pains. In private cases, however, when no such avowal is required and one is confronted with a situation he calls "pain", it is the person who evaluates it to be either pleasant or unpleasant. In such cases it is the knowledge of the person about the extent of "pain", his knowledge about "pain-qualities" and the pragmatics involved in one's private life when one confronts pain. This is not to rule out that private pains are never publicly avowed, but the avowals may be different or even confusing or misleading. In medical science, doctors face such situations of trifling "pain avowals". We shall face interesting questions regarding this after I have said something about 'non-painful' and 'pleasant' pain. This in fact brings before us the peculiar uses of "pain", as a *noun* along with some *adjectives*, when in the literature of physiology the problem of 'pain threshold' is considered to find out the point at which a 'state of affair' has to be adequately ascribed that name. The question is whether or not a sensation, which is only just noticeable, has pain-quality and yet not unpleasant? Physiologists say that experiments measuring threshold of pain suggest that this does happen, although it is important to notice that in saying so they get into the problem of blurring of the distinction between 'pain-quality' and the emotional reaction. Such blurring by the physiologists results in the peculiar uses like 'non-painful pain' and 'pleasant pain' etc. G.H. Bishop in "Physiological Review" mentions such uses. In such uses the uneasiness of the physiologists is apparent as they decline to call a state of affair 'pain' by qualifying it with an adjective (non-painful) to mention that which is 'not unpleasant'. It appears that once we use "pain" with regard to a sensation, it is extremely difficult to accept that it is not without an unpleasant sensation or without a pain-quality, but here we are faced with a situation in which we do not like to attach emotive reactions. The physiologist's dilemma is clear when he is drawn between the distinction of "pain really so-called" and "threshold pain". The former is "pain" when it is really "painful" whereas the latter is "pain" but not "painful pain" or better said, is "non-painful pain". This is, however, *not* "pleasant pain". The expression 'non-painful pain' thus wants to save the case of self-contradiction by clarifying simply the possibility of threshold pain cases where emotional protests are not helped by pain-qualities even if distinct sensations are there. The noun (pain) refers merely to sensations where the adjective refers to our reactions to it, which, however, as it normally should be, is *not* so disagreeable. The physiological use is owing to the obsession that "pain" must *logically* be "unpleasant" otherwise its definition is not possible. But in the foregoing discussion we have tried to get over this difficulty by saying that definition of pain need not beg "unpleasantness", yet, generally speaking, "unpleasantness" is an important key in understanding "pain" as distinct from "sensation". What is more crucial is to take into account 'pain-qualities' in this regard to make such distinction. But many physiologists face this problem of "pain threshold" and an adequate use of "pain" in that regard. We may consider the reports of C.A. Keel in this matter.[16] Keel's experiments on exposed blister base with amounts of chemical solutions reveal that it is extremely difficult to describe the point at which the sensation caused by chemical applications becomes unpleasant and thus painful. No doubt there is a point at which even the sensation becomes pleasant. Keel has thus coined a new word 'metaesthesia' for the range of sensation before it becomes unpleasant. He thus conceives, with the use of this word, the possibility of state of affairs, which is neither pleasant nor unpleasant. Hence, 'metaesthesia' is not *true pain,* which is again by definition always 'unpleasant'.

Prof. A. Forbes' case is somewhat face-saving for the physiologist[17]. He gives us the example of inserting sharp fingernails on the skin, first gently and then pressing it hard to find that gentle contact evolves touch sensation and then there is sharply defined change in the quality of the sensation. It is difficult to ascribe a name to this naive sensation, which is unpleasant (as does Keel). Forbes differs from Keel to call the naive sensation "pain", which is definitely and easily recognizable. To Forbes, "pain" *must* be *unpleasant* by definition but he still prefers to call it "pain" throughout even when it is pleasant or neutral, may be due to its later transformation into a state that follows emotional protests. From all this we find that in physiological use, in case of threshold pain, the presupposition that "pain" is what is an unpleasant sensation necessarily is the basis of explanation. But this will leave us indecisive as to how to describe abnormal or unusual phenomena. People like Trigg are thus emphatic in mentioning the difference between sensation and our reaction to it within the concept of "pain". The conclusion, which seems obvious to him, is that with the concept of 'pain-quality' after all, we are less bewildered about classifying sensation and differentiating it with pain experience. 'Pain-quality' is thus crucial in the discussion of the possibility of some pains, which are still labelled 'non-painful'. Similarly, it will be too cumbersome to speak of 'pleasant pain' although it is not like 'square triangle'. The basic idea may be that in particular situation it is difficult to use the concept "pain" without qualifying it, for in this case, contrary to unpleasantness, pleasant feeling is what at best we can distinguish. Extending what Forbes says, if "pain" has to be used throughout his experiment about pain threshold, the naive touch of finger-nails and even gently scratching the skin may be pleasant and if it is pressed and scratched beyond limit, the same may be unpleasant and thus adequately called "pain" (or really "pain"). Again, the problem is with the apparent loss of use of 'pain quality' in this context. In the later case of 'real pain', one has to really look at the emotive protest or reaction in terms of expressions like 'the nails cause scrubbing pain' or 'the nails cause cutting pain' and so on to clearly know the difference between why it should be called "pain" disregarding the qualifier "unpleasant" along with it, whereas in the former case, it is difficult to identify 'pain-quality' except for the word 'gentle scratch', which, however, is not as we have said a 'pain-quality' and thus is not a classified pain sensation. Hence, it will be sufficient to call it the feelings of touch, mild finger scratch and so on but neither pleasant scratch nor non-painful scratch etc. It is really pointless.

Let us now leave this discussion here to return to another interesting physiological problem regarding pain, that is, the problem of *public avowal* of pain and related questions. It is important to consider these questions because the medical use of "pain" and the communicative *public* image of "pain" are closely related in so far as in-pain patients or persons quite often than not come out of the private shackles to seek medical help or management of pain and for that reason avowal of pain is essential. It is a two-way traffic, the one who is in pain and wants to avow pain to the other who is the practitioner, most hopefully the one who will help the person. The avowal of pain may be related to mind or body and the other party need not be doctors alone, rather sympathizers, nurses and so on. But let us consider doctor's case here. Another factor to be kept in mind is that, in such cases, the levels of understanding of "pain" are different. Also knowledge about pain phenomena and use of pain words may be vastly different, yet with this drawback, the public avowal of pain and its management has to work. Public avowal of pain covers problems like expressions of inhibited pain, blurred and bluffed information of pains and misreporting of pain. It cannot be ruled out that the public avowal of pain is of great importance in the medical science in particular. Thus the public avowal of pain is purposeful, although the *harmfulness* of it is not ruled out altogether.

In modern medicine "pain" has gained the status of a communicative concept. But it has concentrated more on pathological pain and, therefore, a tendency to use the concept 'pain' to refer to signal indicating some bodily disorders. But it may be extremely dangerous to try to avoid the psychological disorders as well, particularly in cases of communication of complex pain experiences and inhibited pain experiences. Nevertheless, the primary model of reference is 'bodily disorder'. Communication of pain (in case of human beings) is often addressed to someone whom we expect assistance or we think that we can depend on the person. It follows that what is communicated and to whom is of great importance to correct understanding of the phenomenon. Hence, the communicative use of "pain" arises out of a *need*, which may be that of a bodily disorder (mainly), or it may be another need. The experience and expression of pain is an attempt to satisfy this need. While the nature of experience and its expression depend on physiological pain, the actual meaning of the experience differs essentially from that. Thus, in case of pain-avowal, "pain" points as a referent first to the body, ambiguously to both body and other people and some particular person. This takes us much deeper into the recognition of complex use of "pain" in pain-communication and the fact that the use is limited only if we explain it in the context of communication of pathological pain.

We may thus consider the practical problems in diagnosis and treatment in medicine only if we consider the trifles in pain-expressions not merely from pathological angle but from the communicative angle as well. Why is it that a chronic patient of gout complains of *severe* pain even though he is showing clear signs of recovery? "Pain patients" whose complaint is chronic and yet benign, its experience, etiology and management demands attention in medical science, equally important is to consider the inhibition and expression of pains, which are chronic. Let us shift our attention towards these chronic pains and pain patients. If we want to know about chronic pain, we ought to know its difference with acute pain, which increases with our anxiety until a certain point when we do something to obtain relief before the pain becomes very severe. The acute pain experience is thus a good example of the growth of anxiety with pain and our immediate hurried needs for management. The experience with chronic pain is different because the pain persists and causes the defensive reflexes to diminish because they do not help. 'Help seeking' is a behaviour, which is more routinized and hopeless. It thus crosses the boundary of mere pain to become a *suffering* which is long lasting and patients start inhibiting it and live with it. At later stages, public avowal is not clear, a psychosis grows, and the patient may even end up exaggerating pain and curse doctors, medicines and so on.

The chief difficulty with chronic pain is to ascertain the *meaning* of "pain". The patient more often than not fails to give meaning to chronic pain. The patient may *understand* the meaning of chronic pain, which the patient confronts through the explanation given by his doctor, but the pain makes no sense as a warning signal, since it cannot be avoided or treated. Even when the underlying disease or pathology can be specified quite precisely in most of the cases, there may be no effective treatment. The pain in this sense gets no meaning, that is, it becomes dysteleological or non-purposive. It is not unnatural to have chronic pain cases, in which normal people would cry but the patient finds it difficult to use the word "pain" any more, he almost hopelessly takes it as a state of affairs which perhaps has no answer. This is not the case with acute pain when the patient is worried about his pain experience, the nature, location, intensity of pain and its management. The management is relatively easy as well.

There is another sense in which the patient finds it difficult to ascribe meaning to his pain, and that is in trying to find the *reason* behind his state of affairs, which perhaps he has stopped calling "pain". "Why on earth should I suffer from gout?" "Gout" in the meantime might have become meaningless physical deformity for the patient as he hesitates to talk about "gout-pain", he is rather worried about why he should suffer from such things. This attitude may lead to fatalism and scepticism. As such, pain is associated in our minds with punishment for carelessness or wrongdoing, patient's soul-searching, we may say, is to undo pain to get relief. Tragically, seldom are the reasons found and the patient experiences confusion as to the meaning of his pain and he also experiences bitterness that others who are more sinful seem to be better placed. Chronic pain thus results in three attributes, as Le Shem says, "meaninglessness, helplessness, and hopelessness". Apart from being fatalistic, the extreme sceptical nature becomes part of nature as one becomes, for instance, worried about a particular time of aggravation of symptoms and even asks, "what if"? This "what if?" is serious as it spells out patient's worries about the nature of pain and the type of pain. Was it not cancerous pain or something else? What if the doctor did not understand it properly? What if the doctor does not understand any more? Shall I live any more? In chronic pain therefore, "pain" is often the other name of "worries". "Worries" become painful to bear any longer.

In cases of chronic-pain, pain is often looked upon as an *embodiment* of evil, which is relentless and all-powerful and it is, therefore, taken as something to be eliminated and not simply cured. The word therefore, signifies *something* natural or unnatural which has to be eliminated. In bearable cases of 'gout' the patient may thus forget that there is anything like 'gout', it is the *evil called* "pain" which has to be won, has to be eliminated. 'Chronic pain' is thus the cause of suffering, and "pain" is something that has to be countered. It is natural that any discussion, which is much deeper, should enter into the psychological effects, but we shall not consider them now. What we have come to know is that it is extremely difficult to ascertain a definition of chronic pain and with it the clumsiness of using "pain" in this expression grows worse. It may at best be a kind of pathological pain having serious psychological accompaniment but what is the significance of "pain" in this expression is difficult to ascertain. Is it an "unpleasant feeling? Or is it a "persistent evil"? It is pretty easy to call acute pains cases of pains in which "pain" signifies experiencing "unpleasant sensation" at its worst rapidity and intensity. The "unpleasantness" is marked by pain-qualities. But in chronic pain cases, is it possible to experience distinct pain-qualities, which are obviously "unpleasant"? The answer may be heavily subject-dependent. We have to consider the pain-patient, his experiences and his public avowal (of course if he comes out of his shackles). The public avowal of chronic pains may be eluding, fleeting and even bluffing. The inhibition level may be so intense that the avowal may be completely misleading at times—"well, I live with it, do you have an answer to it?" It is not that chronic patients do not start off well with the descriptions of "pain experience" as "unpleasant". "It is bursting", "It is burning", "It is pulsating" and other such "pains" may be common reply and then with the lapse of time these may increase, the doctor may face a lump of unpleasant expressions called "pain", every bit of "unpleasantness" may be portrayed now and then. The visits may be regular, if you neglect them, they complain. But then I believe these "unpleasantness" is replaced by "hopelessness" and "despair", "anguish" and "worries" and then "curse" the "fate" or the "palpable evil". "Pain" is a lost expression, pain-qualities not to be of help for public avowal of "unpleasantness". However, we have little doubt that in cases like chronic pain, "pain" and "suffering" are close allies as the result of pain is suffering for the pain-patient.

Let us now consider the physiological explanation of suffering and with it the uses of the concept "suffering". I fear that nothing much could be said in this regard because pathology of suffering is preferred not to be so fruitful a discussion because normal reference in physiological literature is "pain" and not "suffering". Physiology has been predominantly concerned with beings that are valuable to us and to the nature as a whole, hence, it is natural that it takes interest in not only how they are constituted, but also in how they feel. There are two aspects: what happens at the mental strata when one feels pain. Every time the mainframe of reference is 'pain'. The reality is that we, who are gifted with language and with the power to communicate, communicate our feelings, and when we communicate some "unpleasant feelings" which we experience to be quite distinct as they are qualified with some disagreeable qualities, we have picked up from the repository of English usage, a term called "pain", which is believed to be a concept best suited for this purpose. This concept is thus used in physiological literature as borrowed from the common human language use (in English) to go deeper into the question of how, for instance, human beings feel "pain". We may discuss it in the same way about animals and although they do not use "pain", even they may feel it. That they possibly feel it as we do (something utterly disagreeable), we prefer to use the same concept for further physiological use. If using "suffering" was not that inconvenient, then why didn't we use it? The question is that in physiology it was not preferred with a reason, perhaps. In physiology, pain has been used to refer to a phenomenon that affects us, whereas suffering has been used in the sense of not a phenomenon needing physiological explanation, rather a psychological (emotive) state of affair, which is the result of pain. Physiology goes for the basis of suffering and not straightway for the emotive aspect, which, they believe should be better considered by other subjects. It will be too harsh to reject 'suffering' from scientific discussion. Psychology certainly takes greater interest in it as well, but physiology has a qualified interest in so far as 'suffering' has been considered not for a detailed pathological scrutiny. The definition of "suffering" "from physiological point of view is, therefore, difficult to arrive at. However, what Trigg says is interesting: "in *connection with* pain, "suffering" *implies* distress or a high degree of *dislike*. To ask if someone suffered much as a *result of the pain of a disease* is to ask whether he was distressed or whether he found it *exceptionally unpleasant*."[18]

First thing that we have to notice is that this is not a definition of the concept "suffering". In physiology, as I have said, a definition may not be needed at all. Definitions are never without a purpose. The question is, if "suffering" is not at all a theoretically as well as practically important concept the meaning of which has to be clarified, then why should we be so keen on defining it? It is not the first order task of physiology to clarify the meaning and significance of the concept "suffering", nor is it important to clarify its different uses because this task may be performed with greater interest by a logician for instance. Hence, the need for defining "suffering" is not urgently felt in physiology. Nevertheless, physiology bears the characteristics of positive science and as such takes greater interest in causal questions related to an event or a phenomenon. It is natural that they consider "suffering" to be a concept, which has been shaped through abstraction, no doubt. The basis of such abstraction, according to such sciences, must be concrete events or phenomena. The phenomena which present them as stark reality are what we experience outside our consciousness, several object, things, events, which cause different *sensations* in us, some of which are noxious or utterly unpleasant which we further classify in terms of different qualities called "pain-qualities" to *call them* "pain". Thus "pain" is one abstraction that physiologically speaking, refers to "unpleasant sensations". In so far as pain-phenomenon is concerned, that is, how "we experience pain", we must find its cause or its origin and from thereon we trace exact physiological mechanism that leads to such experience. We may further classify pain experience according to the pain-qualities. But that is not the end of all, because one who experiences "pain", either fleeting or fixed, we call them (even the animals) "suffering", that is, the one who suffers from "pain" or the one who "suffers from pain experience". "Suffering" thus refers to a state of affair 'which is due to' or the 'basis of which is' or 'which is the result of' experiencing pain. What Trigg says is pretty clear in this context He makes it clear that "suffering" has to be better understood "in connection with" "pain". Interestingly, suffering reminds a "state of affair", whereas pain reminds us of an "experience". Hence, any talk about "suffering" is not possible without relating it to 'pain experience'. We must not get confused and start thinking that the meaning of "suffering" is possible only in relation to pain because physiologically speaking, clarifying the strict meaning of "suffering" is not the main objective. Rather, clarifying the natural concomitant of one who is in pain. The word 'implies' in Trigg's assertion need not be taken in its strict logical sense, otherwise it would read as "in connection with the term 'pain', the term 'suffering' logically amounts to or mean....", and then it would be a hopeless case of defining 'suffering' in terms of 'pain'. Here we only understand that the concept "suffering" may be meaningfully understood if we relate it to pain- experience, what naturally follows is that *like pain*, it amounts to a 'state of affair of distress' or 'extreme distress'. "Suffering" is thus an abstraction resulting from states of distress and extreme dislike caused by 'exceptionally unpleasant' sensation elicited by factors like 'distress'. Taken in this sense, it is very difficult to understand the basic difference between the two abstractions, "pain" and "suffering" because both refers to "unpleasant sensation" elicited by certain factors. The difference lies elsewhere. The abstraction called "suffering" may not be meaningfully understood if we disregard the fact that a person (or an animal) is *in pain*, the causes of which is evident, whereas the abstraction called "pain" may be used even if we do not relate it to another abstraction "suffering" or even a fact that somebody suffers because the clarity of the meaning of "pain" is deeply related to "unpleasant sensations" qualified by certain "qualities", such as "pricking", "punching" etc. We do not, for instance, speak of a "thrashing suffering" or a "bursting suffering" but any pain experience, which is qualified by any pain-quality whatsoever is our experience such that one experiencing burning is said to be in "suffering", i.e. the general reference of which is "suffering". Hence, "suffering" is not a phenomenon, it may be a state of affairs, a fact at best, which may not be without a reason—the reason or the basis is pain experienced and not an abstraction called "pain". Both pain experience and the fact of suffering takes us to the level of subjective experience and thus to the mental strata of man and yet pain may be physical here and there on parts of body to be identified (which however may be quite meaningless to do so), but suffering engulfs the 'whole-man', the entire 'personality'. "Pain" and "suffering" both refers to emotive aspects of man, yet suffering may have a broader frame of reference of sustained distress, agony, anguish and helplessness. It is uncommon to speak of the 'pain of man' or 'human pain' when we wish to refer to the general distress of human beings or mankind. We thus speak of 'the suffering of man' or 'the human suffering' or 'the suffering of mankind'. 'Pain' finds a relatively narrower extension which is particularly inadequate to explain the unpleasant experience of a man elicited by sensations, whereas "suffering" has a much broader extension so as to cover the states of despair, anguish and distress of man. It is, however, difficult to find out in Trigg's assertion what he means by 'exceptionally unpleasant', for 'exceptional' has distinct vagueness. Moreover, there may not be much reason behind 'exceptional unpleasantness', to be called "suffering" and not "pain". It is a matter of situational difference with great degree of subjectivity involved that we determine the exceptionality of unpleasantness. Interestingly, when we bleed owing to a small cut and do a lot of ooh! ouches! we are said to be in pain and we really experience pain and it need not be compared by others or by us with the terrible stomach pain we had a few days ago. To say that the terrible stomach pain is a stomach suffering, and bleeding is a pain, is gross misuse of language. It blurs the real distinction between the two conceptual uses as well.

We should better realise that in any meaningful sentence the occurrence of the word 'pain' is not essential for the meaning of 'suffering' to be clear. Hence, we may have causal assertions in which 'suffering' may be directly related to a noxious stimulus. For instance, when we say "this suffering is due to cancer" or "he suffers from cancer", the pain element may be absent and lurking in our mind when we read this sentence, which is perfectly meaningful. The semantic behaviour of "suffering" is thus independent of "pain". We therefore, need not unnecessarily be saying, "He has cancer which causes unpleasant sensations such as burning blisters and pulsating head, and these experiences of extreme pain is the reason why the person is in suffering". He suffers from cancer cannot be translated into, for example, "He experiences the pain of cancer". In statements like these where "suffering" is causally related to a stimuli, we find a cause of a state of affairs called suffering, which does not make any specific reference to pain of the pain-patient. Much wider than that, we know what cancer can cause, something that engulfs the 'whole man', irrespective of whether or not at the moment he is in pain. That the person is in deep trouble, in a state of despair and distress is conveyed to us clearly. No doubt it is an assertion with a purpose, to state the condition, the cause etc., of a person's present position, but it arouses an emotion as well. Using "pain" in this way is thus not uncommon. Like "pain assertions" therefore, "suffering assertions" may be purposive as well. They may be purposive in order to evoke emotion, state a condition, find a solution etc. One may, on the other hand, try to find a purpose of "suffering" when it is taken not merely as a concept but a fact. Like "pain", therefore, "suffering" too has both conceptual and factual use in statements in which they figure prominently. The foregoing example of the independent use of "suffering" as a state of affairs in a statement is not enough to counter Trigg's assertion that the concept "suffering" may be meaningfully used with at least a reference to 'pain-experience', if not the concept "pain".

Let us consider the statement of Jack Beompard. He says, "suffering may be *defined as* the *experience* of organism in a situation that involves physical and mental pain, usually attended by a sense of loss, frustration and vulnerability to the adverse effects".[19] It is clear that those who want to have a strict definition of "suffering" normally refer to pain experience and to the subjective emotive states. The subjective elements in the definition are clear. Hence, even a definition of "suffering" may not be possible without reference to pain phenomenon; however, it is clear that such definition, if at all needed, must be *causal* in nature. The ostension of "suffering" and the ostensive definition of "suffering" however may not be possible because like "pain", "suffering" cannot be shown or produced *per se*. We may produce unpleasant situations or conditions resulting in unpleasant sensations and thus pain experience as also the state called "suffering", but we cannot produce suffering, the thing we have not seen before. Hence, "suffering" appears to be like "pain" not perceptually presentable and yet these abstractions are perfectly meaningful and they are differently used. To learn the use of this abstraction called "suffering" it is not necessary that we kick or prick etc.; no body does that really to teach the uses of these concepts. We learn when we ourselves are affected by unpleasant pain experience or when we suffer. We learn also when we go through the English language usages. The definition of the concepts "suffering" is thus not needed in physiology in relation to pain experience, the concept may be meaningfully used to make it clear what the abstraction stands for. In so far as suffering is taken as a state of affairs, in physiology, there is no way but to refer to its genesis.

I have just stated that accompanying pain-qualities are not needed for classifying different kinds of suffering, for as I have said it is no use talking about "pricking suffering" and so on. Then is it true that even though suffering in relation to pains is obviously related to unpleasant sensations at least, we may still not speak about qualities of suffering? How is then classification of suffering possible? Indubitably, we do speak about "suffering due to ignorance", "suffering due to poverty", and "suffering due to exploitation" as also "suffering due to intense burn". But such classifications of suffering are not classifications in the same way as we have seen in case of pain, these classifications stem out of pain-qualities, which is not the case when we consider suffering. Moreover, when we speak of "suffering due to..." we are in search of or we are in need of etiology of a state of affairs called "suffering" because, I have said, the genesis of suffering may be unavoidable in this regard. This may be true of pathological suffering, one may say, for instance, in case of "suffering due to intense burn", but is it true for cases like "suffering due to ignorance" and so on? What I think is that when we speak of non-pathological suffering, we still need to find a causal explanation for not strict classification of suffering, rather for the *clarity* of what suffering is *due to*. Such cases of non-pathological suffering even takes us to consider whether or not pain element must be prominent in expression relating to suffering. Because "suffering due to ignorance" if translated into more clear-cut terms as "one is in a state of suffering because he is ignorant of the Reality", one does not find whether or not there is a pain reference. It is difficult to make out whether or not the person concerned is in some pathological or psychogenic pain because he is ignorant of the Reality. We often tend to refer to such pains, which is said to be implicit in such assertions. But the vagueness rules out its confirmation. Nevertheless, the assertion is emphatic about a state of affairs, as the person who is said to be suffering from ignorance knows clearly what is the cause of such a state. However, it is debatable whether or not the person is an advanced psychopath. But there is no doubt *we find* the person suffering or we call him a sufferer not withstanding the fact that the sufferer likes it or not. The real issue is that without pain reference, we have "non-pathological" assertion about suffering (not a definition), which still begs a causal explanation. One may infer, however, that certainly in cases like these the broader significance of the abstraction is clear as it covers the 'whole man' and his 'personality', which understandably is in a state which is utterly disagreeable to him or to other persons. Now if pain reference may be absent, is somebody in suffering? We shall have this question here as it takes us to the psychology of suffering. Thus in the next section, the psychological use of "pain" and "suffering" will be considered.

"PAIN", "SUFFERING" AND PSYCHOLOGY

The psychological explanation of pain and suffering has no doubt revealed that in particular the word 'pain' is used to explain very many different psychological experiences from physical sensation to and including intellectual and emotional states. In the foregoing discussion, we have constantly been encountering the psycho-physical double nature of physical pain; this is fundamental to the *psychological explanation*. But we will not immediately indulge ourselves in the history of such explanation; rather, we shall first of all try to concentrate on the problem of definition, i.e. the possibility of a psychological definition of "pain", which may be aimed at clarifying the concept in use.

We find several definitions of "pain" in Psychology; one may be classified as predominantly physiologically based, which is a mix of the physical and the psychological reference, yet the former is more prominent. It goes on as: "by *definition* the *pain experience* must include pain sensation; associated phenomena, although important, are given secondary considerations".[20] It is extremely clear from the assertion that its purpose is to clarify the *meaning* of the term 'pain', and, therefore, a definition has been given unhesitatingly. The remarkable feature of this definition is that although it wants to clarify the meaning of "pain" to give it a physiological orientation, it has been clearly defined in terms of experience, which must have its origin in 'pain sensation'. Such assertion takes us to the more psychologically important factor, yet not discussed with great interest. The definition of "pain" in terms of experience makes it closer to the "public" avowal and not merely "private". The physical aspect of the origin of pain sensation has been carefully avoided to cover such pains, which are produced by no apparent stimuli. It thus covers the possibility of those pains in which indeed no pain is experienced. One good example is the 'phantom limb' experience. Such a definition may be due to the crisis-crossing of borders of physiology and psychology, in which, however, psychology is much interested in not leaving out the physiological basis. This definition is liked particularly because the definition of the concept of "pain" in terms of emotions and attitudes not only clearly tells us that in fact what is basic in pain experience is emotions and attitudes but the imperative presence of 'sensation' in any case is not left out. This definition is *causal* in nature as it traces the immediate genesis of pain experience in terms of pain sensations. The imperative used in this regard clearly states that "pain" ought to be defined in terms of sensation at least. There is no indication however that in this definition, *anything* has been defined in terms of other *things*.

Ripley provides an excellent definition of 'pain', which is more inclined towards psychological basis of pain. He writes: "pain is a *sensation* which is dependent on the *consciousness* of the individuals. The highest integrative centers participate in its integration. In addition to the common *origin* through *noxious stimuli* acting on peripheral nerve endings, it may *originate* through the activity of the individual and intellectual function of the *thalamus* and cerebral cortex, as in pain of the thalamic syndrome or in psychogenic pain".[21] This definition of "pain" is even better in its synoptic understanding. The psychological overtone is clear in the mention of pain being a 'sensation' depending on the individual's 'consciousness'. However, these need not be taken as synonyms of "pain", the latter half of the definition is a hurried addition about the origin of sensation and the status of the noxious stimuli. No reference is, however, made to mention the non-noxious stimuli. The attitude in psychological definition of pain to still hold back the neuro-physiological basis is clear. In this definition as well, with the growth of information owing to research in these fields, definitions are ever changing and ever growing. An absolute definition is thus a distant dream. This is a healthy misfortune. But unfortunately in psychological definition, the *causal* element creates a lingering sense of abstraction. Why *should* the definition of a concept beg causal explanation? The tendency appears to blur the conceptual treatment of "pain" to the mere phenomenal explanation. Should we define like that? Does it serve our purpose of definition of pain? These are questions to be left aside now.

It will be interesting to analyze the psychological definitions, the one by Hardy and others, and the other by Ripley. The former trying to accommodate under 'pain experience' the element of "public" more than the "private" as well as those cases of 'pain experiences' that appear to have physical stimuli, whereas the latter trying to accommodate sensations and consciousness of such sensations as basic, notwithstanding the noxious physical stimuli. The former tends to underplay emotions and attitudes with regard to pain experience, whereas the latter is not so outspoken. Let us continue with the first view. With regard to pain experience we ask 'where is the pain'? This is central question to the medical man concerned with pain experience.

As I have already said something about the public avowal of pain experience (the pain patients' avowal of pain to the doctor), it appears to be a kind of social contract, which unites patients and physicians. The physicians' expectations are about the quality, location and duration of pain. Now if the pain-patient cannot tell where the pain is, he is either taken to be a bluff master or an insane. Whether or not it is proper, the localization of pain plays a vital role for even the medical man, and this is largely due to *semantic* habit. Russell says: "when you feel pain in the leg that has been amputated, where is the pain? If you say it is in your head, would it be your head if the leg had not been amputated? If you say yes, then what reason have you ever for thinking you have a leg?"[22] Russell refers to the peculiarity of 'phantom limb experience' in which the experience of pain is without pain really speaking and the noxious stimuli and the immediate unpleasant sensation are all absent. Gravity of the problem lies in the question 'is phantom pain experience so private to the pain-patient that its public avowal is impossible or even if possible, need not be taken to be literally true, and if it be the case that it is not true, do we have any right to make assertions about pain-patients as we normally do i.e. they are insane or bluff masters?' Or do we say that it is a mistake to neglect the private element inherent in pain experiences, of which a glaring example is phantom experience? We may not limit this discussion to the phantom limb experience but to *causalgic* and *hyperalgesic* pain experiences. The former refers to persistent *burning pain* experience whereas the latter refers to pain experience owing to originally *non-noxious* stimuli or in which noxious stimuli produce more pain than they *normally* do. The former experience may be an aftermath of peripheral nerve injury, whereas the latter may be due to tissue damage or as a result of nerve lesions, In the latter case, the primary type often vanishes with healing process, whereas the treatment of the secondary ones may not be that easy, only temporary healing may cause some relief. But causalgic pain is often not relieved by any surgical means or other medicines. In both cases, however, in so far as some management has not become effective enough for cure, they resemble phantom limb experience. The basic problem being the private experience of pain which may not be or need not be made public or if made public, may cause several conception in the mind of the people.

In all these cases of pain experience, however, at some point of time, physical, nerve and tissue injury or damage have been sustained, the only problem is that long after that the experience may linger in the patient's private life, particularly in cases of phantom limb and causalgic pains. Then do we say that even if one had a leg no doubt (and he agrees) and that long after a painful amputation and horrifying experience of losing a leg, the pain is *in his* mind? If it is so, is it imaginary or painless pain? If such pains are essentially private and also imaginary, we have a natural tendency to classify some causalgic pains as different from these and call them *psychogenic pains*. I must remind here that "painless pain" is not the same as 'non-painful pain' because the latter, we have seen, is *pain which is not unpleasant*, where as the former is *pain wrongly so-called* because there is no pain at all. Many thinkers however consider this distinction of somatogenic and psychogenic pains artificial as also unnecessary.[23] These people have projected the descriptive aspect of the causes of pain in psychological or physiological *languages* as more important. Categorizing psychogenic pain as such is nothing but an effort by the medical man to become entangled in a discussion of how experience of physical sensations can arise from *mental events*. However, if we refrain from such thinking, it is better to say that such categorization is an effort to describe the pain experience in the *language of psychology*. Translating pain experiences (of a long part perhaps) into the 'language of psychology' is, as Graham says, a kind of 'linguistic parallelism' applied to a spectrum of the so-called psychosomatic disorders. Hence the current coinage that phantom type cases of pain experience are "psychogenic" in the sense of "due to psychological causes ", carrying with it the meaning of the "imaginary" and the "painless pain" and thus peculiarly private and *not* public, had better be replaced by another description of "psychogenic". It is "pain which is better described and understood in psychological than in physical language". This is a good example how the term "psychogenic" with the increment in information has been more clearly described and expectedly, in what manner this word has to *function* in psycho-physiological literature. This is not the meaning of the term or the definition of it, rather the analysis of its meaning. In this sense when we call phantom type pain experience as "psychogenic" in practice, we usually understand it as pain experience, the physical explanation of which should be replaced by an adequate explanation in psychological terms. If we follow this, the integrity of the patient's pain experience is restored and we do not say that the pain-patient is "imagining" his pain or that it is not real or that it is not really pain or that his private experience has made him a neurotic. What is interesting is to notice that in all cases of phantom type pain experiences, which are allegedly private and misleading, because the person is neurotic, we have to understand the *meaning* of "pain", i.e. we have to further analyze the meaning in this context. The first level meaning of "pain" is "pain as a symptom", which the phantom limb type represents, and then we come to the second level of meaning which is communicative in which pain is a form of interpersonal behaviour used as a means of soliciting help. These two levels of meaning of "pain" are important for a medical man where as the third level, which is *symbolic*, is also important, for it covers passive-aggressive behaviour via pain complaints. The first two levels of the meaning of "pain" project the private and the public elements of pain experience. It will be really difficult for us to divorce them from each other.

Let us come back to Russell. He maintained that bodily feeling, whether painful or pleasurable, may be considered as both public and as private data. According to him, all scientific inquiries have treated them as public data and have approached them accordingly, from the 'point of view of physics'. The best example of this approach to bodily feelings, especially pain, is to be found in medicine, physiology etc. He complains that in these sciences a tendency to overlook the private elements of pain experience with regard to the purpose of informing other persons about such experience is clear. If we follow this, he argues that the notions of "physical pain" and "mental pain" become meaningless. What we have seen thus far provides enough ground to say that Russell's way of speaking may not be safe either. It is desirable that we limit ourselves to find out an adequate explanation, either physical in terms of psychological or *vice versa*.

Gilbert Ryle argues against the sharp distinction between public and private elements in pain experience. The argument rests mainly on Ryle's view of the nature of "sensation". Ryle thinks that having sensation is not the same as identifying any object or a stimulus it is thus a source of providing data for experience which is very much personal and private to the person no doubt but to call it public is needless as the same sensations cannot be identified and detected like things or episodes by others. But we have been talking about the public avowal of pain in terms of pain-qualities in which the crucial factor is not merely "sensations" rather it is "experience". The problem is not whether or not private sensations are reproduced publicly, rather the way the publicly produced experiences are to be interpreted and understood. We can do it in both ways, finding out an adequate psychological or physical explanation. In so far as phantom experience is concerned, its being private or public is all misleading, the best way is to know how to interpret such experience, in what terms to say so. If we do this, the meaning of "phantom pain" becomes clear. Now, if we attempt to search for an adequate psychological explanation of so-called psychogenic pain, we find many explanations according to different tones. This does not interest me for the present purpose. What interests me more is that "pain" in the context of "phantom pain" and even persisting "causalgic" and "hyperalgesic" pains has a dual or antithetical meanings. "Pain" may signify that this part of the body is lost or it may signify just the corollary, the body part hurts, and, therefore, is present. This paradox of an antithetical meaning of "pain" for the *ego* reminds of Freudian theory of the psychological significance of the anti-thetical *meaning* of primal words like "pain". But the anti-thetical meaning of the concept "pain" and the implication that one who uses pain in an anti-thetical manner, uses "pain" in proper contexts is a neurotic, is serious. The anti-thetical uses in real life situation has to be particularly evaluated by the medical man in psychological terms and not physical. There is no doubt that such patients are send to psychologists and psychiatrists by either neurologists or surgeons. This is not a hindrance to an adequate understanding of pain-patients and pain avowals.

Getting back to Russell's anxiety to give meaning to "physical" and "mental" pains even though the sharp distinction between the private and the public elements in pain experience is not to be overplayed, as was done by Russell. We may say that the crucial factor in this regard is the "emotional" component, which is usually a part of the pain experience. I would like to recall what I have said before about 'physical pain' in particular. When we talk of such pain, we are talking of a sensation with a particular quality. We have maintained that the genus of what we call pain sensation covering bursting pains, cutting pains and so on, there is something in common other than that we usually dislike them. But having these sensations does not constitute the *whole experience of pain.* The whole experience of pain that coagulates the physical and the mental pains does not depend on the mere presence of the sensations but in the *emotional* factor. In fact, mental and physical pain each involves the *same* emotion of pain or distress, but the type of the 'object' they take differentiates them. With 'mental pain', the distinction between emotion and 'object' is far more clear-cut than in the normal experience of 'physical pain'. The distress we feel at the loss of a relative or a friend is quite a different kind of thing from the loss of a relative or a friend, which we certainly do *not* feel. A sensation of pain, on the other hand, is not so different from the distress we feel at it. Both are experiences of a person, and it is reasonable to suppose that if both occur simultaneously, there will be no clear boundary between one and the other. This has led many to assume that when one is in pain, there is only one experience. With this, the paradox that pain appears to be both a sensation and an emotion arise. The argument is that pain is a sensation in so far as it can be localized and has its origin in a stimulus, and it is an emotion in so far as it disturbs one and makes one think of it as bad in some way. This paradox is removed the moment if two strands are separated, and we realise that the usual experience of pain involved both a sensation and an emotion directed at it. This is the second point, which was not so clearly focused in the so-called definitions of pain, the reason was that the definitions may not tell us these things, they often miss a number of points. The causal definition in particular may miss these points as knowing the genesis of pain experience synoptically is not to know pain experience itself.

It is important to notice that the concept "pain" fuses many components, which may be expressed in various ways. If it fuses the private and the public feelings and avowals, emotions and sensations of feeling, the physical and the mental, then it coagulates dualities into unity. Brentano strongly suggested that in pain, such fusion is easily noticeable. It may not be an imperative to literally follow what Brentano says but what is indisputable is that the distinction between emotion and sensation can become very blurred. Wittgenstein also denied that emotion and sensation could be cleared in whole pain experience. He said that pain behaviour in this sense might be taken to be behavioural manifestation of distress, as 'the expression of sensation'. The word 'expression' in this context is not the same as 'expression of emotion'. Yet, those who have been confused with the use of the word "pain" in physiology and psychology is due to the fact that ambiguity is not in the word itself but in its disposition to refer to 'simple' sensation and to the whole pain experience—the combined sensation and emotion. The ambiguity of reference may be really misleading in scientific literature and there is every possibility of a contradictory usage. However, as we have been maintaining, if "pain" basically signifies a "sensation with a particular unpleasant quality", the assertion may be straight enough and even true, but it does not take care of the whole pain experience—emotion and sensation combined. Hence, the above as we have been maintaining is still *not* the *definition* of pain which is satisfactory, nor is a satisfactory meaning of the word 'pain'. Again, we are sceptical about definition of "pain", but we shall again leave it aside. But the duality of pain does not rule out the occurrence of the different parts of the whole pain experience separately. The emotion of distress does arise with of course an 'object' of some kind. Such a case is often what we call "mental" pain, whereas it is possible to have sensation of pain in one that is not distressed by it. May be for this, we have in mind what we call "physical" pain. But the point is that when we speak of "pain experience", we speak of 'unity in duality". However, when we use "pain" as a concept, it may be a different story.

Using this concept in perhaps an eccentric manner is to speak of "the enjoyment of pain". Is this statement an embodiment of gross contradiction? Our normal belief is that "pain" is a "sensation which is disliked"; then the person using the above has to be first taught what pain is and then he would not speak like that. Unfortunately, we cannot perhaps teach the person what pain really is but we can teach him how to use this concept any way. But do we use this concept in any grossly mistaken fashion when we speak about, for instance, "the enjoyment of pain"? Do we say that the user must be a masochist? On the basis of our foregoing discussion, if we use the notion "pain" to cover the whole pain experience, then obviously it is difficult to see why "the enjoyment of pain" is a contradiction in terms. But we may argue that the emotive aspect in pain experience is one of distress, suffering and so on and not one of enjoyment. Hence, the user of "pain" in the manner of "the enjoyment of pain" is either not fully aware of how to use this concept and what it really signifies or one fully grasps this concept, and yet suddenly uses it *eccentrically*. At best we may find an excuse like, "the person feels pain, but reacts to it in an *abnormal* way". Then we find a way to say that it is perfectly intelligible for a masochist to enjoy a sensation of pain. Hence, the analysis of the meaning of a masochist's abnormal assertion from the psychological angle enables us to know that using "pain" that way may not be a nice way or even a desirable way. The use of the notion "pain" in any statement whatsoever does not only depend on the grammatical rules of constructing a statement or on the fixed lexical meaning that has been ascribed to it, it depends on many things. One is the *analysis* of the meaning of the notion as it is used in a statement either from the physical or from the psychological angles, whichever is adequate. Perhaps we could only in this way be able to know whether or not for a person who has grasped the notion properly and is not a masochist at all, uses this notion in the manner we have mentioned. This is not to say that any talk about such assertions is absurd because we may sensibly analyze the meaning of such assertions, rather it is not desirable for us to *use* the notion in that manner in a normal fashion when we have the basic idea of the notion. Basic idea of the notion amounts to not only "sensation", which may be liked, disliked and so on, rather sensations qualified with pain qualities, which are experienced by us and we express our emotions through various behavioural patterns. Thus, if the masochist for sexual reasons, inhibits extremely disagreeable pain and yet shows faint signs of behavioural dislikes, the masochist cannot be said to have enjoyed pain but the masochist's psychic condition is extremely abnormal. It may be reasonably understood that the masochist may speak of enjoyment of pain but this needs care as well. It will be thus extremely harsh on our part to disregard the several interesting uses of the concept in physiological psychology. Sauerbach and Wenke says, "Age-old human experience findings, its expression in linguistic tradition tells us exactly what modern physiological psychology has arrived at its own way. The word 'pain' expresses that 'unity in multiplicity' which is characteristic of the emotional reality of pain itself, and it presents itself to us at every stage of human experience in constantly differing forms[24].

Much of the confusion about the term "pain" is due to the historically important theories in psychology. We had a glimpse of it so far in the forms of behaviouristic and holistic theories about pain experience, pain expressions and the use of the terms. To know more about the use, we have to trace the history further. *Logical behaviourism* for instance, begins with an interesting idea which emerged in our discussion earlier on, i.e. about the *ostension* of pain or to produce something sensibly when we want to know what "pain" means. The risky effort attempts at showing that 'mind-word' like "pain" are not taught by showing examples of things as we do in case of teaching 'red' because one cannot point to a standard pain. The only way is to point to some piece of behaviour and to ask to compare the feeling somebody is having with this one. If two feelings have identical quality, then your feeling is legitimately called feeling of *pain*. But in that comparison, can I have exactly that feeling which the other person has? Obviously not, and, therefore, to say that the *intension* (connotation) of the word "pain" is a certain 'quality' which I know from my own case must be wrong. But the behaviourist may say what I know from my own case is *not* the intension of the English word "pain", but only that I experience the *referent* of the word. Hence, the referent of the word 'pain' is a piece of pain behaviour no doubt. But what is the intension of "pain"? To speak of the intension of the word "pain" is problematic because knowledge about this matter is ever growing and as such we may not have an ideal definition by connotation. The logical behaviourist may prefer to call it a *cluster concept*, i.e. the application of the word "pain" is controlled by a whole cluster of criteria which are essentially *synthetic*. The result is that there may be *no* satisfactory way of finding the exact meaning of "pain". We may try a synonym or say that it is a feeling accompanying a pain-quality or something else, but unfortunately we do not have the meaning of "pain". The behaviourist would however, say that "pain' is a cluster concept no doubt but it stands for a *cluster phenomena*. Is this the case? What the logical behaviourists want to say is that we may *explain* the *meaning* of the word "pain" by referring to overt behaviour, but what *we mean* by pain is not the presence of a cluster of responses but the presence of an event or condition that normally *causes* those responses, We have seen before that in the event of the ostension of pain *per se*, what at best many scientists do is show or produce the cause of pain eliciting sensations. This may be partly true, as pain is not the only stimulus or cause of pain behaviour, but only one of many. But is it acceptable that what we mean by "pain" is but the cause of pain and what we mean by "pain" is *not* clear when we talk of responses? Certainly 'pain talk' would not be translatable into 'response talk' because "I have pain" means "I say such", are not one and the same assertions. Following that it seems legitimate to say that the *effects* of pains (i.e. behaviour) are not the same as the *causes* of those effects (i.e. what I mean by pain). Hence the possibility of 'pain-talk' does not necessarily presuppose either 'existence of pain' or 'pain responses' but it may be talking causes of pain when we want to convey what we mean by "pain". Causal explanation is thus an imperative. It will be very difficult for the scientists to reject this because as we have seen that one cannot sensibly talk about pain without refering to its genesis. But again one has to notice that one can define or talk about the meaning of "pain" without any such reference. Nevertheless, we have also seen that when we talk about pain or pain experience, more clearly, we *ought* to talk not only about its genesis because that will be leaving out other *components* that make the talk possible as well as more adequate. Such talk leaves behind the scar of 'mind-body' (the "physical" and the "mental") duality which is basic to the behaviourists and which we have tried to 'fuse' in the 'unity' of "pain". It is thus difficult to accept that 'mind-talk' or 'pain-talk' is a logical construction out of 'response-talk', and that 'pain-talk' is reducible to 'cause-talk'. But there is no doubt that "pain-talk" covers all these 'talks'. But what if we imagine a peculiar world in which even 'talk of pain' has been suppressed? Hilary Putnam in an essay[25] imagined such a case to show that despite the possibility of a *private* way of *thinking about* pain, knowing that this abstraction is sensible enough to be used that one may use it to convey an intolerable situation of unpleasantness, one may *not* necessarily avoid or admit to *having pains*. Such suppression leads to pretension not to know to what it refers. Then what the logical behaviourists would argue, Putnam says, is that, if pains are logical constructs of our behaviour, then it is perfectly legitimate to imagine such cases of not having pains because behaviour reflecting them is totally absent. This amount to saying that some people do have pains, and they know perfectly well that they have pains but as they do not show pain behaviour, they do not have pains. This fantastic imagination of the logical behaviourists is what is repugnant, says Putnam. Hence, the translation of "pain-talk" into "behaviour-talk" is false. The logical behaviourists are also mistaken in so far as they think that pains analytically entail certain kinds of behaviour because from the statement 'I have a pain', it *no* behavioural statement follows. Hence, behaviourist attempts to show that in imaginary cases of suppression of pain for instance, the meaning of the word "pain" may significantly change because unlike its ordinary meaning, "pain" ought to be used to refer to a 'pain behaviour' only and not otherwise, is refuted. Using "pain" in one way or the other is not to change its meaning. 'The behaviourists' account should be thus refutable on two grounds, 'unreasonableness of linguistics' and 'unreasonableness of scientific method'.

Leaving aside logical behaviourism, let us return to the materialists. This will give us an opportunity to upstage the linguistic and methodological critic of the causal theory, which is basic to them. The materialists base their argument on a philosophical intuition that "mental" phenomenon are really a species of the "physical" since physiology is the strongest support for that claim, whereas drawing blood from contrary intuition, the logical behaviourists hold that mental phenomenon is essentially non-physical, psychology is the strongest proof for such claim. The contrary claims with regard to pain are that inciting pain cannot be a physical phenomenon nor can it be a mental phenomenon. We have been dealing with the problems involving the behaviourists account so far, what is crucial now for further discussion is to recall that any claim the behaviourists make is really a claim not only about pain phenomenon, but also about the reference to the notion of "pain". The linguistic turn of this matter can be extended now with the regard to the materialist's claim that 'pain events' are in fact, 'physical events'. We could now say that the notion "pain", which is a scientific notion, ought to have a clear physical reference, otherwise its meaning is not clear. As such "pain" would have as its meaning certain physical phenomenon. Thus, many materialists hold that for the general term of classifying a mental state called "pain", we ought to have an identity statements in terms of some general description of a physical state, supported by physical (or physiological) facts, for instance, the excitation of C-fibers owing to certain stimuli[26]. But the materialists have to agree that if this be the case then although "pain" and "the excitation of C-fiber owing certain stimuli" have different meanings, their identity is supposed to be contingent, not *a priori.* Now if pain and the excitation of C-fibers owing to certain stimuli are identical and yet have different meanings, then, the identity statement must be necessarily false. This criticism is very common against what materialists hold. But many materialists insist that contingent, non *a priori* identity statements are sometimes true and certainly known to be true, of which, 'Water is H_2O' is a good example[27]. However, some modern materialists find an excuse in the assertion that identities are "theoretical". Hence, for theoretical reasons if we identify two terms whose ordinary rules of usages are so different, it is not 'strict identity' we are talking about, otherwise, the fact that some "pains feel vaguely cold" would imply that 'some C-fiber excitements feel vaguely cold,' which is obviously not the case. Thus, some of the modern materialists are at pains to find out whether or not it would be reasonable in the light of current physio-psychological discoveries to change our *linguistic convention* to say that without any self–contradiction, "pain" is "the excitation of C-fibers owing to some stimulus". The real issue is the reasonableness of the adoption of a new linguistic convention to identify (at least at the "theoretical" level) these two expressions. We may call it an issue of "linguistic choice". But this is a hopeless attempt at hiding an apparent mistake the materialists have already made, i.e., pains (phenomena) simply *are* the excitation of C-fibers owing to some stimuli and as such, although the physical and the mental are cleared dimensions, in so far as pain is concerned, it is explainable in terms of excitation of C-fibers etc, i.e., in terms of physical. Hence, the "mental" is really the "physical". In fact, the face saving attempt of this basic materialistic claim is distorted by such modern efforts. Nevertheless, I have called this an explanation and not definition because explanation of 'pain phenomena' in terms of excitation of C-fibers etc. or replacing one term by the other is no definition really, but as we have seen that in so far as materialists try to clarify the meaning of the notion "pain" in terms of excitation of C-fibers etc. it may be called a definition which is causal in nature, and as we have seen, there are obvious difficulties in accepting this as well. But to return to our discussion, if we go along strictly with what basically the materialists want to claim about pain (phenomena) is that some identity statement like "pain is excitation of C-fibers owing to some stimulus" is necessarily true. Following that, since excitation of C-fibers etc. is a *composition specifying term* that names a kind of physical phenomenon, there could be no pains in any possible worlds in which there is no material stimulus. Moreover, it has to be further defended that it is impossible for there to be a world in which some excitation of C-fibers is there without a pain being felt, To attempt at defending these demands, materialists have to fall back on intuition, which may not be very desirable. Kripke in his paper "Identity and necessity" argues that although there is solid scientific materialistic defense in favour of identity of 'water and H_2O', there is hardly any in favour of identity of "pain" and "excitation of C-fiber owing to some stimulus". However, on the basis of information from physiology and psychology, what the materialists assert in the statement we have seen may be interpreted differently. In fact, it can be possibly shown that the problem, which the essentialist criticism and Kripke's criticism of materialism have, lies in fact that for them, materialism entails mind-body identity statements, which it does *not*. This also goes against the empiricists analsis of materialism that it syntactically reduces mind-statements from body-statements. Whereas the modern versions of physiological psychology, which is believed to be championing materialistic psychology, shows that mental and psychological states are *not definable* in physical terms. Mental events, states and processes, in particular differ from uncontroversial physical events, states and processes only in the particular arrangements or configurations of matter and material forces that constitute them and as such, as Boyd says,: "Pains are quite different from earthquakes; but the difference is configurational, not constitutional".[28] But, as we have seen, materialists' search for the exact physical causes of pain (phenomena) is not enough unless we go on meticulously describing the exact way in which the physical causes incite such and such sensations in us and further we experience pain. In this sense, the materialists may face an insoluble methodological dilemma in so far as "excitation of C-fibers owing to some stimulus" does not successfully lead us to explain the actual experience of what we call "pain". Does materialists have to offer any more in plainly physical terms to explain *the experience of pain*? This is often thought to be not defective but an unfinished methodological explanation of pain experience. Instead of the linguistic trifles, if we move into the methodology of pain, it will be difficult for us to maintain that the concept "pain" is explainable (if not definable) in either physical or mental terms. What is crucial is to notice that in physiological psychology any discussion about pain may be incomplete if we do not have an explanation that takes care of both these factors. This may, in turn, enable us to more adequate explanation of the notion "pain" as used in the modern scientific literature.

Many modern psychologists prefer to move away from the reductionism of both physicalism and behaviourism and advocate *functionalism* with regard to the resolution of the problem of "pain". However, 'functionalism' is stranded in mystery owing to the variety of its user in psychology and philosophical psychology. In one sense, 'functionalism' stands for a theory according to which a system may be decomposed into component parts, each having importance and each contributing to the system according to their capacities and are thus integrated with one another. In this sense, functionalism is a kind of holism that tends to coagulate both behavioural and mental components involved in the explanation of pain. Robert Cummins, for instance, supports this theory (Cf. "Functional analysis" in Ned Block edited, *Reading in philosophical psychology*). If we follow this, then there is hardly any reason for thinking that pain can be explained either in materialistic or behaviourist terms, but what is crucial is the involvement of *both*. Apart from this, we have metaphysical functionalism, a modern variety, and more closely followed these days. Metaphysical functionalists are not concerned with how mental states account for behaviour, but rather with what they *are*. They hold that mental states are in fact functional states, meaning thereby the clear avoidance of mental states being reduced to either physical or behavioural. It is thus concerned with mental state *types*, not tokens. It is concerned with *pain* and *not* kinds of pain. Metaphysical functionalists gladly agree with the physicalists that *particular pain* is a physical state or event, and for each type of pain feeling organism, there is a single type of physical statement which could be easily seen in that type of organism. Nevertheless, the functionalists disagree with the physicalists in that what is common to *all* pains in virtue of which they are pains is not only a type of physical state of organism. Similarly, metaphysical functionalists would agree with the behaviourists that a particular pain is a behavioural state or event and yet disagree that pain *per se* is *not* that. The functionalist says that what is common in calling something "pain" is that it is a functional state. Thus, the functionalists' disagreement hinges on the *metaphysical* without being ontological. Metaphysical functionalists characterize mental states in terms of the causes of those states. Hence, they would like to say that pain might be characterized partly in terms of its tendency to be caused by tissue damage owing to noxious stimulus, by its desire to get rid of it and by its behavioural patterns to isolate the painful part from the noxious substance. Hence, explanation of pain demands care for the genesis, management and behavioural reactions.

Any way, the functionalists' attempt at putting isolated factors together in the explanation of pain faces a setback when their minds divert towards the relationship between functionalism and physicalism, because their basic adherence to genesis of pain cannot but rule out the physical completely. It is due to this that different kind of functionalism surface. Many functionalists, like J.J.C. Smart, believe physicalism is probably *true*, whereas others, like Hillary Putnam, hold that it is probably *false*. Such an odd disagreement is mainly due to ambiguities in 'functionalism' and 'physicalism'. We can dispel the composition by just making in clear that the dispute is really whether or not pain is to be treated simply as a kind of physical state. Those who agree have no hesitation in accepting that physicalism is *true* and indeed they are quite right because the phenomenon of pain feeling and pain experience does invariably relate itself to physicalism, the account provided so far by the sciences may not be absolutist any way. However, if we consider the concept "pain" and think about qualities that make "pain", real "pain" we have every reason to doubt the physical account or even the behavioural account. In this sense, to negate physicalism appears to be correct. I have maintained that "pain" as such can never be "noxious eliciting specific disagreeable feelings". To know about "pain" one needs is know many more things. Alas, metaphysical functionalism too may fall short, because it does not really show great interest in the different ways in which the concept "pain" may be used and meant. To delve into what "pain" really is and to reach the domain of "functional state" is not to reach the complex, intricate and interesting domain of the uses of the concepts and its meanings.

One may not find too many things within the terms of explaining "suffering" in psychology because the main interest is twofold, 'the phenomena called pain' and 'talk about pain'. Yet, in terms of trying to define "suffering" in psychology, we find Hiltner and Meninger saying: "Sufferings are such relatively complex and high level *modes of consciousness* as regret and anxiety and despair".[29] The interpretation of the notion in terms of subjective consciousness is thus clear. Again, I must say that although the authors intend to define the notion, the purpose is not to formulate its exact synonym, rather an explanation of how usually in psychology it is used. The common uses are clearly spelt out as 'modes of consciousness', namely, "regret", "anxiety" and "despair". However, in this explanation, the main frame of reference is such that its ostension is not possible. Nevertheless, its outward physical expressions may be present. Even the public avowal of such suffering may be extremely vague in both behavioural and linguistic terms. In that sense, this high level complex, subjective experience *resulting* from the whole involvement of human organism in feeling pain may be really difficult both to explain and understand. What human beings do or how they behave while in suffering may *not* be determinable in clear terms. What degree of throwing arms or snatching hairs expresses suffering from say an extremely complex variety like the loss of the dearest friend, is not easy to say or in what understandable human words could this be expressed is an enigma. Hence, one has to be in such mode of consciousness to know what it means. The meaning of "suffering" is thus not determinable in behavioural, linguistic and definable terms. One has to be in that state. But how can one is exactly in another person's state of suffering at different times or at the same point of time? Hence, all experiences of suffering are subjective modes, most likely not to be expressed or understood by others. Still people do use this notion to say that one suffers, not because the user of the notion has realized other suffering, but because when one sees expressions of pain in bodily or linguistic terms one uses this *broader notion* that perhaps covers what "pain" cannot. The common understanding is that transcending pain experiences, the person who undergoes or has undergone such an experience, is at an enduring modes of consciousness that lingers long although scars of pain diminish. With this *endurance of pain experience* in the 'mind of man', the whole personality is affected, which pain could not perhaps effect when it was at its hurting best, such level of consciousness that affects whole personality of man (not merely behaviour or his language use) is what is covered by this broader notion called "suffering". May be that *not* all pains have lingering effect on human personality so that they suffer, but we do not know really what is there in the Machine's mind, do we? So the temporality of pain, irrespective its intensity, we often use this notion so that it may cover the now and thereafter of pain experiences, involving not just the body and the mind but the whole person so to say, the person who is a social being, who lives, acts, influences, gets influenced and fizzles out. May be, in doing so, every moment the suffering element lingers, but how to get rid of it is another question of interest which psychology may approach from a different angle.

One is sure to believe from this that any behaviourist and materialistic claims of explanations of suffering may not be satisfactory at all because suffering is neither due to such behaviours initiated owing to pain aversion, nor it is anything necessarily explainable in terms of material configurations. The former takes us to the possibility of knowing that "suffering-talk" is not translatable in terms of "behaviour-talk" or *vice versa.* A person may be said to be suffering his entire life owing to *ignorance* of the Reality *not* because the person at least sometime shows a set of related behaviour like shaking his head vigorously, muttering an unknown name, weeping profusely etc. Even the behavioural patterns like going to the Himalayas, sitting under a tree, with eyes closed and postures erect not doing anything but concentrating on something unknown, are not what implies suffering from ignorance. Unfortunately nor is there any clear physical excitation that resulted in pain experience and further, deep suffering. Hence, "suffering-talk" *may not* be translatable in terms of "physics-talk" either, causal explanations are unsatisfactory. But can it be "pain-talk"? It appears to be if "pain" naturally goes along with "suffering". Is it the case that all modes of consciousness we have termed "suffering" are translatable in terms of "pain" or more clearly "pain experience". As "pain-talk" is neither purely mental nor purely "physical-talk", it may not be "suffering-talk" either even if the functional account is taken into consideration; and if in pain experience, the unity of the mental and physical is considered seriously. In the common parlance, however, pain experience is taken to be the *cause of* suffering and, therefore, the causal nexus of explanation is not given up really. This may lead us to another linguistic trifle, that is, does "pain-talk" imply "suffering–talk"? We may now face a situation when it is imperative for us to distinguish physical from mental suffering (if not metaphysical suffering); "suffering-talk" covers all these because it will be unnecessary to speak of "all sufferings are only mental". But the distinction may be going back to hopeless reductionism we faced before. How can physical suffering really mean what it is if it is not something related to modes of consciousness and thus to the mental level? Can we speak of "mental suffering"? How can we undesirably do so when the ghost is really in the Machine? But still the ghost may suffer not due to any physical suffering, which often is a literal cause of physical pain or bodily pain clearly speaking. Hence, we may speak of mental suffering without any physical accompanying facts. This may be further extended to cover "physics-talk" as well. The reason is that in the example of "suffering from ignorance" there is really neither physical nor physics-talk involved, and yet we perfectly sensibly use this expression. One idea may be that it is 'psychotic-talk' not 'mental-talk' because the suffering is clearly not normal. Is it so? It will be a fearful account of psychosis to cover all sufferings like these as psychotic because the whole gamut of metaphysics and religions using such expressions may turn out to be not only the garbage of the positivists, rather madman's expressions. It will be creating insoluble scepticism leading to the crunch of meaningful language use in which such expressions involving "suffering" has to be rejected. Let us then consider this expression as sensible and then analyze its reducibility to "mental-talk".

The question is not one of reducibility, rather intelligibility and interpretability of such sentences from an adequate angle. "X suffers from the ignorance of the laws of nature" and "X suffers from the ignorance of Reality" are really different expressions both involving the notion of "suffering". The first is meaningful only if we approach the *analysis of its meaning* from *empirical level* (which I think involves physics-talk) whereas the meaningfulness of the latter depends on the analysis of its meaning, from *metaphysical level.* However to have such sufferings is not to analyze these meanings; rather to *have* them at the *consciousness level.* Hence, "suffering-talk" does not imply "mental-talk" or *vice versa*, but "to suffer" is "to have" particular subjective modes of consciousness. But we have to still resolve the basic problem: Is "suffering-talk" impossible without "pain-talk"? It is perfectly possible only if we remember the nature of the "talk". Any "suffering-talk" like "X suffers from the ignorance of Reality" does *not* refer to "pain-talk", where "pain-talk" is what is taken in the modern holistic sense. It also does not refer to "pain-talk" in the reductionist sense either. Hence, "pain-talk" does not imply "suffering-talk" or *vice versa*. But we may still argue that 'pain experiences' are understood in holistic terms, but even then the former does not imply the experience of suffering owing to ignorance of Reality. The involvement of both the "physical" and the "mental" factors are not necessary for suffering experiences.

"Suffering" thus appears to be a much wider notion than "pain" and the consciousness of suffering not reducible to such and such pain experience. "Suffering" may be really the consciousness of *distress* rather than "unpleasantness" which is basic to "pain". But these are not definitions of these terms. As such, for suffering we need not refer to any pain-quality. The transcendence of suffering beyond consciousness is *not* possible although its explanation in purely mental or psychological terms can be transcended. Similarly its purely physical explanations may be transcended. Nevertheless, any naturalistic explanation as these may lead us to a causal nexus no doubt, and, therefore, to find an impending causal definition following these lines may be lurking around. It may, however, be seriously questioned whether such definitions serve any purpose in the understanding of what suffering *is* or how it *ought* to be used. But we leave this problem here.

As I have maintained that the involvement of suffering in our consciousness may not be transcended, we come to clarify it when we speak about neither the suffering of our selves nor participating in the sufferings of others but inferring suffering in perhaps all members of the nature; this also results in an *induction* which is very common in the existentialist and other writings. There is no restriction, therefore, to use "suffering" in sense of "The Ganges has suffered a lot due to the whims of man", "The soil suffers damage because we ruthlessly cut trees", "I am suffering from chicken pox", "The players suffered a humiliating defeat", "The saint suffers from the ignorance of Reality", "The student suffers from the ignorance of basics of algebra" and so on. It will not be wrong to speak of accompanying pain experience with the consciousness of suffering in some cases mentioned above, whereas in others both the "physical" and the "mental" factors are involved. Still, we have cases when no reference of pain experience is needed. However, we may ask, but what about the first two assertions? In those cases, neither do I suffer nor do others but members of the nature, namely, a river and soil suffer. Obviously in these cases, "physics-talk" is involved and the causal explanation prominent but can we speak of the 'pain experiences' and then the consciousness of suffering? It will be really difficult. Can we speak of suffering? It is difficult. But we do speak like that and these are not insensible. In such cases, we may be really 'inferring' suffering as we infer pain in case of animals. But animals may show some signs or symbolic expressions, which may help in such inference which the Ganges, and soil does not. Still we infer suffering in their cases, in cases of inert things as well and it is not peculiar that further induction may lead to assertion like: "The whole nature suffers" or "The whole nature is in pain". These are instances where "physics-talk", "our consciousness of pains and sufferings", "analogical inference" and "induction", all mingle. "Suffering" in this sense may be a notion which never loses its consciousness stronghold, and basic tonality of which is "distress". In this sense, there is nothing in language to prevent us from extending this notion beyond the human locus. Whether or not the whole personality is always affected is a hopeless question with regard to suffering, but it certainly carries with it a sense of distress that may suggest many things to us, for example, these inert things may have lost their basic structural properties. But can we speak of "a knife suffers at the whims of man" or "a whip suffers due to human cruelty"? What is wrong in the grammatical structure? Are these assertions insensible? If we refer to suffering of rivers, soil, hillocks and so on, why not 'knife' and 'whip'? All these assertions could really imply that these are loosely and childishly constructed sentences that speak about the damage of a knife or a whip; may be we understand the sense that a person has perhaps knowingly and wrongly used such things so as to damage its basic properties or qualities (of cutting, whipping etc). In this sense then we have better alternatives in our language, such as, "The knife has been damaged or blunted by such and such man knowingly" and so on. It is not a grammatical or linguistic mistake to write that "the knife suffered a damage" either because in that sense although "suffered" does not carry the basic tonality of "distress"; what has been used through a meticulous analogical inference (comparing the damage of our useful organs perhaps which are always at mercy), rather to convey the sense of extreme structural defects incurred by a useful object owing to an irresponsible human act. There is no problem however if we delete "suffered" and write simply "The knife was damaged". The use of "suffered" and its meaning has to be thus analyzed from *linguistic angle* now. Dragging physiological, psychological and philosophical explanations into all cases of knowing how English word "suffering" has been used and why it has been used like that is hopeless. This English word has many more peculiar linguistic usages than one. But what notionally "suffering" means in physiological, psychological and in other contexts depends on many factors we have been discussing. Nevertheless, its basic tonality of "distress" may be very important to remember and its consciousness is what is crucial.

Our discussion might have revealed the possibility of talking about "non-painful suffering", which is however not "pleasant" suffering. If "suffering" does not inherently carry the sense of "distress", can we speak of "pleasant suffering" and even "enjoyment of suffering"? Are all "distresses" not "unpleasant" and, therefore, if "suffering" amounts to distress at least, is it not "unpleasant"? If it is, will it be adequate to speak of "pleasant" suffering and also "enjoyment" of suffering? This is a debatable issue and if we have in our mind cases of Super Yogis who teach us how to live *in* distress and live *with* distress and yet *not* show the slightest blink of unpleasantness in terms of "talk" and "behaviours", then is it true that we find distresses pleasant or is it that whether or not we express distress, it is there very much, of which no machine may have any record. We may record "pain spikes" in pain situations recorded by machines, but how to measure or record distress and associated mental and physical reactions, particularly when we have Super Yogis? One way is to say that for Yogis, "suffering" is never "distress", it is a "pleasure". Therefore, for Yogis at least, we may speak of "pleasant suffering". I fear it is not the same as "enjoyment" of suffering, for then the Yogi is *not* 'Yogi', he may be nevertheless a 'bhogi' (gross enjoyer), or much worse, a 'rogi' (abnormal person in this context).

We have seen that "suffering" being basically a mode of consciousness, the basic tonality of which is "distress", it is not merely a state of feeling pleasure or pain, but is much wider than something that affects the entire personality of man. Hence, "pleasure" and "unpleasantness" may not be necessarily seen to go along with "suffering". The notion may be perfectly sensible without relating it to these feeling states. Hence, for a yogi who tries to or learns to live in suffering and with suffering, yet it does not affect his personality in the least, the 'yogi' is not 'pleased' or 'displeased', his level of consciousness is such that suffering has no accompanying modes of behaviour. For him suffering is there no doubt, that is, he accepts that he is conscious of such a state of affairs and as such in distress, but then, he is neither pleased nor displeased with it because he has learnt not to link it to such feelings. A state of "distress" is thus most likely not a state of being pleasant or unpleasant because one may inhibit such feeling to enter into consciousness. Can one *inhibit* suffering, yogis so to say? Perhaps *not* because people like yogis learn how to inhibit suffering because that mode of consciousness is perhaps beyond control so as to be inhibited. Ordinary people live in suffering and learn to inhibit, to go pale in unpleasure or to blush in pleasure, for ordinary people are not Yogis. However, suffering with its inherent property of distress affects their whole personality, and not merely is the ordinary man conscious of it, he may be easily linking it to pleasure or unpleasure. An ordinary person, for instance, may find some pleasure out of the fact that he suffers a lot during his research work, whereas at the same time, despite all suffering, it may be quite unpleasant that he is not getting the desired result. From these two cases we could infer that it is both possible that with "suffering" there may be no accompanying feelings of pleasure or displeasure and there may be such feeling strongly present. It demands how the consciousness of suffering has been linked to the inhibitory management of feelings like pleasure, pain etc.

"PAIN", "SUFFERING" AND SOCIOLOGY

Apart from psychology, sociology pays great attention to the problem of 'pain' because person's physical pain is not simply warped in the existing person's mind or his solipsist world, it tries to be *public,* and when it does so, it affects others, the fellow beings and society as whole. Not only this, the person's existence itself becomes problematic as several social and political stress factors tend to crunch the person in pain. Thus, in-pain person and his finding a voice on the one hand and the socio-political and perpetual complications on the other hand are related, for that reason, it is not out of the way to expect sociology (particularly existential sociology) to be interested in this matter. The readers are perhaps aware by this time that I will not unnecessarily indulge in finer details that sociology offers; rather concentrate on those that demand philosophical reflection.

Physical pain is one of the most interesting feelings to a sociologist because they believe it to be basic to life. We have seen that as per medical science for most physical pains, we can have definite causes and that we can manage to either prevent or cure pain. We have also seen that for some physical pains, finding a definite cause and preventing or eliminating it is not so easy and the situation is worse with "mental" pains. Hence, pains continuing for a long period and affecting the whole being as such change our lives, our views of medicine, medicine itself and even our body images. Pains have thus great personal and sociological ramifications. The problem is no less complex and disturbing when *another person's* physical pain is experienced. Thus, when one speaks about "one's own physical pain", one might almost appear to be speaking about two wholly distinct orders of events. The reason is that a person effortlessly experiences *his pain* which experience is not so effortless of the one existing outside his body. Even if a person grasps the pain of others, it may be 'fictitious' and not 'real'. For an in-pain person, pain is "having pain" and for an onlooker, who hears and sees the person, knows about pain with some "doubt". In the existential situation, therefore, a person's pain is in the midst of something undeniable and something not conformable. More distinctly, pain is also *unsharable* in the sense that one person's experiences of pain are unsharable. One reason for this may be language itself. Virginia Woolf writes, "Let a sufferer try to describe a pain in his head to a doctor and language at once runs dry"[30]. This is not peculiar to English speaking people, but to all language users. Prolonged and chronic pains do not only resist language but also destroy it, it surpasses language to upheavals of cries and sounds, which may be historically prior to learning languages. This is not to say that no variation in pain expressions can be seen in cross cultures and languages, but the clarity persistently lacks.

The shattering of language is thus basis in which we consider an existential being in pain, of course in relation to others. This exceptional character of pain is understandable if we realize that our habit to recognize all interior states of consciousness being regularly accompanied by objects in the external world may be healthy because once we react to physical pain, unlike any other state of consciousness, it has no *referential* context. It is not *of* or *for* anything. It is precisely because it takes no object that it, more than any other phenomenon resists objectification of language. Yet if we attempt at objectifying pain, we are at risk of inventing linguistic structure that will accommodate this area of experience normally so impregnable to language. Nevertheless, socio-linguistic researches[31] reveal that at least five groups of people are engaged in the process of 'creation' of pain language. We have individuals themselves in pain whose pre-language groans and cries surpass the level of destruction of language to project into speech the pain they experience or have experienced. The other group of individuals is better placed. These individuals are not so bereft of language, as are those in pain. They speak *on behalf* of those who are in pain despite the impediments to expressing another person's pain. Any way, the public avowal of private experience enters through at least four channels. Medicine is one. Ronald Melzack of 'Gate control' fame along with W.S. Torgerson has developed "McGill pain questionnaire" that is used and liked in many hospitals and pain clinics. Melzack's effort is to replace the conventional medical vocabulary ("moderate pain", "severe pain") by an arranged coherent group of "pain words" used quite often by the patients. Placing any such words in company of certain other commonly occurring words one coherent dimension of felt experience of pain is understandable. We may thus have "temporal", "thermal" and "constructive" groups merging together the "sensory content" of pain, whereas other may convey the "affective" and the "cognitive" content of pain. Interestingly, these words conveying the "sensory" content of pain are those which, we have seen, are basic to label "pain" as an unpleasant experience. These are the 'pain-qualities' like throbbing, burning, pricking etc. The choice of these words no doubt tells the doctor about the unpleasantness of pain apart from dimensions characterizing some disease rather than something else. But this does not forever solve the problem of pain or the problem of expressing pain in medical contexts. This may be nevertheless an external image of interior events. Another channel through which 'creation' of pain language is possible is the *publication of agencies* like Amnesty International which provide us with the transcripts of personal injury trials, the poems and narratives of individual artists. These enable pain to enter into a realm of shared discourse, which is more social than the patient-physician situation. Thus amnesty attempts at communicating pain language to those who have never under gone physical pain owing to torture so that they realize pain owing to torture and thus compel the international citizens to stop torture.

The fourth channel is the courtroom where not only visible physical injury but also pain experience and constant suffering are vividly pictured through *legal language* structured for the purpose of seeking justice. This is neither effective for prevention nor a cure for physical pain, nor useful in raising public voice in favour of one who is in pain, rather an effort (may be ineffective) to bring legal justice to one who has suffered due to physical pain inflicted by others. The lawyer may be thus a sincere person to create language depicting pain or speak on behalf of pain, not knowing however what it is like.

Finally, creation of pain language may be through *art*; literary art so to say. The literary representations of pain are perhaps the last attempt at being dismayed with how to express pain. Fictional analogies, a paragraph depicting a real life crisis etc. may bring out the pain language in much modulated style. Psychological suffering in particular, which is difficult to objectify may even find a place in literary creation through which it may be authentically expressed.

Nonetheless, objectification of pain experiences in all clarity and vividness is a near impossibility. The expression of physical pain in language remains an enigma. The difficulty results in *political* complications as well and a sociologist truly shows interest in this as well. A person who is incapable of expressing pain may be seen easily succumbing to another person's *power.* The person having that power may be the one who rejects pain, tends to overlook other people's voices, groans and moans, deconstructs language so overwhelmingly that body in pain is lost from everybody's sight unless some reconstruction takes place.

Further, verbal non-objectification of pain does not amount to simply something which is less easy to express than some second event, but something so closely impossible to express so flatly invisible that the problem flees the possibility of expression so that other phenomenon occupying the same environment will distract attention from it as if pain were not there. The result is that in cases of torture, the powerful agency politicizes the case in a manner that the physical pain which is perceptually veiled and verbally lost, stands as no ground at all in favour of the sufferer. The pain is thus something not there at all and the powerful agency may still go on with torture. War is another instance of political complication owing to the language shattering in cases of physical pain. Although the central activity of war is injuring and the goal of it is to injure and outclass the opponent, the fact of injury inflicting pain tends to be absent from the strategic political descriptions of war. The act of improperly *describing* torture or war, either intentional or unintentional, is thus made possible by the inherent difficulty of accurately describing any event whose central context is bodily pain or injury.

The sociological analysis of pain thus stands out to be clearly the induction of pain through noxious stimulus, the hopeless verbal objectification of the subjective attributes of pain and political complications due to language shattering. A moment's reflection shows us sociological explanation of pain having a close affinity with the physiological and psychological explanations already discussed at length. Clearly, sociological explanation begs the image of the weapon or wound or noxious agents who induce physical pain in exactly the same manner that we have seen. Explanation of pain is in fact explanation of pain phenomena and not a thing, the crux being the experience of a sensation called "pain", which brings the psycho-physical double nature of man at the center. The irresistible impulse to start from weapon or wound is due to the fact that the very word "pain" has its etymological abode in "punishment" reminding us that even the basic act of naming this most interior of events entails an immediate mental gymnastics out of the body into the external social circumstances that can be pictured as having caused the hurt. But sociological explanation of pain perhaps falls short of those pain experiences allegedly not owing to physical hurt or weapon etc. However, we have seen at the very outset of this explanation that the ostension of pain *per se* is ruled out as it is not a thing to be produced, rather an experience which implies that certain damage producing agent or agents might have elicited it and that it has far reaching verbal and political complications. Despite clear avoidance of ostension, the explanation no doubt enters the genetic account of pain, much advocated by physiology and psychology. The distinction of such an explanation rests on the fact that beyond the physical and mental setting of the existential being, it takes us to consider the actual position of the sufferer vis-ā-vis other persons, society and power. In doing so, interesting deconstruction and construction of 'language of pain' goes on, of which we had only a glimpse in the early explanations.

Accepting the verbal non-objectification of pain, what sociologists get is that first of all most *essential* aspect of pain is its *aversiveness.* Scarry says, "If to the person in pain it does not feel averse, and if it does not in turn elicit in that person aversive feelings towards it, it is not called pain".[32] Further, he says, "*pain is* a pure physical experience of negation, an immediate sensory rendering of "against" of something being against one, and of something one must be against". Even though it occurs within oneself, it is at once identified as "not oneself", "not me" as something so alike that it must right now be gotten rid of[33]. What Scarry says is not any different from what Trigg and other physiologists have said.

What the physiologists have in mind is not difficult to understand. They conceive a necessary *empirical* relation between "feeling averse" and "pain" and in that sense, generally speaking, with the experience of pain, aversion occurs; however, it is not that all cases of aversion are logically, necessarily, cases of pains. There is only an empirical necessity and there is possibly no *logical* necessity between "pain" and "aversiveness" because with the experience of pain other feeling may occur as well and that aversiveness may even seem to be absent at times. Hence, if pain is the *necessary* condition of "feeling averse", then it will be perfectly all right to speak of "If *no* pain, then *no* averse feelings" or "If averse feelings, then we experience pain". Scarry's assertion lulls us to believing that "pain" is the necessary condition of "feeling averse" because invariably when "pain" occurs, "averse feelings" occur or to say that if there is *no* averse feelings, then there is *no* pain. This is going too much with 'averse feeling', because what is *empirically* necessary is that "if there is averse feeling, what goes along is "pain experience" but to say that "if there are no averse feelings, then there are no pain" is not what the physiologists would say. Otherwise, the word "pain" loses all meaning without "averse feelings". This is not a happy situation as it may lead us to "averse feelings" being the exact synonym of "pain" or that "pain" may be defined in synonymous terms like that. Scarry's intention is clear when he provides a definition of "pain" (if he seriously meant it, of course). He takes "pain" as a "pure physical experience of negation". He is going along his basic presupposition that "pain" is *invariably* a negative experience (of aversion so to say). But for one moment, why it is a "pure physical" experience is difficult to understand because pain experience need not be merely "pure physical" as we have already seen. Hence Scarry, like many other physiologists, holds that genesis of pain must be explained in physical terms Yet, even if physiologists may be bogged down with such genesis, they do not always call it necessarily "purely physical" experience, because there are instances of absence of physical factors in pain experience. Moreover, sociologists may be right in thinking that pain is something which is not the corporeal being itself or something else, but something that troubles the self, acting negatively against it and it is desirable to get rid of such negative thing. The sociologists may be wrong in holding that "pain" is an embodiment of "pure disvalue" because the teleos of pain experience is key to the "against" it and to "get rid of it". One interesting question arises from the sociologists' position, i.e. if "pain" *elicits* "aversiveness", what does it signify? Does it signify that "pain" is the *cause* of "aversiveness"? If it does, is "pain" the *cause* taken in the sense of logical necessity or constant conjunction or sufficient condition? We have seen that both the physiologists and psychologists feel reluctant to call "pain" the *cause* of "aversiveness" and as such, "elicits" may *not* be taken as *cause* either in the sense of necessary or sufficient condition. It must be made clear that pain is not to be taken as cause in both the senses of logical as well as empirical necessity because "all pains elicit aversiveness", is not logically, necessarily true, and empirically speaking, "all pains elicit aversiveness" is not necessarily, verifiably true. But generally speaking, it is quite natural to empirically prove that "pain" does elicit a feeling of "aversiveness". This is clear when we use "pain quantities" to express our "aversiveness". Following this, the physiologists and the psychologists play safe by not speaking of "pain" being the cause of "aversiveness" in the sense of 'constant conjunction' because their constant conjunction cannot be established. Rather, *exceptional* cases may be easily found when pain and aversion are not constantly conjoined. I think this is perfectly wise because taking "pain" as cause in the senses of either necessary relation or constant conjunction will be prone to contrary instances far easily. Things are all the same when we consider "pain" as cause in the sense of sufficient condition because "if pain, then aversiveness" or "if no aversiveness, then no pain" will be a difficult alternative to accept, because *without* any distinct pain experience, we can well imagine "aversiveness". The problem is, what kind of pain experience could precede the averse feeling we have while taking stale food? Or if a holy soul feels no aversiveness while sleeping on a thorn bed, would it be that he is not in physical pain?

Sociologist like Scarry is caught on the wrong foot in so far as he may actually hold that "pain" is the sufficient condition of "aversiveness" at least. In his mind, "pain" as the cause of aversiveness, exactly in the sense of sufficient condition is lurking, for the words "elicit" and "not called pain" in Scarry's foregoing assertion, is testimony to it. Hence, according to Scarry, "pain" *must* be considered as a sufficient cause that elicits the feeling of aversion, which, however, I have said, is not proper to maintain.

Moving further along sociological explanation, we discover two more aspects of pain closely related to the first aspect. These are the *double* experience of *agency*, the *internal* and the *external*. In case of physical pain, the 'external' agency is the noxious stimulus, knife, pin and so on, which are said to be "against" the body. Whereas, the 'internal' agency is the body of the sufferer itself, which is "against" the whole existing being. Even if the external agents are absent, we may still *imagine* one such agent present and construct in our common usage pictures like, "knife like pain", "pinching pain" and so on, Hence, the very sensation of pain, is basic to pain experience, and the body of the sufferer itself is the agent that carries it. All this may sound too good but in sociology the urgency for having an external agency in pain is very much there. This may fall short of explaining the complex psychological pains in which the sufferer is hardly the self pain producing agent or there is any external agency so to say. There is no doubt that in cases of causalgic pain, the external agents are absent (knife that amputates), nevertheless, we do construct pain vocabulary in which mentioning external agents are common. However, it is not implied that therefore, the body itself (the amputated legs) is an agent producing pain. Rather, the very painful or traumatic experience may be the cause of pain. Here, the very memory of pain is the source of recurrent pain. In this sense, if we call the agent's mind "against" the agent or the mind to be an internal agent, we may have good reason for all that. Notwithstanding such belief, if we think that pain itself is a sensory rendering of "against", we may have some reservations because it will be wise to fix up this issue only after the success or failure of management of pain.

This focuses on another aspect of pain, namely, the conflation of the private and public. Pain experience, says the sociologists, brings with it all the solitude of absolute privacy as also the self-expression of the utterly public, which, however, has perhaps no sharers. The solipsistic and the public, the inner nourisher and the outer projector, the internal and the external of the sufferer get mingled in pain experience. But as we have seen, there is hardly any comrade who can share the inner or the outer of the suffering self. Nevertheless, the verbal objectification, however inept it may be, tries to bridge the gap and tries to prevent and /or cure, if not share the pain experience.

Still further, we have physical pain being able to destroy language, the power of verbal objectification, a major medium of self 's attempt at making the inner world public. We have seen something about it but here we have at hand something more. The sociologists believe that before the actual shattering of language of the sufferer, pain experience appears to monopolize language, i.e. the *mode of speech* becomes prominent. This is "complaint" or more clearly, "complaint speech". This becomes evident in case of chronic pain in particular. Eventually, in many deep and agonizing cases, like physical torture, pain deepens so much that the sound alien to learned language displaces the coherence of complaint. Pain thus may have no language in particular until any one undertakes serious reconstruction effort. What may be more interesting is to notice that even the body in pain may tell such stories as may be as vocal as speech, but it is difficult to understand all that.

Another element of physical pain, particularly that which is deep and agonizing, is that it shatters or destroys the contents of consciousness. Pain shatters not only objects of complex thought and emotion but also the objects of the most basic acts of perception. Pain may thus destroy one's ability to see, for instance. This is well projected by assertions like "blinding pain".

Yet another aspect of pain is its "totality", i.e. its total spreading in the entire body and mind, the taking over of the *whole personality*. This is again in agreement with the psychological explanation of pain. The physiologists agree with it. This totality is equally descriptive of felt-experience, particularly the chronic pain experiences. In prolonged and acute pain, the body begins to interpret all sensations as pain.

Finally, pain, as we have already seen, poses a stiff challenge to objectification. Even though the inner aspect of pain is obviously real to the sufferer, it remains unreal to public even through some accompanying visible body damage is there. Pain has thus a tremendous doubling and redoubling power of deobjectifying through lack of public acknowledgement and recognition. It thus grows in quantum proportions with all sorts of rejection and negation and the aversiveness of pain increases with it.

Something special could be mentioned about chronic pain experience because the sociologists hold that (a) 'monopolistic' speech which is "complaint speech" is fundamental to the avowal of chronic pain experience; (b) the objectification through such speech may be hopeless if not misleading as well and (c) such pain experience covers the whole personality of man. The last two points have been projected in psychological explanation as well. But let us now move a bit deeper into the understanding of chronic pain. The pain experienced from few diseases, complications, disorders etc. becomes *chronic* because it does not respond to conventional modes of treatment. Most sociologists thus believe that chronic pain is the one resulting from the failure of particular mode of treatment and not from special psychological reasons, for instance, when the apparent failure of medicine is taken as real failure or to believe that the medicine must fail because the pain is not really due to any physical factor, rather due to mysterious or metaphysical factors. Nevertheless, they say that chronic pain affects one's activities, social interactions, self-image and worldview. This is to cover the whole personality of the sufferer. A chronic pain patient's experiences of pain may thus have far reaching social implications because his personality and his behaviour affect society to a great extent. Society ought to take care of this fact. Moreover, we have to accommodate in this explanation such chronic experiences for which often *no* definable source of pain may be identified. But one thing is for certain, that is, in sociological literature, like the physiological and psychological literatures, the person having chronic pain experience or the person having prolonged pain is referred to as "sufferer". Hence, "suffering" has been largely used as a noun that covers not merely feeling states or levels of consciousness, but also a state of a person who may be distinguished clearly from others on social grounds, i.e. on the basis of the person's interaction with other people in the society. Any way, if we consider chronic pain as the one in which pain itself may become a disease and not just a symptom and that such pain need not be necessarily linked to failure in treatment or physical pain management, then apart from various reasons of such pain, its social implications become clear. It is, therefore, not a useful sociological venture to link chronic pain to cultural differences. The argument that culture determines a person's reaction to chronic pain is suspect because differences within cultural groups are greater than differences *among* cultural groups. Thus the linking of chronic pain to the patient's state of mind, his behavioural patterns and social implications may be more useful.

Once we relate the chronic pain patient to society as a whole, a group of people become immediately closer to them, in so far as relief or management is concerned, and they are the doctors. Yet, the perspectives are different, the patient is a nagging person whereas the doctor a silent mocker. The one who is more akin to take things physiologically and is less interested in the mind of man often tends to see these patients coming to them as those having 'ass-like' pain. But the frustration may be written large on their faces as often because they have no answer to such pains with the so-called painkillers and muscle relaxants. Hence, to brand pain patients as misfits, sociologically and medically, is only one hopeless way of looking at chronic patients. Of course, it is a great mistake to imagine that all sick people would fit into the rule-governed behavioural patterns conceived by the sociologists, because many sick people may be clearly beyond such expected. Hence, any sociological explanation of chronic pain in particular must consider, apart from the peculiar behaviours of sufferer, the emotive and situational factors. Thus in understanding chronic pain, the objective and the subjective aspects of pain experience have to be kept in mind. The subjective aspect in particular helps us to know the existential nature of the pain experience.

Proper sociological understanding of chronic pain may thus reveal that chronic pain is a bodily sensation that is *unique* to the *self*, much like feelings and emotions. It is experiencing of oneself that is not generally visible to others and in most of the cases its intelligibility is defeated, as its expression is vague. It is due to this helplessness that it is often patient's own decision whether or not to make *public* his personal feelings of distress and attempt to communicate a sense of his pain to others. Hence, a chronic pain patient may appear perfectly behaviourally just as we are, but once they decide to change the mode by objectifying such pain, the social ratio changes. The question of acceptance, understanding, sympathy, empathy all come into consideration. Public avowal or objectification of chronic pain is often due to the emotional support one expects from family and friends. The patient quite often is apprehensive that the pain's de-objectification may affect his relationships with nearest ones or may be he thinks that this will normalize his relationship. Such divulgence to doctors may be also when the patient is in danger of suffering beyond limit. He may widen the net more and more, may be he tells some of the neighbours, teachers and so on most because doing so is beneficial. Nevertheless, the chronic pains are kept secret when the self is the only audience, for several emotive reasons, fear, guilt, discomfort and so on. Thus chronic pain may be too devastating to deconstruct the self and relation with other selves because it is mostly de-objectifying and unshared.

In any case, the search for a cure although time consuming and financially burdensome is only one facet of chronic pain in the sufferer's life. The urgency to maintain his daily activities forces the sufferer to restore parity between his most personal feelings of distress and the expectations of the world around him. The existential nature of the self to become rather than be determined results in a continuous process of accommodating the private reality of pain to the public reality of identity, management and social interaction. This process is difficult owing to shattering of language and sharing problems as I have mentioned. As such, the sociologists agree, unlike what Talcott Parsons believes, other people cannot allow a chronic pain patient to depend on them until they recover because these people understand the health problems of the sufferer. In fact, the "sick role" of the sufferer can never be automatically granted in society. Kotarba writes: "The chronic pain sufferer, however, is stigmatized as being sick only when his overt activities justify that reaction this becoming of self is fundamentally influenced by his personal experience. With pain and only secondarily by the interactive evaluations of pain by others".[34] Yet, the interactive evaluation of pain by others may not be acceptable to the sufferer because that may destroy the self itself, for the individual would then have to negate to himself his personal and real bodily feelings. Although it will be very difficult to continually disregard the evaluation of others, particularly that of the doctor, but the basic relationship of the self to one's own body is primary. But the sociologists stress this verbalization and communication of pain, no matter how obscure it may be, has to be focussed. Thus symbolization of existential pain is socially useful and it is mostly based on interpersonal love. Sociologists would not like to speak of a purely sympathetic type of relationship mostly expected from those conceiving "ass like pain". It is empathy, which is more desirably empathy that conceals element of love in it. Hence, social interactivity and not inactivity leads to the real cure of chronic pain.

The sociological explanation of chronic pain thus comes closer to the realization that pain *per se* may not be necessarily thought of as elicited from physical stimulus, for the basic "inner" structure of the chronic patients suggests that the persistence of the feeling of pain itself is the *cause* of pain, i.e. chronic pain appears to merge within the body. As if pain were an *entity* in itself and not a sensation emitted by the body. Hence, the genesis of pain may lead to several factors, but genesis of pain is extremely important no doubt. What is most important is to conceive that chronic pain experience is first private, further public and when it crosses the existential boundary, all problems start. Yet, to resolve these problems, the social interaction and element of love, should rule supreme.

We have been constantly noticing the objectlessness of "pain" as pain is not of or for something. Pain is thus bereft of all referential contents and yet this may give rise *imagining*. Imagination is thus the state which sociologists take as strongly *anomalous* to pain. While pain is a remarkable state of objectlessness, imagination is remarkable for being the only state that is wholly its objects. Imagining is thus not a state inseparable from the objects of imagination. Hence, when one is imagining, imaginary objects appear before one's minds but while in pain, no objects material or verbal are before our minds. It is due to this that it will be extremely peculiar to think of knife as pain or pin as pain. There is no object called pain, of which we can speak about. Any genesis of pain experience, if it objectifies pain in something, is a great mistake. The ostension of pain *per se* and even the ostensive definition of the concept "pain" are thus ruled out. Pain is thus not by nature something that can be objectified.

Nevertheless, the objectification of pain or production of pain is, in the common parlance possible. But the possibility stems out of imagining. Although in imagining, as Gilbert Ryle says, there is *no* object. We ought to clarify that what he means is that there is *no sensed* object in imagining. Hence, it is impossible to imagine without imagining *something*. Imagining "unicorn" needs *no* sensed unicorns, the imagining is possible only when at least we imagine something called "unicorns". Now "pain" being objectless can it be objectified through fertile imagination, which does not necessarily need sensed objects for imagination? More precisely, can we imagine pain in such and such objectified manner? Yes, perhaps at least sociologists would believe that in work, pain is objectified quite often than not into sustained discomfort elicited by such and such noxious agents. Hence, objectifying pain through the imagination of noxious agents and /or pain-qualities is quite natural and they are inseparable components of human nature and pain language used by us. The image of the 'hurting things' or 'weapons' is thus common in the objectification of pain. Similarly, the typical modulation of descriptive words to an "as if" construction of pain language that may have a weapon on the other side, indicates how in our language we do attempt at imagining pain and thus objectify it. It is *not* a question of whether we should do like that or what we get out of that; for these questions lose significance in the face of the irrepressible human nature to do just that. More relevant questions may be, "should we define 'pain' in terms of those imageries?" What else do we get if "pain imageries" are taken to be valuable enough? Do we really know *about* pain or even if we do not know about pain, do we know how we imagine the existence of pain, something to be never sensed? Sociologists find no great interest in the *should* questions. They are concerned with unfolding what we people in society really do in the context of the avowal and objectification of pain. What they say is true only if we remember that imageries and objectification of pain nevertheless demand cultural, racial and other factors to be considered seriously.

As I have already mentioned, in sociological explanation, we hardly find any detailed discussion about "suffering"; nonetheless, it has become clear that the moment we refer to the "state" of suffering we are said to be in that state owing to pain, mainly physical pain. As such, our basic involvement with pain will be sufficient. What I have in mind is that, as such, suffering may end up in the same de-objectification and language shattering as is the case with pain, but instead of "as if" type of objectification, we are better placed in this context to explain the state in more lucid terms by referring to "owing to", "what happens when" and "how are we placed" etc. Any way, I would like to drop the discussion here to further analyze the ethical and the metaphysical uses of "pain" and "suffering".

NOTES AND REFERENCES

1. Keele, C.A. et. al., (eds.), *"Samson Wright's Applied Physiology"*, O.U.P., 1989, p. 4563.
2. Sauerbach, F. and Wenke, H. (Trans. E. Fitzerald), *Pain, its meaning and significance*, George Allen & Unwin Ltd., London, 1963, p. 102.
3. *Ibid.* p. 102.
4. *Ibid.* pp. 101–105. (The authors have enlisted the reactions of Leriche, August Bier, Zumbusch, Strimpell, and Charles Richet, who have contributed to medical literature by raising the issue of biological purposefulness of pain, particularly as a warning signal against health threat, and thus as a 'preserver of life'. Although their views differ widely in their evaluation of the purpose of pain, they agree in so far as pain has been taken as a preserver of life. However, contrary to these views of the authors mentioned, Auersperg also mentions the destructive value of pain signal. Whereas special mention of Rene Leriche is to present an extreme view that the limited and partial usefulness of pain is really useless. The authors remind us that one may object against the idea of purposefulness of pain because 'purposefulness' belongs to quite a different sphere, which Hartmann calls 'an organic' or 'psychological' sphere, and not 'inorganic' or 'physical' sphere. However, the authors are of the opinion that for the doctors, "whilst pain can be used diagnostically, sole reliance must not be placed on it. Thus it would be quite wrong to assume that because there is no pain, there is therefore, no disease" (p. 109). Taking clue from Hartmann,

may be, efforts have been made to supplement the physiological explanations from a psychological angle.)

5. *Ibid.* p. 101.
6. Merskey has provided this definition covering the epistemological along with the psycho-physical double nature of pain; it also classifies the meaning of "pain" in terms of a specific "experience". I have taken Merskey's definition from R.A. Sternbach's book *Pain-patients: traits and treatment*, Academic press, NY, 1974, p. 28.
7. Sauerbach P. & Wenke H., *Op. Cit.* p. 102.
8. Keele, C.A. *et. al., Op. Cit.* p. 102.
9. Hospers, John, *An introduction to philosophical analysis*, Allied Publishers, India, 1998, p. 28.
10. *Ibid.* p. 23.
11. *Ibid.* p. 57.
12. Keele, C.A., *Op. Cit.* p. 395.
13. Prof. C.D. Broad expresses his view in his book *Examination of Mc Taggart's Philosophy* and I have quote from R.Trigg's book *Pain and Emotion*, Oxford Clarendon Press, Oxford, 1970, p. 23.
14. *Ibid.* p. 28.
15. *Ibid.* p. 33.
16. *Ibid.* p. 145.
17. *Ibid.* p. 145.
18. *Ibid.* p. 149.
19. Jack Beompard's definition may be seen in M. Eliade (ed.) *The Encyclopaedia of Religion*, Vol. 14, Macmillan, NY. 1987, p. 99.
20. Hardy T.D. et al. (eds.) *Pain Sensation and Reactions*, Williams and Williams Co. 1952, p. 24.
21. *Ibid.* p. 169.
22. Russell, Bertrand, *Human Knowledge, its Scope and Limits*, Simon and Schuster, Inc. 1948, p. 176.
23. R.A. Sternbach in his book, *Pain patients: traits and Treatment*, *Op. cit.* pp. 20-21 writes: "following the suggestion of Szasz, we can do better by not insisting on classifying pain as psychogenic or somatogenic, but rather by seeing whether a description of cause in psychological or physical languages is more helpful. Merskey and Spear independently advanced the same view.
24. Sauerbach F. and Wenke H. *Op. cit.* p. 75.
25. Hilary Putnam's essay "Brains and Behaviour" in Ned Block (ed.) *Readings in the philosophy of psychology* (Vol. I), Methuen, London, 1980, is a thorough going critique of Logical Behaviourism and Materialism. In an example, Putnam tells us about behaviourist orthodoxy of translating all "pain-talk" into "behaviour-talk". He gives us the example of "Super Spartans" in "X-World" capable of suppressing all "pain-talks" and thus claiming of having 'no pains'.
26. The Physiological explanation of pain initiates from an injury which may induce pain and continue for sometime as the intensity of the nociceptive stimulus is

far above the threshold and capable of tissue damage. After receiving a nociceptive stimulus, two types of nerve fibers are stimulated, namely A and C types of nerve fibers. The former fibers are relatively thick and finely myelinated with a fast rate of conduction but the latter fibers are very thin and non-myelinated with slower rate of conduction. Nevertheless, the latter type of fibers is greater in number and pain sensation due to the fact that stimulation of nociceptive agents are felt at a much longer interval due to the sluggishness of conducting of C fibers. Pain sensation felt due to A fibers are thus called 'fast', whereas those felt due to C fibers are called 'slow' pains. Usually, the pain felt owing to C fibers stimulation is particularly unpleasant and is long lasting. It is thus called *pathological pain* and is not merely localized. Hence, in our discussion (as does Putnam) we have referred to pain owing to C fibers terminate at SGR or Substanatia Gelationosa Rolandi (the tip of the dorsal horne). It is from this junction the next order neurons arise and cross to the opposite form, the STT or Spinothalamic tract which reaches the thalamus, wherefrom the next order neuron arises to end in the sensory cortex in the parietal lobe. The pain-pathway is thus complete.

27. Hilary Putnam and Ernest Nagel in their early writings (1960 and 1965 respectively) supports the materialists' account of "theoretical identity". Cornman suggests cross-categorical identity. Feyerband and Richard Rorty also suggest that "identity thesis" is not really an identity thesis when we consider the issue of predicating mental predicates of brain states and physical predicates of mental states.
28. Block, Ned (ed.) *Readings in Philosophical Psychology*, (Vol. I), Methuen, London, 1980, p. 85.
29. I have taken Hiltner and Meninger's definition from John Hick edited *Evil and God of Love*, Macmillan, Basingstoke, Hampshire, 1985, p. 318.
30. Woolf, Virginia, *On being ill in Collected Works, Vol. 4,* Hartcourt, NY, 1967, p. 194.
31. One such socio-linguistic research into objectifying Pain through 'Creation' of pain-language has been conducted by Elaine Scarry, whose book, *The Body in pain*, OUP, NY, 1985, is remarkable in this regard.
32. *Ibid.* p. 52.
33. *Ibid.* p. 52.
34. Joseph A. Kotarba argues in *The Chronic Pain experience* in *Existential sociology* edited by J.D. Douglas and J.M. Johnson, Cambridge Univ. Press, Cambridge, 1977, p. 268.

2

"Pain", "Suffering" and Some Branches of Philosophy

"PAIN", "SUFFERING" AND ETHICS

Moving abruptly to some branches of Philosophy has a kind of urgency as if. "At the end of scientific explanations, the philosophical explanation should start", is perhaps loaded with some kind of urgency and a hang over of self-satisfaction cannot be ruled out. But I have another excuse. The sudden move is to unfold the uses and meaning of the words "pain" and "suffering" as found in the two branches of philosophy, viz. ethics and theology. This does not rule out many more interesting uses in different non-philosophical literatures, but to refrain from being encyclopedic, it is better we start with a philosophical discussion regarding these issues as found in ethics and theology. But one should be careful about nourishing any self-satisfaction like the one mentioned above or nourishing the idea that 'philosophy is the nursery of these concepts'. Nevertheless, philosophy does nurture these concepts within its vast literature. I have therefore, planned to devote the rest of the book to these oft used concepts in the philosophical literature. First of all, in this chapter, I shall concentrate on the ethical uses of these concepts. This is not merely explaining what different ethicists think about these concepts: rather in what ways in ethical discussion they have figured prominently and what these concepts signify. We may enter into the question of the possibility of satisfactory definitions of these concepts and consider the uses of these concepts in the sense of "motives of actions". I shall move further to consider the 'theological' use of these concepts. However, I shall leave out aesthetic explanations as I have already left out anthropological explanations. This chapter therefore, proposes to analyze ethical and the theological uses of "pain" and "suffering" and the meanings they acquire thereby.

To start the discussion, we first of all notice that I intend to speak about the concept "pain" as it is used in ethics. We shall thus concentrate more on "pain" in particular because "suffering" plays a second fiddle to the former in ethical literature. To begin with "pain", Nowell-Smith says, "words such as "pain" and "hurt" that are normally used with a "con-force can also be used as generic expressions to refer to those sensations and bodily conditions to which most people normally have a con-attitude"[1]. It is very clear from this passage that we can consider the notional use of "pain" in ethics from two angles. First of all "pain" as a 'sensation' and second, the 'attitudes' which people have towards "pain" as a phenomenon. The focus was on the former in chapter 1 (covering to some extent the latter as well). But we saw that to speak of 'pain sensation', its origin etc. will not be enough if we do not have a closer look at those who have the sensation or are said to suffer. Once we take care of the conscious moral beings, we cannot neglect their attitudes towards the facts called pain and suffering and the way people respond to. A deliberate human response either to counter or to nourish pain may be wide spreading as it may affect other beings too. We may thus stand at the brink of moral judgement of such responses. It is therefore, clear that to make an inquiry about the effects of pain and suffering is very important. If we are careful about it, we enter the fringe of ethical discussion. The more we move towaıds the core, the more peculiar and interesting uses and meaning of "pain" in particular we discover.

To start with the attitude of human being towards pain, we find that it is not pro, rather con, says Nowelt-Smith, To make it clearer, in the common parlance, "pain" is taken as some such sensation towards which we show hatred and the *reason* for which is *not known.* There can be no reason perhaps to justify why a man hates pain. Pain simply does not recommend itself to our sentiments and affections. Pain is simply hateful for its own sake. Yet if we argue that we hate pain because it is a disagreeable feeling resulting from tissue damage, we have seen that not all pains are owing to tissue damage. Then we have to give another reason, perhaps mental or even metaphysical and every to give another reason, perhaps mental or even metaphysical and every time we shall not find the reason for calling it hateful. But we may say that not always are pains hateful and as such not always should we understand pain in that terms. Yet, we may skip the masochists who hanker after pleasant-pain and find that even if some pains are non-painful (physically), they are nonetheless 'hurtful' or disagreeable to us. Ethicists often call it undesirable, i.e. pain cannot be the end of human life or the desirable end of life. If one asks, why no reason can possibly be given? Hume, for instance, argues that giving reasons is absurd because pain is an ultimately undesirable end, and, therefore, cannot be justified, for it would involve showing pain as a means to an undesirable end.

But pains *cannot be* an end of human life, what to speak of its being an ultimate end. Nor is the pursuit of *avoiding* pain an ultimate end human life. Ends are what we try to bring about or prevent, and principles are rules guiding them in the selection of ends. What a person tries to prevent is not pain rather, some factors in eliciting a disagreeable feeling. Moreover, if one tries to avoid such things and thinks that what he is trying to avoid are pain, still that cannot be the ultimate end of life. Hence, it is absurd to hunt for reason of pain being undesirable. Kurt Baier writes: "A person who asks such a question must be said not to know the meaning of the words or the point of 'why questions'; remarks such as, 'I hate pain', are empty, uninformative, tautology"[2]. The problem is that the moment we want to be more informative about pain, we have to say, for instance, 'I hate hot water poured on my hand' or 'I hate the death news of my friend' and so on. When pains are controlled as specific feelings or sensations like these and have properties like 'positive or negative feeling tones' we may at best say that 'I hate pain' gives us information about my predilections. It is thus the allotted fate of 'pain' that it becomes hurtful, disliked, disagreeable, undesirable and so on. Gilber Ryle says that in this sense, "a pain is a sensation of a special sort, which we ordinarily dislike having".[3] What Ryle says is not fully acceptable to ethicists like Baier because pain is not the name of sensation of a special kind (i.e. which is disliked). Rather, this word is used to indicate how a certain person *responds* to certain things such as sensations. The reason is that the things we call 'painful' are pursuits, activities, undergoing, experiences, and sensations. Hence pain is *not* a special sensation which we 'dislike', rather is indicative of how a certain person responds to some sensation for instance. There is thus a basic difference between 'I find this painful' and 'this is painful'. The former is subjective and personal whereas the latter objective and impersonal. The former tells our predilections whereas the latter states the nature of an object. Hence, 'I find this painful' tells others my particular *response* and implies nothing about others response. On the other hand, 'This is painful', expresses that every normal person finds it so, that is, one who does not find so, is abnormal. Hence, when we call something 'painful objectively', "pain" stands out to be noxious stimulus most generally unacceptable for its damage producing property, and if we call something painful subjectively, 'pain' stands out to be merely a person's response to certain things. Thus in 'I find this painful', 'this' refers to pursuits, activities, undergoing experiences that this was something which caused the *sensations* which I found painful or that I found this *painful*. But if we ask, 'why do you find this painful?' i.e. if we ask for the reason, the answer is mere tautology because it causes, a *sensation* which *I find* painful. What is important is to notice that claiming that something is painful and claiming that it is also unpleasant indicates a person's *negative* response or attitude to something (a pursuit, activity, sensation etc.) What distinguishes both these claims is that the former implies the occurrence of a characteristic sensation while the latter does not. It may be correct therefore, to say that pains are 'sensations' which *we find painful,* and incorrect to say that they are 'sensations' which we obviously dislike having. Finding something 'painful' may be finding something 'hurtful' and hateful also but to say that '*pains are disliked*' (as says Ryle) is unacceptable because this implies that it is merely an empirical and not a necessary proposition that we dislike having the sensation which we call pains. If we accept the truism that 'whatever we call pains are those which we dislike', then those sensations which we ordinarily dislike but on some occasions like them as well, then we should not call them pains. The martyrs may be normally disliking their nails to be plucked off and find all sorts of tortures inflicted on them painful but when they are tortured (their nails are plucked off etc.), the painful sensation remains very much there barring the martyrs disliking it. This, however, does not imply that the martyrs like the painful sensation of plucking the nails etc. In this sense, we see that if we say that pains are sensations of a certain sort (as says Ryle), then we cannot go on to specify which sort of it is by just saying that they are ordinarily those disliked ones. Now questions arise, why do we hate pains? Or, why is pain hurtful? We have but no answer than to say that because, '*I find them* painful or hurtful' and frankly saying, there are no fixed properties for calling them painful or hurtful. Nevertheless, we ought to remember that according to some ethicists what is crucial in using the word "pain" is that we have to keep in mind both its subjective and objective aspects. Hence, 'I find pain in this' and 'this produces pain', may be sharply distinguished. In so far as the subjective "inner aspect" is concerned, 'finding pain' involves 'responses' to pursuits (weight lifting), activities (glass swallowing), undergoing (amputation), experiences (accidents) and sensations (sore throat). The other important part is to remember that our attitudes and responses towards pains may be mostly negative, but that does not construe the meaning or the definition of "pain". Pain may *not* be thus defined as a sensation, which is disliked or taken to be something towards which we *ought to* nourish con-attitude always. With this we have entered into the controversy of defining "pain".

Before we indulge into this controversy, let me go back to the point of 'undesirability' of pain. We have seen that ethicists do not generally accept pain as the ultimate end of life nor do they accept the 'avoidance' of pain the ultimate end because it is not intrinsically valuable or good or desirable. 'Avoidance of pain in itself is the desirable end of life', is something which is not accepted unanimously by the ethicists because rather than doing that one may speak about the attainment of pleasure or happiness and many more. This is so because the mere 'avoidance of pain' is not sufficient, what becomes more important, is to tell us about the 'positive aspects' of doing so. What if we avoid pain? Some people would call it a pointless question. To them, there is nothing beyond; avoiding pain is final. But the question does have a positive bearing as it asks whether or not 'avoiding pain' is the *only* desirable goal of human actions? Certainly, ethicists do not agree that 'avoiding pain' is the *only* desirable end because that would leave open a question: "What is attained by doing so?" Hence, 'avoiding pain' may not be sufficient, we still expect yet higher goal to be achieved in life. To say that we avoid it because we hate it, or dislike it, may not be sufficient either for we do not get a positive answer to 'what if we go on hating, disliking in avoiding pain life long? 'Avoiding pain' may be thus a valuable means to attain a yet higher goal. But what is it? Ethicists are not unanimous about it. Ethicists have another excuse. They prefer to say that rather than introducing the 'factors' of hate-love, like-dislike, we could say that we try to avoid pain because that is *not desirable* or morally valuable or intrinsically good. It may be, nevertheless, a *disvalue*. I have said that the 'disvalue' of pain is not an established fact as is its 'value' particularly, when we speak of physical pain, which is crucial to a medical man. What many ethicists have in mind is perhaps the fact, whether pain is useful or not, it is, generally speaking, undesirable because pains may be for obvious reasons sometimes *desired* but not desirable. To be precise, pain may be a 'desired end' but not a 'desirable end.' Ethicists may be thus making an important point for those who cannot distinguish among 'painful pain', 'hurtful pain', 'unpleasant pain' and 'pleasant pain', cannot distinguish a doctor or others desiring 'pain signals' for treatment and so on and a masochist desiring pain because it satisfies his personal whims or desires. For the masochist, pain may be only desirable end rather than being merely desired, because that is what he feels the *only* or *intrinsically* good, for himself for the time being, whereas for the doctors, pain is only desired for the sake of treatment or for a benefit but not intrinsically good or only desirable thing. In this sense, then, pain does stand out as not ultimately desirable as we do not generally prescribe pains or we prescribe merely to avoid it. Pain may nevertheless, be desired for apparent benefit or avoiding pain may be desired to attain a higher end in life. Pain may be thus taken as instrumentally good but not intrinsically good. It may be thus extrinsically valuable but not intrinsically valuable. The real trifle lies elsewhere. What if we avoid pain? What end is realizable therefore? These are not easy question to answer. By avoiding pain, which desirable end is attained? May be even more interesting question to ask. Again this is not an easy question to answer. But one naturally commits seeing the 'beneficial' aspects of the avoidance of pain in the fact that we get 'pleasure'. It appears to be an automatic choice. The history of ethics is a testimony to it.

Once we enter into 'pleasure theory', and move forward by analysing it. We also counter the trifle of definitions of "pleasure" and "pain" and face many things, which go against the views, mentioned earlier. The readers in this regard are fated to face Bentham's oft-repeated *assertion,* which is tragically taken as definition of 'good' in terms of 'pleasure' and 'bad' in terms of 'pain'. Bentham says, "Nature has placed mankind under the governance of two sovereign masters, *pain* and *pleasure*. It is for them *alone* to point out what we *ought* to do as well as to *determine* what we *shall* do. On the one hand, the *standard* of *right* and *avoiding*; on the other, the chain of *causes* and *effects* are fastened to their throne."[4] Bentham starts with the same tone as we have already seen, i.e. avoiding the 'why' question can legitimately accept the obvious truism that human beings try to avoid pain and attain pleasure. At the outset, therefore, it is clear that 'avoiding pain' is not enough; 'to attain pleasure' is what is the end of human life. Next, Bentham carries on with his psychological truism to assert that pleasure and pain are the *sole determinants* of what we actually do and should do. Thus pleasure and pain are the determining causes of moral actions or plainly they are the *motives* or motivating factors of moral actions. In the above assertion the word that has worried the ethicists is 'alone'. Ethicists have thought that Bentham has made it clear that pleasure and pain are the *only* motives and there is none other we can really imagine. Moreover, without these motives no action is imaginable. Hence, psychologism of Bentham enters into some kind of orthodoxy, as it appears that the motives that govern us are exactly those mentioned by Bentham. Next, the ethicists thought that 'attracting pleasure and avoiding pain' is the only standard of the rightness of actions, i.e. 'pleasure seeking' is the only end of life as it only has the authority to tell us what we should do. From this they argued that Bentham could be charged of the 'naturalistic fallacy' as he clearly identified the 'desirable' or 'good' with 'pleasure' and calls it the standard of morality. Others went farther to think that the naturalistic fallacy being basically a *definist* fallacy, Bentham could be accused of *defining* "good" in naturalistic terms, i.e. in terms of "pleasure" and "bad" in terms of "pain". What is morally right then, is to desire "pleasure" and avoid pain and what is wrong, is not to do it. There may be long argument for and against such charges. What is less controversial is that Bentham has claimed "pain" to be a *motive* of action or psychological determinant of action. Pain, precisely in this context, is the 'avoidance of pain'. The question is, 'does Bentham at least propose a definition of "pain" in terms of motives of action?'

Certainly, the ceremonious rules of definition I have already mentioned *cannot* be traced here really. There is nowhere in this statement 'pain = df...' We have instead, it is for them *alone to point out*, what we ought to do, as well as *to determine* what we shall do.' But one may argue that what Bentham holds is not merely that seeking pleasure and avoiding pain is what we in fact do, we (following our nature) *logically must* do. Hence, we must seek pleasure and we must avoid pain if we are called human beings. Hence, the criteria of pleasure and pain are 'desired' and 'avoided' respectively. This logical status of pleasure and pain as motives of desiring and avoiding actions then may be the cue towards understanding what "pain" (also "pleasure") *means* or how they ought to be *defined*. Certainly we may accuse Bentham of naive psychologism (which is basic to his hedonistic doctrine) as he tends to move beyond needless argument of why we desire pleasure and avoid pain and embraces the truism that human beings must necessarily be pleasure seeking and pain avoiding. It is not too odd to move beyond 'needles argument or the why question', what is important is to find an excuse in the form of psychological truism. But does it mean therefore, that the definitions of "pleasure" and "pain" may be given only in terms of 'motives of actions'? We do not think so. Bentham tends to hold that 'pain talk' is not possible without 'motive-talk' and any talk about the rightness and wrongness of actions is not possible without pleasure and pain talks, but this is not the same as saying that 'pleasure is defined' or 'pain is defined' in natural terms. This was not needed for Bentham as he could easily maintain that speaking logically, human beings must desire pleasure and avoid pain. In fact, it is not logically necessary that 'pleasure' and 'pain' must be defined naturalistically. Rather, if we want to understand what these things are or what do they signify, there is no way but to speak about 'motives' (not intentions). Considering Bentham's doctrine as the one that asserts, other thing beings equal, we usually 'seek the pleasant and avoid the painful'. It is true factually but not logically because this does not constitute the meaning of 'human nature' and taken as the doctrine that we always do so, is not merely 'logically false', it is, actually, as a 'matter of fact false'. What, however, is clear is that despite apparent mistakes, 'psychological hedonism' by definition amounts to a doctrine that speaks of the primacy of the motives of pleasure and pain to determine the rightness and wrongness of actions. Hence, though we are not safely placed to declare that Bentham has provided us with a definition of "pain" (also "pleasure"), he nevertheless, gives us an important cue as to *use* these terms in the ethical literature, particularly, in the context of hedonism. The 'use' may appear to be odd, but in reality it is indubitably used like that, without going for the meaning of "pain", therefore, we at least know that it is legitimate enough to speak in terms of "motives" when we speak about "pain". Understood in this sense then, it will be really difficult for us to make out whether Bentham committed the naturalistic fallacy or not? Broadly speaking, it is a definist fallacy because neither did he produce strict logical definition of "good" in terms of "pleasure" nor "bad" in terms "pain" nor "right" in terms of "seeking pleasure" and "wrong" in terms of "not avoiding pain". Well, there is, no doubt, a mention of "ought to do" in the passage. Which intends to make clear that what is *desirable* is "pleasure and avoidance of pain". This is not the definition of "ought" or "should". Similarly, in the passage, "right and wrong" are not strictly logically defined in terms of "pleasure" and "pain", rather what is made clear is that "right and wrong" make no sense if we do not take notice of "pleasure and pain". In the same sense, without taking notice of "motives", any talk about "pleasure" and "pain" does not make much sense. It thus appears that hedonists like Bentham might not be making any analytic claim while considering the notions of "good" or "right" ("bad" or "wrong"), otherwise they would have certainly been based the meaning of these terms on "pleasure" and "pain" and have thus committed naturalistic fallacy. They might be well viewed as those who completely escape giving definitions and committing mistakes, because they may believe that it is better to explain the meanings of these notions rather than defining them. This goes right against Moore's criticism of Bentham and Mill. As such Bentham's claim that '*only* seeking pleasure and avoidance of pain are ultimately intrinsically good' (desirable) has a clear mistake with the introduction of "only", but, no doubt, this is an evaluative statement (not analytic) and commending evaluations to others. What is basic to this evaluative statement is Bentham's understanding of the evaluative terms like "good", "bad", "right", "wrong" etc. If we do not understand it properly, most likely, we are sure to commit the mistake of attributing 'naturalistic fallacy' to them. The crucial message being that one cannot define evaluative terms by purely descriptive ones, but one can certainly *explain* the former by means of the latter.

One who is attempting the task of *explaining* the *uses* of evaluative terms has at least, two choices open to him. He may, on the hand, define more or less entirely new technical terms to do the job, which is undertaken, for instance, by P.H. Nowell-Smith (we have seen that) with his terms 'pro-attitude' and 'con-attitude'. On the other hand, he may use old terms having their ordinary meaning and narrow range of application in a new, special and wider technical sense. This is what Bentham does or has been done by Hobbes ("desire" and "aversion") and A.E. Murphy ("want"). What Bentham is simply trying to do with the terms "pleasure" and "pain", is just the same as Nowell-Smith does with "pro-attitude" and "con-attitude", and Hobbes with "desire" and "aversion". These people are thus not making an ethical statement, but a meta-ethical one. They are *explaining* the way the words "good" and "right" are used and thus in a broad sense 'defining' them as well. But they are not doing so with "pleasure" or "pain" in their ordinary senses and thus committing naturalistic fallacy, but in a special technical sense based upon the recognition of this fallacy and even explaining the ground of the fallaciousness of it as well. In fact, Psychological hedonism cannot be called 'psychological' in the sense of an empirical theory of the study of human behaviour, rather, we may say that it is a *linguistic* consequence of one way of stating a meta-ethical theory. We may thus say that in the statements "Men always seek pleasure and avoid pain", the hedonists are using 'pleasant' and 'painful' as whatever men just do seek and avoid. The tautology has a point however, i.e. showing that men do not seek what they seek simply because of what it is but also, because of what they are. Even if we allow this interpretation to work, Bentham's particular adherence to "only", may be taken as an example of accepting an empirical theory, which perhaps has nothing, much to support.

Yet, Mill has something more to say in this regard, which, apart from the basic supporting arguments in favour of psychological hedonism, tries to show for what reasons "only", "seeking pleasure and avoiding pain for maximum number" is the "only" standard of morality or the only criterion for rightness and goodness. Mill says, "And, now, to decide whether this is really so, whether mankind do desire *nothing for itself but* that which is a pleasure to them, or of which the absence a pain, we have arrived at a question of *fact* and experience. Practical self-consciousness and self-observation, assisted by observation of others can only determine it. I believe that these sources of evidence impartially consulted, will declare that desiring a thing and finding it pleasant, aversion to it and thinking of it as painful, are *phenomena entirely inseparable*, or rather two parts of the same phenomenon—in strictness of language, two different modes of naming the same psychological fact, that to think of an object as desirable and to think of it as pleasant, are one and the same thing, and that to desire anything, except in proportion as the idea of it is pleasant, is a physical and metaphysical impossibility"[5].

That people pursue only pleasure and avoid only pain is a matter of simple experience. Mill being an empiricist and a realist would not allow *a priorism*. Mill fortifies this claim further by saying that our intellectual honesty, self-assessment and assessment by others would easily enable us to see the truth of the above claim. Interestingly, Bentham also speaks of such assessment. But it was not as clear as was with Mill. One who is capable of such assessment could see that 'desiring a thing and finding it pleasant' and 'avoiding a thing and finding it painful' are but two different modes of *naming* the same phenomenon. Again, transcending Mill's empiricism and realism, we may allow the above interpretation to work, i.e. Mill is here using the terms "pleasure" and "pain' along with "desiring" and "aversion" in such a manner that there hardly remains any point in distinguishing them. The especial use of "pleasure" and "pain" is thus clear in hedonistic writings. This is *no* definition of "pleasure" and "pain" and so question does not arise of committing any fallacy. This is to focus a specific metaethical theory having peculiar linguistic consequence. Extending it further, we could say that there is enough reason (empirical) to believe that "rightness" and "wrongness", "goodness" and "badness" should be used and understood especially in the context of hedonism. These terms make absolutely no sense if we do not allow "desired" (pleasure) and "avoided" (pain) to be used along with them. Neither *a priori* or logical justification could be there therefore, to show why we desire pleasure and avoid pain, as there is no need to mention that 'good' and 'bad' go along with "pleasure" and "pain" respectively, and that "rightness" goes with "desiring pleasure" and wrongness with "aversion of pain". What makes Mill different from Bentham is that he makes it clear that he is not speaking of quantity of pleasure rather, *quality* of pleasure.

Worth noticing is that in ethical use, the term "pain", no doubt, has been used in a very special way (technical, if we wish to say), using in fact as a universal term for determination of action or motive of action. Hence, psychological (and even ethical) hedonism provides us with an interesting vocabulary that does allow us to use "pain" in an extremely special meaning along with its ordinary one, which has been used in the common parlance as mere 'sensation'. However, we need not think that they have thus presented a stipulative definition of "pain". Rather, pleasure and the absence of pain are presented as ends, goals or purposes in terms of which all action is to be explained. Hedonism is thus inherently teleological. Its explanation of behaviour is in terms of the object desired. Now, if we are to interpret this teleology as inviting some kind of efficacy of the future upon the present or even as requiring the purpose to be a present *cause*, there would, indeed, be an injustice to the hedonists. Thus, 'avoidance or aversion of pains' is the goal to be achieved and it is not only desired but also a desirable goal and thus motivates or initiates us to achieve it. Again it is not merely a cause having such and such effect. Hence, pain as a motive, is not a cause in scientific sense of the term, i.e. it produces such and such effects or it is historically prior to some effect that follows.

But the questions are, 'what kind of a motive is pain?' and 'what, if any, is its difference with intention? Miss G.E.M.Anscombe in her work titled *Intention* (1957) offers an account of motive, which is different from the cause-effect account of motive. She divides motives into three classes, viz. (a) those which are equivalent to intentions; (b) backward looking motives, such as remorse and gratitude, which assign something in the past or present as the *ground of an action* and (c) interpretative motives, such as friendship and curiosity, which place *an action in a certain light.* She distinguishes between backward looking motives and mental causes. Motives differ from mental causes in being bound up with good and ill. However, Miss Anscombe leaves the question, how do motives *explain* actions?, Obviously, she rejects the suggestion that motivated actions are causally determined by preceding feelings, but she does not answer the main question clearly. The difficulty in giving an account of the concept of motive arose partly from vagueness in the concept itself. The vagueness may be dispelled if we remember that words like 'motives', 'motivation', 'being motivated by' all suggest something dynamic, something containing a force or power acting on the agent. It may be thus conceived as the driving force which, when acts on agents may become 'ground of an action' or it may place 'an action in a certain light'. We must thus remember that when we speak of someone's motives, we imply certain type of explanation applicable only to behaviour above a certain degree of complexity. Hence, when we ask, did he have a motive, we simply inquire whether the person's behaviour was of the required level of complexity. Thus, explanation in terms of the agent's motives consists of (a) the agent's beliefs that about the situation in which he finds himself and (b) the behavioural tendencies to which these beliefs give rise.

We have to distinguish motives from not only cause but also intention as well. The person who explains his action of going near a fire *because* he was *cold* is stating that 'feeling of cold' was the 'driving force' acting on him and this way, we find the ground of his action (going near fire) from this. This also recalls agent's belief in the situation he finds himself that the cold may be dispelled when he goes near a fire. In this sense, motive may be thought of as 'backward looking', but, when a person who explains his action of going near a fire by saying that he does so to get *warmth,* it becomes a report of an *intention.* In this case what is clear is that the agent is giving 'forward looking' reasons for his action (to go near a fire).

Now, going back to hedonistic account of pleasure and pain, and to the basic idea of "pursuing pleasure and avoiding pain', we find that according to them, 'pleasure and pain are the motives of action'. If that were the case, in what sense can we call them 'motives of action'? What the hedonist believe is that certainly human beings are acted upon by both the feeling of pleasure and pain during their life-span and they are well acquainted of the relative benefits and harmfulness of the two. Naturally, the agent's belief in a given situation is 'that which is desirable is beneficial to him (egoists)' or 'that what is desirable to others (altruists)' and what is beneficial, largely speaking, is pleasure and not pain (from experience). Hence, it is but natural that agent would prefer seeking pleasure and avoiding pain. This idea that seeking pleasure is beneficial and avoiding pain is also beneficial, always acts on the agents and initiate them to do definite actions. In this sense, then, pleasure and pain, are definitely the motivating or dynamic factors that influence or drive agents to do actions. These motives may be thus said to become 'grounds of action' or they may explain actions in a particular light. The ideas of pleasure and pain in this sense may be backward looking reasons in so far as an agent may explain why such and such action was done. Actions done are thus mere means to attain the goal or end embodied in motives called 'pleasure' and 'pain'. We do not, therefore, say that pleasure and pain are motives acting as causes of such and such actions. Well, what is interesting here is to notice that the motives of pleasure and pain may be best understood in terms of 'pursuance' and 'avoidance' and with them go the basic ideas of advantage and disadvantage, benefit and harm.

Let us assume the case of a hedonist once more. If we ask one of them why did he act so as to help the poor persons living in a slum? He may say '*Because* I *felt sympathy* for the poor'. He is, obviously giving a 'backward looking reason' or speaking about 'a motive' called 'sympathy' that acted on him to do the required action. Do we think that the hedonist would ever say that he helped the poor *because* doing so he was pursuing pleasure and avoiding pain? We are, in fact, not so conscious about the nature of motives the kinds of motives and the question of benefits or harms that not usually go along with the motive when we face them in a real life situation. But we often make rational choice of actions in several situations which certainly may have some motive behind it and the knowledge of which becomes clear when we are pressed upon to look 'backward'. Normally, however, what happens with us is that when we are in a given situation like the one mentioned above, we look 'forward', that is, we report our intention. We would normally say (if asked about it) that we help the poor *because* in doing so, we shall pursue pleasure and avoid pain, (which we get out of constant touch with the poor people's state perhaps!) or may be someone of us, more generous (as are utilitarians) would say that he helps the poor *because* in doing so, he contributes to extend maximum happiness to maximum number. What I believe is that the hedonistic account of pleasure or pain as motives stands out to be more clear when we go along with the notions of "pursuance" and "avoidance" and such activities find a pertinent explanation when we report our intention, which, however, is exactly the achievement of the desirable goal (viz. getting pleasure and avoiding pain). In this sense then it will be extremely difficult for the hedonists to distinguish the so-called motives from intentions. However, it is nothing odd for motives may be *explained* in terms of intentions, too. Motives may not be thus identical with intentions, as they are not identical with causes or mental causes. The feelings of pleasure and pain are thus considered to be the motives of those hedonic actions which are clear only if we report out intentions, in the form: "I do this because doing so I shall *get* pleasure and *avoid* pain". With this report, the *end* of action is clear and its *beneficial* aspect as well, But the problem is that every member of the goose club may have distinct motives of pleasure and pain affecting him and evoking him to an action and he has every reason to believe that theft and gambling would give him pleasure and thus enable him to avoid pain. Is this beneficial action right as well? The hedonists are not at par with the members of the goose club only in so far as their reports of intention do not merely make clear their goals which are shared by all notorious people, rather *qualified* with the fact that such pursuance of pleasure and avoidance of pain *also* have far reaching social benefits because they cover Socrates but not pigs. But, then with these lengthy report hedonists would turn out to be *refined utilitarians* otherwise, they would face all dangers of being treated as comrades of a goose club. Certainly, the reporting of motives in terms of intention is *complex* but desirable one because that reveals the real motive behind an action.

Now, it is not enough to have motives or intentions, what is crucial are to have "good motives" and "good intentions". Now, the question is, are the hedonists worried about these things? They are certainly worried about these things because when they speak of "satisfaction of pleasure and avoidance of pain" (psychological hedonism) or "maximising pleasure for the maximum number (ethical altruism), they are speaking not only of a motive (and we have seen it may be understood as a report of the intention of the hedonist) just for the reason that this is the end or *summun bonum* of human life but the criterion of moral rightness as well. Hence, "pursuing pleasure and avoiding pain" is a valuable ethical goal or an ethical good, which *ought* to be attained. As it 'ought' to be attained, it has a kind of 'prescriptive force' and an 'emotive force' as well. Hedonic pleasure is thus desirable just because it is an embodiment of 'value or good' whereas, pain is undesirable just because it is an embodiment of 'disvalue or bad'. We may argue about the *teleos* of 'pain' no doubt and its instrumental value, as does the medical man, but what the hedonists have in mind is that the generic sense of "good" is that it is value and not disvalue, and thus it is desirable and not undesirable. Pain being essentially a disvalue and arguably instrumentally valuable cannot be called "good", and for that matter is not intrinsically desirable. We may nevertheless speak of 'pleasant pain' or of 'non-painful pain' but the hedonists would commit that it is not uniformly and generally valuable, as is pleasure. They become more clear as they add saying that in fact, the very 'disvalue' of pain in its being is *not* beneficial to us and the very 'value' of pleasure that lies in the fact is beneficial. Hence, even if the generic sense of "good" is valuable, hedonists find no sense in isolating 'valuable' from 'beneficial'. In this sense, "good" is "beneficial good" according to hedonism. It is not equivalent to instrumental good however. More clearly then, according to the hedonists the end or goal of human life being "pursuance of pleasure and avoidance of pain," ought to be a valuable or good goal for the simple reason that 'pursuing pleasure' and 'avoiding pain' are both valuable or good in themselves or are very intrinsically good. We have already seen that if we allow our interpretation of hedonism, there would be least sense to consider "pleasure" and "pain" isolatedly. The feelings called "pleasure" and "pains" are not taken that way by the hedonists. They would like to believe that with "pleasure" goes "pursuance" and with "pain", "avoidance" and as such, with "pleasure" goes "beneficial" and with "pain", "not-beneficial". Hence, putting the 'pursuance of pleasure' and 'avoidance of pain' together, the value of the complex whole is certainly 'valuable' or 'good'. Such value may be called 'beneficial value' or 'beneficial good'. Hence, "pursuance of pleasure" and "avoidance of pain", both are intrinsically valuable and thus desirable end of human life. They are intrinsically good because they are not an instrument or means to a higher good but are good in them. We thus do *not* "pursue pleasure" and "avoid pain" because we get this and that out of it, rather we do so because doing so is valuable or good. Nevertheless, hedonists would allow that the feeling called 'pain' is bad because it is not beneficial and the feeling called 'pleasure' is good because it is beneficial and the benefit is not to be *a priorily* understood or justified, it has to be 'experienced' (rather it is experienced) only if we have great degree of intellectual honesty. Not only this, "avoidance of pain" along with "pursuance of pleasure" is ultimate good or highest good as well. To the hedonists, therefore, 'pleasure and pain' should be better seen as motives and, pursuance of pleasure and avoidance of pain are intrinsically good because they are highly 'beneficial'. We may disagree with the hedonists on several accounts like, 'every man ought to pursue pleasure and avoid pain always' or 'every man ought to do these things' only. But without going into what is correct or incorrect, logical or illogical, we have here peculiar use of "pain" as motive and as "good" motive; the latter idea becomes clear when we know that with "pain" goes "avoidance of pain"(as also with it goes "aversion"). With the sense of "aversion", the hedonists believe that there can be no rational desire for "aversion". Hence, "pain" *per se* is not a matter of rational desire, if "pain" is here looked upon merely as a sensation. But if we do not forget hedonic vocabulary and conjoin "avoidance" with "pain", it is certainly a matter of rational desire and thus it is almost the same as saying that it is intrinsically desirable. Thus the feeling called "pain" may be intrinsically undesirable or it is not a matter of rational desire, but the "motive" called "pain" is in fact the motive of "avoidance of pain" and that is certainly a matter of rational desire or for that matter intrinsically desirable. One who is, however, worried about the rational desire of "non-painful pain" and "pleasant pain", rejects the claim of hedonism; he rather accepts that some state of affairs, as mentioned above, do not fall in the category of "pain" which must not be "avoided"; rather, be avoided. If he accepts this at least, no pain as such should be nourished, is the natural answer.

We thus have in the field of ethics disputes about the values of pleasure and pain as 'feelings' and about the value of standard of morality based on the notion of pleasure and pain as 'motives' or more clearly, motives of "pursuance" and "avoidance" respectively. What is also crucial in this controversy is to answer whether or not 'value' is what is 'beneficial' and 'good' or 'desirable' is what is 'welfaristic', and whether or not only 'the pursuance of pleasure and avoidance of pain' is what is beneficial or welfaristic. An interesting discussion has been initiated by G.E. Moore in *Principia Ethica* (PE) about the basic *value* of good, (both unmixed and the mixed) *vis-a-vis* the *disvalue* of evil, (both unmixed and the mixed). Moore thinks that like great positive goods (wholes having *no* evil elements), there may be greatest positive evils (whole having *all* evil elements), this makes it clear that he would like to stipulate intrinsic evils as essentially "ugly" *vis-a-vis* intrinsic good, which are essentially "beautiful". The stipulation clearly forces the senses of disvalue going along with "ugly" and value going with "beautiful". Moore goes on to classify the greatest positive evils into three viz. (a) enjoyments or admiration of that which is intrinsically either evil or ugly, for instance, cruelty and lasciviousness; (b) emotion directed to an inappropriate object, like hatred for the poor and (c) the class of pains.

In PE, Moore writes: "The third class of great positive evils appear to be the class of *pains*"[6]. He writes further, "it is not pain itself, but only the *consciousness* of pain, towards which our judgments of value are directed ...pain, however, intense of which there was no consciousness, would not be evil at all".[7] It is, therefore, clear that it is not pain rather the "consciousness of pain" which is intrinsically evil or one of the great evils (and for that reason a disvalue). Several interesting facts, in this way, become clear. First, Moore has no doubt that "pains" ought to be classed under "evil" and "evil" being stipulated as "ugly", "pain" acquires the basic meaning, viz. "that which is ugly". Further, "that" has been clearly stated as not an corporeal object but consciousness of a feeling and for that reason, "pain" is "the consciousness of a feeling which is ugly."

As we analyze Moore's assertions, it would be a necessary precondition that one has the consciousness of a *feeling* called "pain" or that somebody's feeling state of mind is uniquely distinct from many other feeling states because it is essentially "ugly". The stipulation of the meaning of "pain" may be valuable, if and only if it could successfully clarify the meanings of several cases of pains, particularly, the 'non-painful pain' the 'pleasant pain' and the 'enjoyment of pain' or the 'masochistic pain'. One thing that becomes sure here is that a conscious state of mind is very important and we are conscious about pain, that is to say, we are conscious about not a thing called pain but a *feeling* called pain. Hence, whatever may be the causes eliciting pain (physical, mental, metaphysical etc.), what is basic; is 'to be conscious about a feeling called pain'. It is clear that

Moore would not like to call "pain" something which is out there in the nature rather, a 'feeling state of mind' of which we *ought* to be conscious (*not* that we *are* conscious, because we may not be conscious at all). This is perfectly in consonance with the idea that in so far as we call some pains "non-painful" or "pleasant" or "enjoyable", undoubtedly, we are speaking of such feelings about which we are conscious but we may still have different accompanying *attitudes* in being either *not* finding it hurtful or finding it pleasant or even enjoying it. But if we follow Moore's stipulation seriously, can we really be conscious about a feeling called pain which is essentially "ugly" and yet not hurtful"? Two other cases do not pose great problems because being conscious of an "ugly" feeling and having attitudes like finding the feeling "pleasant" and "enjoying it", are perfectly all right with many psychopaths. We have to keep in mind that if we stipulate "ugly" to "pain" then an athlete finding the pain of hard work "pleasant" would be certainly in a feeling state of mind, towards which one has a pro-attitude, which, however, would be labelled "abnormal" according to Moore because as we have seen earlier, any pro-attitude like this one would rob off "pain" the basic *disvalue* that it carries. But if we do that as we have already seen, we would be deprived of finding any physiological value or medical value of pain no pro attitude would ever be possible in case of feeling called "pain", "pain" would be an essential "disvalue" and prone to "con-attitude". To call "pain", "ugly", would be falling into the absolutist trap of the stipulative meaning of a term, which, however, looses all its inherent flexibility of uses, and meaning. What I have said just now may be the basis of understanding why ruling out the possibility of "non-painful pain" as impossible or absurd, would be carrying too far with a stipulation which does only limit uses and meanings of "pain" rather, limits the usages and meanings of "ugly" and "disvalue" as well because we know that "ugly" is *not* only "pains" and "disvalue". If we try to assimilate in the range of the uses of "pain", the usage of the notion in the sense of "hurtful", we would understand that it is perfectly all right to speak of "non-painful pain" which amounts to the consciousness of feeling of pain, which is, nevertheless, *not* hurtful (as in the case of an athlete or a student or a researcher working hard and bearing pain). And if we know that pains may be also not hurtful, the pro-attitude towards it is always there and with it, to speak of value (and not 'disvalue') of pain seems to be sensible. However, Moore's stipulation works sensibly as well within the framework of explanation of "pleasant pain" and "enjoyment of pain".

Moore's opinion that 'mere cognition of pain is a great evil' is questionable on account of calling it by that name ("evil"). The problem is only if you follow Moore's stipulation of "pain" ("ugly"), the very cognition of pain as a *phenomenon* would amount to the cognition of a wanton "evil". Moore has thus clearly associated himself with these ethical thinkers who had no doubt about the fact that "pain" or "the consciousness of pain" is nothing but "evil". Hence, "evil" would be a broad 'generic notion' coagulating "pain". This tends to further jeopardize the conceptions the value of pain and non-painful pain as found in medical usages and elsewhere. Moreover, it seriously jeopardizes the clear distinction between the meanings of "pain" and "evil" which these notions acquire on account of a variety of uses in different philosophical and non-philosophical literature. To repeat, the stipulation, viz. "ugly" and "evil" shall force out the different uses and meanings of the notion "pain". This is not to say that "pain" is sometime, "good" because you have to first clarify what is "good". If we follow Moore's stipulation of "good", "pain" cannot be called "good" rather "evil", whereas if we do not forget the medical man's notion of "pain" or of athlete's pain or student's pain or yogi's pain, we think for a while, to call it "evil" (and also "good" in the sense of "beautiful"). But, we may not hesitate in calling it "good" in the sense of "beneficial". Now, if we keep the doors open and do not opt for a stipulation of either "good" or "evil" or "pain" or "pleasure", we are at the brink of knowing the wide range of the uses and meaning of these notions. May be, we learn how to distinguish the ethical uses and meanings from the metaphysical or the physiological as well. Perhaps only then we shall know in what ways are "pain" and "evil" differently useful and meaningful concepts. I would like to consider the crucial point only at the end of the book.

Nevertheless, Moore makes it clear that he would like to conceive the possibility of good and evil combined in an 'organic whole'. In that case the beautiful and the ugly would make a whole called 'mixed good'. But, before we come to that, we find Moore saying, "In the case of pain and pain alone, it seems to be true that a mere cognition, by itself, may be a great evil... it is a less complex organic unity than any other great evil and then any great good, both in respect of the fact that it does not involve, beside the cognition, an emotion directed towards its object, and also in respect of the fact that the object may here be absolutely simple, whereas in most, if not all, other cases, the object itself is highly complex"[8]. It is clear that Moore would like to call "pains" less complex wholes on the ground that it involves no emotive aspect, because the cognitive aspect is sufficient enough to call something "pain". I have already mentioned that it would be absurd, nay impossible, to rob off the emotive aspect from "pain" because the mere consciousness of pain will *not* do, our emotion and attitudes towards the objects of consciousness matter greatly. If we overlook this, we forget why it is perfectly sensible to speak of "non-painful pain" and why some people speak of "pleasant pain", "psycho-pathic pain", "enjoyment of pain" and so on. Even causalgic and by hyperalgesic pains along with metaphysical pains find enough explanation. The mere cognition of pain may *not* be sufficient at all to call it "evil" or "ugly" or even "good" or "beneficial".

But, Moore would not like to stop arguing that the intrinsic disvalue of pain in being an evil stems out of the fact that any feeling of pain when combined with one or the other evil state of mind, would make no difference to the badness of the whole, because the inherent badness of pain is so great that it hardly matters whether or not some other bad elements gets conjoined to it. Hence, there is no way but to argue that "pain" is an evil and is essentially bad and ugly. It is very difficult to understand why pain has to be taken as intrinsically evil for the mere fact, that pain plus other evils make no greater evil whole. That something is intrinsically bad or evil or good does not depend on such artificial imagery of confining pain with other evils. One way is to say that the immediate cognition is sufficient, which we have seen is not good enough without combining the emotive aspects of a person in pain or a person cognizing pain. Those who speak of the immediacy of pain as evil and the immediacy of pleasure as good, have to fall into the paradox of intuitionism and say that it is imtuitively true that pain is evil and ugly and if one asks, how do you know all that? The only answer is, "from intuition". The vicious circle grips us, it is worth commending that Moore refrains from calling "pain" the only evil and "pleasure" the only good, but the way he argues that "pain" is *always* an "evil" and it is *always* "ugly", is difficult to accept.

Moore does not seem to be in a happy position at all because this idea has been lingering in his mind and it is evident when he himself raises the point, that in some cases, the addition of pain, even though, it is inherently an evil, serves a *good* purpose. Hence, the teleological value of an infliction of pain (Moore likes it to be not too intense), is indubitable in so far as such pain cures a worse evil state. For instance, punishment of some form (not too intense) may be valuable (even though, inherently "ugly") for the person who is in a very ugly state of mind and for the society at large. It appears that we may not overlook the value of pain, even though he calls it inherently evil. This is a peculiar position where both the 'value' and 'disvalue' of pain have been clearly projected. With this, Moore shifts to consider the possibility of "mixed goods". What interests us here most is that if this were the case, hardly Moore's arguments in favour of intrinsic badness of pain from immediacy of its cognition is at all proved beyond doubt. We are again reminded of the importance of the emotive factors that play the most vital role in either calling "pain"as either "ugly" or "beneficial".

We have thus seen how in ethical literature the notion of 'pain' in particular has been differently used. We may, if we wish, generalise the issue by saying that so far as the notion "pain" is concerned in ethical literature, we have been either using it having an essential 'con-attitude' to signify 'disvalue' or we have been using it having an essential 'pro-attitude' to signify 'value'. However, this is true if and only if, the notion is taken to be the one standing for a "motive" and not a "feeling" because we may be, in ethics, more interested in the former and not in the latter. Nonetheless, if we cannot reject the role of 'feelings' in ethical discussion, there is still a controversy about whether according to people like Moore, "pain" has to be taken as a 'disvalue' and be used having an essential con-attitude.

We also find that in ethical discussion, whether taken in the sense of either feeling or motive, no strict definition of "pain" could be found easily. Refraining from giving a definition of pain stems from the benefit that most ethicists derive out of the basic knowledge they have about 'definition of ethical terms'. Most safely, we may say that like fundamental moral terms such as good, bad, right, wrong etc. the terms 'pleasure' and 'pain' are simple and indefinable mainly because a strict logical definition of these terms always leads to 'naturalistic fallacy'. Yet, when we explain rather than define these terms in a highly technical and abstract way, (as do the hedonists) we are doing nothing odd basically because we are, at least, not committing the naturalistic fallacy. Explanation of "pain" is so technical and abstract and so different because there is no common agreement among the ethicists about how uniformly it should be used. If we keep the options open, the uses are varied, as is its meaning (that we have seen). Let us leave this discussion now.

We have been neglecting "suffering" from ethical discussion. One reason for this, like "pain", "suffering" is neither a 'feeling term' nor a 'motive term' and it is peculiar to use it as an 'end term' either. Now let me clarify this point. 'Suffering' is not a 'feeling term', rather a term signifying 'a state of affairs' that covers feeling term like 'pain'. It tells us about the state of a 'whole person' who is undergoing the pangs of pain. Hence, it is the feeling of pain and not the state of affairs that may be crucial in the discussion of the morality of action. The same is the reason for why 'suffering' is not a 'motive term'. It is actually 'pain' and not 'suffering' which is used to mean that we are under the influence of a 'motive' demanding evasive actions. But I must say that this may be true only in case of Western ethics because in Indian ethics, suffering itself is the most important motive demanding moral actions that evade the state of suffering. We shall come to it later on. It is an interesting way to evaluate the relative disvalues of pain and suffering. In 'existential ethics' suffering has been given more importance. The same is in the case when we consider 'suffering' as an 'end term', that is, when 'avoidance of suffering' along with 'attainment of pleasure' has been used as the end of moral actions. In fact, 'avoidance of suffering' along with 'attainment of pleasure' is a queer possibility. It is, practically speaking, impossible to avoid suffering and if we do allow it, it does not go along with the attainment of pleasure rather with the attainment of 'eternal bliss'. However, the western ethicists do not allow such possibilities but in Indian ethics, these things may be the most crucial ones. We shall not consider either the position of Indian ethics or existential ethics in this regard right at this place because we have separate chapters to do so. For the present purpose, we shall accept that in western ethics, the term 'suffering' does not figure prominently mainly due to the reason that the term 'pain' is believed to be sufficient enough to convey the sense that suffering is a state covering pain. However, we shall know more about it when we consider the positions of Christian Ethics, Existential ethics and Indian ethics at respective places.

"PAIN", "SUFFERING", "EVIL" AND THEOLOGY

From the foregoing discussions we are now at a position to understand that there is no need to think that 'pleasure' and 'pain' are the opposite qualias of the soul and that avoidance of pain does not automatically end up in pleasure. Pleasure is a psychic condition, which prevails when we do not feel it (like pain) and show a pro or con-attitude, rather, when we pursue it. To be in an active state of mind is essential to both of avoiding pain and attainting pleasure. The opposite state of pleasure may be at best 'unpleasant' but not pain. What we understand further is that both may act as motives because we are in an active state of mind to pursue pleasure or avoid pain or something more than or quite different from that if other motives are also effective. Yet, we do accept that suffering is neither a psychic state of pain nor a psycho-physical state of pain. It is broader than that. Normally, pain is thought to give rise to suffering. However, suffering is not simply our reactions to physical pain. It is our reaction to many kinds of events and circumstances of which physical pain is the one and generally, not the most dreadful. We may suffer also, for example, from fear, anxiety, remorse, envy, humiliation, famine, ignorance, injustice, death, love, personal estrangement, boredom, frustration, poverty and many more. Indeed, emotional and metaphysical suffering, quite unconnected with physical pain, can grip us more inwardly and more vehemently and be comparatively less endurable than physical pain.

As we now move on to consider the theological explanation of pain and suffering, we will realize that we are moving closer to the notion 'suffering' than 'pain'. For this, then, 'suffering' has to replace 'pain' to which it has so far played a second fiddle. The reason is that theologies are not merely concerned with what pains do persons have, but also with what effect wholesome suffering has on the existence, the existence which is not merely looked upon as physical, built out of inert building blocks. Broadly speaking, the whole nature may be conceived to suffer human beings inclusive. Pain in this sense may be referring to an extremely complex state of affairs, which is better replaced with terms like 'misery', 'distress', 'anguish', etc. and not merely by 'pain'. It does not amount to 'human misery' or 'human distress', rather 'phenomenal misery' and 'phenomenal distress'. Escaping the difficult question of whether or not animals are conscious of such misery or distress, we, at best can say that our consciousness is testimony to *universal* (or in my terminology 'phenomenal') misery or at least, we are quite well placed in using the term in this sense as well. Another fact of suffering is that human beings are perhaps better placed both in communicating this state of affairs and in managing it. At least, we violently wish that our state would have been otherwise (may be sometimes at the cost of neglecting others). The state of suffering is thus a state of not nourishing or lingering or over avoiding, rather alleviating or blowing off.

Theological interest in pain and suffering may be thus more inclined to suffering, yet with obvious inclination towards human suffering. 'Theological problem of human suffering' is the main theme with which theologians have been engaged, notwithstanding their basic approval that the whole existence (which is very special) may be said to suffer. Theologians interest in suffering thus, apart from focusing human suffering, does make things complex by reminding us that all the suffering is at the mercy of God, who is the creator of the whole existence and one who is omnipotent and good. May be, evil is a function of 'sin'. Hence, we have more complex notion, for example, 'sin', and also 'evil' (which is more popular), because 'suffering' is a notion easily subsumed under the wider generic notion called "evil". "Evil" may cover "pain" and even "sin". Hence, theological problem of human suffering is also understood in terms of 'theological problem' of human evil (at least this is the way theologians discuss with few exceptions). Hence, in the present discussion, with the concept of 'pain' and "suffering", 'evil' is introduced. Human concern for suffering (theologians are humans), is complex. First, they want to know what is it? Why is it there (particularly when God is the creator)? And can we manage it? The last question focuses the self and the other regarding concerns for human suffering. The pattern of discussion that I shall be following now concentrates especially on these issues which have been most efficiently and broadly covered by the Christian theology. But that is not the last answer. We have to take care of what the Islamic and the Judaic theologies have to say. I must remind the readers that the focus of attention now has been thus shifted to "suffering", as it is a more inclusive concept than "pain" and to consider "suffering", without calling it an "evil", is impossible in theological conception. I must remind here that my aim is not to explain all the details and the intricacies of theologies regarding this matter, rather to concentrate more on what has been done with the concepts "pain", "suffering" and "evil". I have deliberately left Hindu theology here because it has been dealt with in the forthcoming chapter.

Whatever may be the difference among the religions of the world regarding the management of pain and suffering or so to say evils like these, the most nagging question ever lived is that 'why is there such evils'? I have said that not in all religions is this 'why' question so prominent, but only in *theistic* religions this has become extremely prominent because the focal points in these religions are God and the attributes of God, which taken together with the existence of 'evil', do pose a lot of problems and so the 'why' question proves to be an ofshoot. Often this 'why' question sounds to be too odd, even discouraged as rebellious and blasphemous, but the modern mind has always been encouraging it. Hebbelthwaite observes: "the urge to try to understand has nearly always prevailed, the doubts and questions sooner or later coming to the surface and demanding an answer. The bare appeal to faith and trust has not been felt to be enough. In every theistic religion we find some explanatory framework in terms of which the presence and extent of evil and suffering can be understood."[9]

To start with Zoroastrian concern about the problem of evil, one finds at the outset that the "problem of evil", which is more fundamental, covers with it the "problem of suffering" because the latter is a subspecies of the former problem. Hence, "suffering-talk" could hardly be severed from "evil-talk". What is quite distinct from it is the "good-talk" because the corollary of "evil" is "good" and not "pleasantness" or "well-being" or "benefit". In fact "evil" has been considered along with "good" as the two are equally ultimate principles that constitute the whole existence. They are not only 'equally ultimate'; they are "belligerent" too. This lays the analytic nature of Zoroastrian religion. It is theistic in so far as it accepts Ahura Mazda, the "Wise Lord', and the source of all good and the creation. It is dualistic in so far as there is an uncreated 'spiritual force' acting against him, the Angra Mainyu. Its thesis is thus not to be taken as 'mono-theism', rather 'dualism', and its account of suffering is pretty clear. It is an embodiment of "evil" as against "good". Hence, it is an expression of the ultimate principle of uncreated spiritual force counteracting the 'principles of good'. "Suffering" may be thus understood (not defined) not as merely physical pain or noxious substance of the metaphysical force of "evil", which is basically meant to act against what has been divinely created, or what exists as an expression of divine creation or an act of the Good. The entire existence is thus viewed as the one, which is a battleground of the two belligerent metaphysical principles, the "good" and the "evil". It is noteworthy here that what is good is the Lord Himself and thus the existence being His creation, it is He Himself; nevertheless, the ever dominating power of "evil" which may last till doomsday, prevails at times to counter it. The goodness of God and His supremacy becomes established everytime when they win the final battle. Perhaps, "suffering" as an expression of "evil" has been used to remind us that in so far as existence is concerned, the reality of evils like suffering cannot be avoided (and it will continue to be there), nay, its supremacy may not be accepted as suffering is something manageable (only if good prevails).This reminds me of two things; one is that the state of suffering has to be identified in the entire existence and not here and there or in the individual self only and the other is that suffering is a notion, subsumable under the principle of "evil" and thus understood. It is corollary of "good". The former reminds me of the "existential sense of suffering" or the existentialist use of the notion of "suffering", which is much broader than any technical use; it also transcends the ethical use to enter into metaphysical use. Nevertheless, the principle of Good being predominantly metaphysical, the ever going war (as if) between good and evil and the prevailing of good over evil projects the ethical tone in Zoroastrian issue. The principle of good is the divine principle unfolded in multifarious ways (as the world) and also in the ethical actions, whereas the principle of evil is the non-divine principle unfolded in many ways (as suffering and pain) and also in unethical actions. We are thus reminded of the fact that "suffering" is a concept used to express the state emerging from wrong moral choice. When one chooses to do something under the influence of the non-divine principle, or the principle that is right against the divine principle of good, we say that he chooses to do something which amounts to suffering or which is an embodiment of evils and such, it is a wrong choice or morally wrong. Suffering may be thus more than mere pain or nagging physical disturbance, rather a state that pervades the entire existence because the moral beings may be favoring Angra Mainyu and not Ahura Mazda. Human beings have that tendency. This is an important presupposition in Zoroastrianism.

Proceeding from the dualism of Zoroastrianism to Islām, which is overtly monotheistic, "suffering" has been treated not as a theoretical problem. Suffering is not a theoretical problem in Zoroastrianism also; it is practical so far as the importance of managing such evil is concerned. But every management approach has to first answer the 'actual ways' in which suffering usually occurred. The Quran is no exception in this regard. It starts where other religious doctrines also start. The existential element is strongly present in all these theologies in so far as suffering is looked upon as a state of affair. It stays alive proving to be a persistent problem. I have said that with higher level of consciousness, perhaps, the problem is discovered by the human beings. Hence, suffering is an ever-exiting human problem or it is theological problem of human evil.

The most striking feature in the Islāmic theology is that suffering has been treated as a 'dissolved problem', that is, a 'problem completely saturated in the problem of God's omnipotence with a claim that it exists in the whole nature'. Although, Islām speaks of God's Love (like Christianity), yet, unlike Christianity, it does not raise the problem of suffering as the one, which contradicts God's Love, rather God's omnipotence. Thus, God's omnipotence and the problem of suffering so coagulate that it hardly makes any sense to make an absolute separation. The problem of suffering thus dissolves in the problem of accepting God as omnipotent. Now for one thing, if God's omnipotence is indubitable, then 'suffering' becomes quite natural to occur with it because the all-powerful God must also create that and if this is not the case, then 'why it is not?' Is the real issue! So, it is clear that "suffering" in Islām, is a concept used to express a state of affair that permeates the whole nature and signifies something metaphysical as even God's attribute of omnipotence has to do something with it. The Quran seems to be least troubled with the notion of going God's omnipotence together with suffering because it would say that if we do not imagine God to be too small, suffering also will occur within creation which is divine, and with His omnipotence, it is always under His *control* and not beyond Him. If this be the case, then, we have to accept the existence of suffering with God's omnipotence and yet, believe that this does neither disparage God's nature nor have a permanent negative effect on the existence as such because the suggestion may be like Zoroastrianism that "ultimately suffering has to suffer at the hands of omnipotent God." It is due to this that suffering is not a great disturbing problem. It may nevertheless, raise questions about the *nature* of God.

Quranic use of the notion "suffering" is peculiar amalgam of the 'natural' and the 'metaphysical' in the sense that on the one hand "suffering" has been used to signify 'misery', 'pain', 'death', 'anguish' etc. to be accepted as a harsh truth, and on the other hand, "suffering" has been used to signify as a 'state of affairs' perfectly under the control of God. The existence of suffering is with God and its control also is with the same God. Such use of "suffering" does not focus suffering as 'theological problem', rather than posing greater problems for the conception of "God" in Islām. In this sense, suffering is a problem only in so far as it poses trifling questions about the nature of God's omnipotence. More clearly, it raises great problem at the face of the assertion that 'God has power over every single thing'. In fact, the Quran does devote substantiating and exemplifying this assertion exactly. The reason behind the existence of suffering may be interesting enough. What is more interesting is that the teleos of suffering has been accepted here indirectly mainly because God's omnipotence may lose significance if it fails to play its vital role in controlling suffering at least. Suffering is thus purposeful. The instrumental sense of "suffering" thus emerges in the Quran as well. All these things may not be too comforting for the Islāmic theologians. John Bowker says, "But this poses serious questions about the character of God; to think of God as having created suffering to be an inherent fact of creation might be impressive in terms of omnipotence, but not of compassion. In conjunction, therefore, with the fundamental assertion of the control of God, there is almost inevitably a constant exploration of ways in which suffering can be understood as purposeful. It is this which leads directly into the quest for ways in which suffering can be understood as instrumental"[10].

The ways in which suffering can be understood as instrumental is that suffering is a *punishment for sin* and it is a *trial or test*. Thus, with suffering and God's omnipotence the concepts of "sin" and "trial" enter. The metaphysical sense of suffering becomes more clearly by now and its non-corporeal or non-phenomenal purposefulness is also clear. To support the purposefulness in terms of punishment for sin, the Quran appeals to experience and to the knowledge of the past. But this is hardly a pertinent philosophical reply. There is no doubt that suffering has been taken as a consequence of evil or that, which has to be taken as palpable sin deserving divine punishment. Hence, it is through this that the 'divine being' punishes the evil. But it may be too hasty to declare all cases of suffering as cases of evil and that, suffering must be looked upon as a state when nothing but punishment is forced for the sin committed. Most of the physical and environmental sufferings are not in fact due to our sins. What sin this nature has done, is difficult to understand and what punishment shall do to the corporeal nature, is difficult to realize.

As for the other explanation in terms of 'test or trial', i.e. to test the truly good human beings, God quite often inflicts suffering in many forms, and who assail the suffering or sinners are the truly good human begins (so to say Moslems). Thus suffering becomes a necessary part of the purpose of God that helps to create a faithful disposition and helps to make a difference between the sincere from the insincere. Suffering is, in this way, conceived to be something that forms a true character; it also exposes it, i.e. reveals the true nature of man.

From these explanations several questions arise. First is that Islāmic theory of suffering revolves round human evil and what has been said is hardly applicable to the nature as a whole. Further, if we consider suffering as a punishment, it follows that suffering, endured faithfully, helps in acquittal, in the final reckoning, of the sins by God, and that, it leads to life or exposing oneself voluntarily to suffering in the cause of God can be commended or even enjoined. The effects of suffering are thus important in so far as they help to produce an equal and balanced character and conversely, fear of suffering is a mark of inadequate trust. We may also think that the teleological understanding of suffering is, sometimes, stated in terms of the belief that God uses suffering in order to bring men to their senses, though, often it does not have the desired effect. Extrapolating Quoranic view of the instrumentality of suffering, it is unwise to be worried about the inequalities of life since all comes from God and there is no point in trying to achieve uniformity. Similarly, there is no point in lamenting the fate of those who suffer in the cause of God. The concept of "suffering" is thus rigoristically used in the teleological theology of Islām to convey the sense of 'strict justice' of God. A reward based exactly on the balance between good and evil awaits all. Hence, "suffering" may be taken as term signifying a 'warning signal' and a more immediate 'punishment'. The former use of the term is not much different from what medical man takes "pain" to be but the latter use of the term is the metaphysical use, which is special.

Islām has basically optimistic theology because its attitude to suffering is utterly positive not passive acceptance, and rather constantly contesting in order to alleviate it. In the Quran, therefore, these two attitudes of acceptance and action are woven together. Acceptance that God's control over suffering is established and actions within the context of his creation is desirable. Islāmic notion of suffering is reflected in Sufism, the mystic philosophy of which encourages voluntary suffering undertaken in the cause of God. The mystic view, which is the instrumental view of suffering, reinforces the practice of ascetic rigorism.

In so far as "suffering" has been used to refer to human evil, a distinct sense of sin owing to disbelief and immorality comes into mind. The unbelievers who are prone to think that suffering is not due to human misdeeds rather physical and those who are immoral beings deserve punishment in the form of suffering. Islāmic metaphysics of suffering in thus closely connected with the morality of man. Hence, man makes evil and he is the one who unmakes it as well, is written large in Islām. The goodness of human acts thus lies in the belief that we ought to do such things that help eradicate suffering and realize why it is there. The *free will* of man to act fervently so as to counter suffering, rules out an absolute deterministic theory according to which God's design is everything for the existence of suffering and the eradication of it.

Like Islām, Judaism has been consistent enough to propagate monotheism. Religiously speaking, the inner urge towards an ethical monotheism makes Judaism more and more difficult to affirm equally ultimate powers independent of God and thus, compromising his omnipotence. Philosophically speaking, the inner urge towards the recognition of an infinite source of all, there is a fight against every ultimate dualism. Brian Hebbelthwaite says that "the combination of these religious and philosophical pressures has led the theistic religions, both in their scriptures and in their theologies to affirm doctrine of creation, in which all finite beings depend wholly on the creative will of God."[11] The theistic spirit of Judaism is also distinctive in maintaining that God has shown his hand in the very history of existence and at the same time, history is testimony to ever living suffering, which is, obviously, an evil; and if, God participates in history, he has to be responsible for suffering. The 'why' questions arise naturally, 'Why does not God intervene during the wanton suffering of man'? Jewish tradition reflects a number of approaches to an assessment of the nature and meaning of suffering and provides with options for overcoming painful experiences. Judaism thus mainly undertakes human suffering as 'real' and his vulnerability towards accepting it and living with it, and yet to find a way out of it. Suffering is something beyond His control and thus simply from being human. The offering of "suffering" as notionally applicable in case of *humans* is clear. In the Rabbinical Jewish literature, the problem of suffering is not presented with the deep existential fervour. The actual existence of suffering, whether or not, it permeates whole existence, and why, at all, is there suffering, are not extremely disturbing problems. These questions were rather prominent in the opening chapter of Genesis. But, the fundamental assertion is that the Created order is essentially good, and that, evils such as suffering, portrayed in *death* are consequence of alienated Adam. Suffering is, thus, outcome of the 'choice of man'. There is no second factor responsible for evil. Indeed, Genesis does not portray a single fall of man, rather a 'gradual degeneration' of the human capacity to remain good and corrupt the basic divine nature. The problem is thus not why suffering exists, rather why it affects some people and not others. Hence, the problem of suffering is of its *distribution*. There is also, no doubt, that suffering has been considered as a subspecies of "evil" and it refers to the ethical question with which this conception is closely related.

There is no doubt, however, that "suffering" has been also used to stand for a "state of affairs", which need a 'cause-effect explanation'.

The simplest causal explanation is that "suffering was a 'punishment' and just 'requital' of 'wickedness'. The wickedness is a sin no doubt, which is mainly due to the 'ignorance' of the right path. Suffering is, thus, due to or it is caused by the ignorance, that the fundamental good nature of human beings should be restored and any corruption on the part of the human leads to sin, and thus, to punishment. Suffering is thus evolved as some state of affairs which is mainly due to human follies, the breach of the covenant for which Yahweh repeatedly shows mercy and favour but punishment is deserved. Suffering is thus no simple state of affair, it bears a deep moral and metaphysical significance. Thus according to Deuteronomy and Deuteronomic history, "suffering" should be understood as a punishment for sin. The Islāmic Instrumentalist theory is written *deep* in the classical Jewish literature. This is an unfortunate theory and open to objections. The most cursory glimpse of life makes it clears that wicked do not get cut off while the ruthless flourishes. But, why this should happen, is persistent through the scripture until 'Jeremiah' was made to believe that the flourishing of the handful of wicked (and thus sin) is only apparent and that God will re-establish that original relationship which he had intended all along. This puts back the optimism, despite the threat of discontinuity owing to distribution of suffering. The solution of suffering thus lies with God. The classical 'Jeremiah dilemma' was better settled by later replies, that is, 'suffering is a test of faith'. Again, we find the purposefulness inherent in suffering, a purpose that is not so easily 'understandable' to the human mind. What is essential, is to value suffering as a futuristic good because it enables us to realize the basic truth that God will prize all good people and punish the wicked. Such response could be seen in the book of Job. Yet in Job, there is difference, the prologue of Job offers that suffering was to test man's faithfulness. The epilogue suggests that Job made his suffering *redemptive* by accepting it faithfully and by praying for his friends (Eliphz, Bildad and Zophar) who were non-believers. The crude philosophy of redemptive suffering of Job finds a deeper impact in 'Deutero-Isaiah'. It has been clearly stated that suffering can be made redemptive, so that, it becomes the foundation of better things, collectively, if not individually. This element of redemptive suffering places the value of suffering in order to attend spiritual progress.

We find yet another shift in the Judaic literature when suffering gained new dimension in the 2nd Century B.C. as for the first time, Jews were martyred for their faith. In Maccabees acceptance of suffering is not referent of mere faith, rather an estimated need for sacrifice for such faith. Suffering in its worst form; is an inspirational phenomenon for the fellow men having faith in God's goodness. This is the *sacrificial* sense of suffering. Hence, voluntary suffering, ending up in laying ones life, has been looked upon as good, a good leading to the moral journey of man that ends up in the metaphysical realization. "Suffering" thus comes closer to "death" with no negative linking, the positive side lay in the fact that death does not engulf the good man's life; the life lived after is good. Extreme suffering may thus end up in enjoying the right of living a good life after the corporeal pangs are over. This, again, focuses the value of suffering (as did the apocalyptic) through divine revelation, which, however, is not a matter of common understanding.

The persistent use of "suffering" in 'Rabbinical Judaism' to refer to morality, is very clear. A direct relationship exists between suffering and wrong doing on the one hand, and between right actions and joyfulness (not pleasantness) on the other. But one may suffer not because one has done wrong but on the contrary, because one has done right. Here is a distinction made between suffering that result from sin and suffering that result from acting virtuously. In this respect, suffering is a necessary part of the burden of ascent, since it results from the assumption of tasks that the righteous takes willingly upon themselves. The rightness thus bears the burden of ascent, according to Psalms–"The Lord tries the righteous". This teaching of Judaism however once again, reminds us of the instrumental theory according to which suffering has been instrumental to test the faith of God and to test those righteous people who can bear the pangs of bearing burden of suffering for others. But this does not focus any inherent or intrinsic value of suffering, as inherently, it has been looked upon as very harsh, crippling and disastrous experience. It is perhaps due to the fact that even God is said to suffer owing to the wanton suffering of the common people. The Rabbinic discussion of suffering extended over increasing wide fields. However, the understanding of suffering as a potential means of the individuals and the community of the faithful seems to hold good in the discussion to get salvation.

Among the monotheistic religious responses to the problem of suffering, Christianity is extremely important and there is no doubt, "suffering" along with "pain" has been considered as 'sub-concepts' within the broader concept of "evil". Nevertheless, any discussion with regard to pain ought to be better considered within the general perspective of suffering. Ulf Goerman observers here that "in a broad sense, queries concerning pain and suffering go hand in hand with the existence of human beings and are referred to as the problem of evil."[12] From this, what is clear, is that both pain and suffering have been conceived as kinds of evil and to consider these concepts without the concept of "evil", will be unwise. A large body of responses to suffering found in Judaism is found in Christian thought as well. In the New Testament, in particular, there are many passages indicating that "suffering" is better understood in terms of the function of *Sin.* In its worst form, suffering may appear in the form of *death.* Thus predominantly "suffering" may be understood as *bodily suffering* amounting to harsh punishment, agony, misery and death. Whatever may be the case, in John 9: 3, Jesus himself however, rejects the notion that suffering is necessarily a function of sin. He cites the example of a blind person who is in deep physical agony and says that neither the blind person (his own) nor his parents' sins caused blindness. Nevertheless, in the New Testament and in other Christian literature "suffering" has been used to signify a *disciplinary function.* Suffering stands out as some such phenomena acting as deterrence to the whole humanity to keep well under control. This sense of "suffering" conveys God's unfailing interest in the moral goodness of man and is confirmed in Hebrews 12: 3–13 and in James 1: 2–4. The deterrent of suffering, so to say, is carried from Jewish literature wherein it is considered as a 'preventive dose of spiritual medicine' or to prevent the ever emerging sin.

It is therefore, clear that the Christian responses to suffering covers both the *retributive* and the *deterrent* senses. These responses are, in fact, directed towards finding excuses of why suffering should be there in this world and man, who is created by the divine lord should nevertheless, suffer. These excuses however do not fill out the whole Christian literature, there are other excuses as well. But we get important information about the ways in which the concept has been used in the Christian literature. Bearing close connection with the Jewish trend, we find that "suffering" may be used to signify the wanton misery inflicted on us as a consequence of the direct activity of the devils. The Christian interest in considering "suffering" as a state of affairs, utterly undesirable, and the one having its genesis owing to devil powers, takes us to the more mystic than the realistic understanding of 'why suffering should be there'. In scripture, Satan appears thrice, not as an embodiment of evil, but as a 'member of heavenly court' to test the human faith in God by provocative functions, "Suffering" may be thus understood as a function of *provocation* to test human faith in God and to make sure the moral goodness of man stands firmly. However, in the Post-Biblical writings, we find the Satan's figure fading out and almost like the Zoroastrian trend, stands out as an evil force staging rebellion against God. The ruler of evil power is thus concerned to step into the Garden of Eden to become instrumental in the *origin* of all human suffering. Suffering thus having a definite metaphysical cause becomes a state of affairs. With this alone starts the *fall* of man. St. Augustine, who taught that the state of the world, from which Christ came to rescue men, was caused by the fall of man in the Garden of Eden through temptation by the devil, propounds such an explanation. The result of this first sin was his 'expulsion' from this Garden, the 'necessity' of pain and toil, and the 'fact of death'. The state of original sin was further on the common state of man and the whole world was allowed to fall under the influence of the Satan. The later Christian theological writings thus pose a peculiar question, whether or not demonology of the scriptures and traditions is treated as mythology and a culture-bound figurative expression of the reality of the evil that afflicts human beings in the world. One way to support the mythological status of the devil and the evil spirits, is to recognize the cultural change and the conviction that, no religion need be static in the frameworks of belief of bygone days. Yet, with the advancement of sciences, the demonic, possessions have fizzled out and no literal belief in demons is relished any more these days. Nonetheless, the influence of malevolent agencies in this world cannot be neglected. The Christians these days however resist the belief in the spirits for its negative power to create fear and suffering. The modern Christians rather tend to accept that once the devil is regarded as a *symbolic* figure, the Augustinian explanation would cease to create influence on us. The doctrine of the fall of man and the original sin has become symbolic of human condition.

Why then, the view that physical suffering (in the sense of physical pain) caused by the devil's interference, has not been taken seriously by modern Christians? Mainly due to the fact that such an idea may amount to the encouragement of another objectionable idea nourished by many Christian theologians. The idea is to put the whole weight of theodicy on the *free will defense*, for the devil as a fallen angel, would be an example of mere conversion of a good agent to the bad. All suffering, including the natural disaster, accident, disease and death could be thus attributed to the misuse of free will. In the first place, it is extremely difficult to make theological sense of this supposition. The God permitting His creation to fall into the grip of a supernatural irredeemable malicious spiritual agent, is neither a religiously nor a theologically plausible picture. The idea, thus advanced by some early Christians is more animistic and demonological than that of rational theology. In the second place, modern scientific knowledge of the fundamental energies and structures of the world enables us to reject the idea that the physical world might have had different and less harmful properties, had it not been interfered with by the devil. Appeal to devil and free fall thus stand out to be rejected by the later Christians.

Alternate solution to the problem, which is more philosophically plausible, can be gathered from two arguments provided on the issue of *pain*. From the Jewish trend, we gather the solution provided by Moses Maimonides. He says that man suffers owing to physical pains through the possession of a body. He points out that all bodily corruption is a 'consequence' of the 'ever changing' material structure of the self-propagating creatures rather than the forms into which they are made. But the form should be bound with matter, and God also creates matter as something inherently good (and not bad). Yet, such self-producing creatures made of matter, which is good and not evil, have passed away to give the created progeny a place to grow and multiply. Hence, it is needless thinking that the material man need never die and need never be subjected to pain. Hence, even if created by God, the self-creating man must be thought of essentially different in form, and thus, essentially independent of the creator too. However, Moses' tendency to verify the physical pains into a petty affair, particularly in relation to God's whole creation, has been particularly disliked as an implausible theological argument.

Turning to the Christian solution provided by St. Thomas Aquinas, which seriously considers God's will and providence, and this awareness of the conditions which, by His decision to create an ordered universe, God necessarily imposes upon himself. Aquinas thinks that God permits certain defects so that the inherent good is not hindered. In case of physical pain, Aquinas says that God wills it only in the sense of willing the good, to which *it* is attached, for example willing to maintain the *balance of nature*. God thus 'wills that something should live their constitutional course and die away'. The distinction between God directly willing and indirectly willing or only permitting is clear. The good of the whole is willed directly, the concomitant evils, if such there be, are willed only indirectly. It is thus logically impossible to will the balance of nature without willing the death of the individuals. Thus an ordered physical universe containing organic creatures has all the possibility of suffering from pain. The whole account, however, is testimony to the fact that the concept "pain" has been clearly used to signify only "physical pain" for which there must be a definite cause. The causal theory dwells between the human follies, demonic activities and God's will to restore the natural balance. To put it more clearly to the modern readers, it may be said that God can no more create a balance of nature without the death of individuals. Brain Hebbelthwaite says "there may well be logically necessary conditions which make it impossible to create an ordered physical universe containing organic creatures without the possibility of accident and pain".[13]

This can be justified by our scientific knowledge of the laws of nature and the structure of the physical and chemical components of the natural world. Both these components have led to the evolution of sentient as well as conscious life under the same general laws. The consequence of such evolution is not one directed, i.e. only good or evil, with good and creativity, the evils of pain also is amalgamated. But the theodicist still faces the problem of the creation of the universe having pain and suffering. Analysing this problem may lead us to many trifles, which I do not want to discuss here because they may not have direct bearing on the understanding of the theological uses of "pain" and "suffering". The discussion rather tilts at the discussion of "evil", which we shall consider later on.

Interestingly, in the Gospels there is hardly any theoretical attempt to analyze the implications of the view of the origin of suffering owing to Fall because, therein, Jesus is represented more realistically and practically. It is reflected in the repudiation of the genetic understanding of the fact of suffering, and, replacing it with the sense of *ultimate punishment* or *retribution* or perhaps, sanction to control the misdeeds of man. A passage from Luke here would not be out of place, that suggests this: "At that very time there were some people present who told Him about the Calibans whose blood Pilate had mixed with their sacrifice. He answered them 'Do you imagine that because these Calibans suffered this fall, they must have been greater sinners than anyone else in Galelie? I tell you they were not; but unless, you repeat, you will all of you come to the same end or the eighteen people who were killed when the tower fell on them at Sialoam; do you imagine they were more guilty than all the other people living in Jerusalem? I tell you they were not; but unless, you repeat you, will, all of you come to the same end".[14] (Luke 13:1-5).

The passage recorded by Luke focuses the idea of repudiating unidirectional causal or genetic explanation of "suffering". Here "suffering" has been unequivocally used as a notion covering the notion "pain", particularly "physical pain", in terms of torture and harassment etc. Replacing the genetic account, we get two ways of understanding the Christian notion of "suffering". One is, of course, the retention of the idea of suffering as an ultimate punishment or sanction, and the other is unequal *distribution* of suffering, i.e. distribution of physical miseries in an unbalanced manner, as if, some injustice has been done to. But this is a misconception, which Luke tries to clarify. I feel that the retention of the sense of sanction carries with it a sense of morality because with it, the Lord does not convey the idea of 'teaching a lesson' or 'deterring' the evil doers, rather discipline for those whom he loves. In the New Testament, the author of the letter to the Hebrews say, "It is for discipline that you have to endure. God is treating you as sons; for what son is there whom his father does not discipline?"[15] This is what the Quran iterates. Whatever degree of morality may be soaked in these assertions, it may be viewed differently as well. One may view it as theodicies' attempt at acting psychotherapist in the face of human tribulations or to try helplessly to save their faces by saving the ignominious God. Even one may view such attempt as inherently unethical in so far as disastrous human suffering has been taken so harshly. Nevertheless, the moral function of pain and suffering, those aiming at the holistic development of human character and personality and in the fostering of virtues such as fortitude and compassion is a common feature of modern theodicy. Prof. John Hick, in his book *Evil and the God of Love*, argues that this world ought to be such as something 'potent of contrary qualities', for instance, it nourishes harm and good, and that 'harm' is not without a purpose; it serves 'soul making'. Thus, "suffering" may have a teleological sense as well, here in this context (unlike biology) the purpose is quite different; it transcends the bodily sphere to enter into the realm of character of a person, which is the object of correction or may be a kind of special preparation for fashioning and schooling in the virtues. "Suffering" may thus stand for some state of affairs, which ought to be there for the exercise of character and perseverance of ever ending self-sacrificial love. Without suffering, therefore, we may conceive of a world running short of precious human values. The state of suffering may be thus made more intelligible and justifiable with, of course, a risk of being more emotional and over-moralistic. People like Hebbelthwaite retorts saying that "to see the world as a vale of soul-making is in any case too narrow a world view. It fails to do justice to the profession, variety and exuberant energy of the physical, animal and human creation"[16]. Avoiding the controversy, we can now move on to see the other side of Luke's passage. As I have said, it focuses the problem of 'distribution of suffering'.

The first to be noticed in this regard, is that when we speak of 'distribution' of suffering, the notion 'suffering' has been certainly used as a state of affairs, which is not simply another 'mundane affair' having a physical cause, rather, in an extremely social sense, mostly metaphysical, because suffering is said to be justifiably distributed in the nature as a whole; by none other than God. The question is why should God distribute extreme suffering to those who are ordinary pious people and disciples of God? Luke's problem is clearly present in Mathew as well. The essence of the Christian response to suffering is the realisation of God as Father and it comes out clearly in Mathew's Sermon in the Mount. It makes entirely clear that a disciple's response to suffering is practical and active because it is laid in the pattern of Christ's own life as a testimony to the fact that extreme suffering may be overlooked at the face of the sustained relationship of child and father. It is due to this that extreme physical agony in crucification may give way to deep binding love for God, the Father. Indeed, in some passages in Mathew, *compassion* is said to be instrumental in the relief of suffering and this is the mark of discipleship. John makes it clear that much before extreme physical agony in the form of crucification. Jesus was aware of the future that was awaiting, and, therefore, his suffering ought to be seen more practically, that is, something from which Jesus may not be exempted, although, it was clear that Jesus would ultimately mingle with God. What is more important here is to know that he did not 'lose' God even in the experience of physical pain. The distribution of suffering may thus, apparently appear to be too harsh and unjustified and one may even think about the reality of the goodness of God or even God's existence, but 'suffering' stands out as an acid-test, as if, for the one who never loses sight of the eternal Divine relationship. Clarifying this sense, John Bowker says that "Indeed in a vitally important sense he (Jesus) established the relationship of God, a Father conclusively, because by the willing acceptance of his own innocent suffering and the vindication of that acceptance in the resurrection, he rewarded or transferred the relationship to an arena where no further accident of suffering could threaten it.[17] This focuses the ultimate belief (of John) that suffering may be seen as a state of affairs which is not eternal; it may be rather potentially destroyed by God. Hence, the distribution of suffering does not present a fatal problem. We have to remember here that although physical suffering like blindness etc. need not be necessarily seen as a deliberately inflicted punishment of God; it is, nevertheless, real and tragic with every positive hope that in presence of Jesus one can overcome this and even God is to be found here. Suffering is neither pretence nor unreal, nor it be treated as a real tragedy.

One gets an idea that in the synoptic gospels the way the notion of "suffering" has been used is more symbolic than calling it real or unreal. To be precise, synoptic gospels represent Jesus as a suffering servant, whose physical suffering may be so real to our eyes that we may hardly doubt it, but for that reason, Jesus' divinity is not at stake; this suffering conveys a different meaning; better said, it attempts at conveying a meaning, that is; that painful nature of humankind is most likely to suffer as did Jesus with a difference and if the sinner does not keep faith in the eternal relationship with God, he has to face the ignominy of everlasting suffering. The symbol of suffering is an attempt to usher in the senses of repentance and salvation among God's loved beings. Jesus' suffering in the cross is thus symbolic in so far as a similar fate for sinners may not be meted out if there is no repentance and no love for God. The symbol is, nevertheless, a deterrent symbol and needless to say that deterrent value of 'suffering' persists in synoptic gospels.

The Christian understanding of suffering is never complete without noticing the value of not suffering, rather the risen life of Christ, which is a testimony to the final release from all suffering and attaining God. For this, the Christian opinion is that the avoidance of all behaviour that might cause suffering to others is the most important and to take efficient steps to relieve suffering is desirable. But such practical acts at the face of suffering invite suffering, and this is basic to the understanding why at times, the distribution of suffering appears to be unjust. The idea of using the notion of "suffering" as *instrumentally valuable* for the disciples of Christ is particularly prominent in St. Paul's writings. Paul's view is that although Christ's disciples shall win convincingly in the final run, the discipleship involves suffering. These focuses the identification of our own suffering with that of Christ.

This is the basis of the instrumental value of suffering and practical response to why there is suffering for the most pious man. The same awareness is there also in I Peter that suffering is to be taken positively and be endured. The best suitable example to this is found in Christ himself. Thus, Christ himself as the 'figure–head' of suffering occurs in letters to the Hebrew as well. The instrumental view of suffering, thus invariably, projects the value of suffering rather than rejecting it as an utter evil. But this does not amount to say that suffering itself is good, because the person who faces suffering with view to serve humanity and divinity, at least does so with a clear idea that his life shall, inevitably, lead to a final release from all suffering. Suffering cannot be either moral or spiritual end of human life.

The New Testament line of dealing with the notion of "suffering" brings another interesting way in limelight in which suffering has been symbolically used in association with Christ's suffering. The crucified

Christ, the victim and the risen Christ the victor has been efficiently symbolised in the New Testament to let the nature of *human deficiency*, of which suffering is a part has to be understood. It is to be noticed as a consequence either of an original capacity for goodness, which has not yet been realised, or as an original sin which has had its effect on all subsequent individuals. John Hick traces these related and yet different thoughts corresponding to the two ways in which human deficiency was understood. According to Hick, when suffering is looked upon as an original capacity for goodness which has not yet been realised, it is *Irenean* way of looking at "suffering" because, its prominent version was put forward by Ireneus, whereas when "suffering" is looked upon as an original sin which has far-reaching ramifications, it is *Augustinian* essence, for its clear formulation could be seen in St. Augustine's writings. However, these responses are not much different because whatever both of them essentially want to convey is the Christian idea that if "suffering" be considered as an important symbol signifying human deficiency then the matter of urgency is to eradicate it; to overcome such deficiency by keeping an unflinching faith on leading a *qualitative moral life*. Both Ireneus and Augustine believed that it is not very important to ask for the genesis of human suffering always, rather to go for leading a good life. Perhaps, the symbolic use of Christ's suffering projects the most important message: the message of the value of "good life" and the value of "leading a good life". The symbol efficiently focuses the existential value of suffering in the world as whole, which, nevertheless, has no intrinsic worth.

From the above discussion, one gets an idea that the different ways in which the notion of "suffering" (covering "pain") has been used in Christian theology, is broadly speaking a state of affairs which is as real as our existence in this world, so it would be unwise to call it an intrinsic value and that we have obligation to remove suffering if we have unflinching faith in the summun bonum of life, that is, becoming one with the reality of God. But "suffering", as has been used in Christian writings, focuses another interesting question, 'what is our image of God, if suffering is a *fact* (or a state of affairs)?' We can put the question differently; whether our own sufferings or that of others, disclose anything about God? If the answer is in the affirmative (the Christian writes that way) apart from other interesting things, we may have an idea of how "suffering' has been more interestingly used along with another metaphysical notion, that is, the notion of "God", and both the symbols, as if, combine to reveal interesting things. One interesting revelation is the way the theistic user use "suffering" in order to project his or her images of God or his or her images of the Being *called* 'God'.

The Christian writers are divided sharply so far as the question of human suffering and the involvement of God are concerned. The basic problem is whether or not God ought to be conceived as capable of *sharing* in our sorrows? Some Christians say that God does share with an element of *sympathy*, whereas others say that he shares with an element of *empathy*. Hence, human suffering has a bearing on how God himself participates in this state of affairs. To say, suffering calls either enough sympathy of God or not merely sympathy but God makes himself sure to suffer as well. God is sure to suffer. The tension between the inner nature of God owing to immanence and transcendence evolves the conflicting assertions. We are thus indecisive about whether or not God is impassable or passable. Leaving aside the lengthy controversy, let us concentrate on the understanding of the meaning of "suffering" which Christians attribute to God.

First thing to notice is that "suffering" has often been parallelly used with the word "pain" in Christian writings, particularly in recent works like Kitamori's *Theology of pain of God*. This is not only a parallel use, it is blurring, and therefore, many Christian writers find it important for distinguishing "suffering" and "pain" clearly in order to ascribe a concept of "suffering" to God. The first point of distinction is that pain is bound to the body, which connects it to things out there in the nature. It is due to this that pain is often considered as a physical sensation emanating from an external stimulus, whereas "suffering" is a more complex concept conveying the sense of 'distress' owing to our relationship with other beings in particular, i.e. when the bond of relationship is destroyed, J.Y. Lee says, "suffering deals with the inward disposition of man while pain deals with the bodily sensations of man".[18] To continue further, the recent thinkers hold that suffering deals with psychological and spiritual dimension of life even though, it is inseparable with pain, which deals with the physical dimension of life. Thus pain should be taken as belonging to the sphere of bio-physiological study. However, in human life, pain and suffering are intimately related with each other that we couldn't separate them. To the Christians, therefore, the intensity of suffering is to be measured by the bond of human 'relationship', whereas, the possibility of pain is measured by the 'acuteness' of the physical stimulus of sensation. Nevertheless, as Christians consider human beings as an entity of body and spirit united, the experience of suffering and pain is intimately united with each other, but this is not tantamount to their synonymous use. This is really an interesting attempt to *evaluate* the meanings of "pain" and "suffering" and without going for definitions, the meanings have been differentiated mainly on the basis of a stipulation, viz. pain and suffering are really state of affairs, former more clearly understandable on the basis of bio-physiological descriptions, whereas the latter, understandable on the basis of the inward disposition of man. What we learn from this criterion of evaluation and whether or not we are really able to distinguish them this way are different issues to be considered later on. Hence, taking Christian evaluation of "pain" and "suffering" cursorily, it is easily understandable that when we speak of human relationship with divine being, we cannot apply the same notion of "pain" because "pain" being essentially understood in terms of sensation bound to the physical body, does not belong to "God", which is a metaphysical notion meaning a Pure Sprit. Therefore, the concept of "suffering" is an ultimate form of divine experience.

So far as human relationship with God is concerned, it is actually a relationship of eternal *Love*. It runs the risk of wholesome suffering of entire creation, and also, the Divine Being immanent-in-creation, suffers as well. The Divine Being has the potentiality to suffer owing to *empathy*. Empathy is thus participation of Divine pathos. Likewise, the potentiality of human suffering is owing to the depth of human love for God. Thus, one who is afraid of suffering is unable to love God or others. Kikegaard puts it beautifully as, "the distinguishing mark of religious action" for "this suffering means the relationship or love". Thus suffering is experienced actually when, the possible or actual threat of the destruction of loving relationship is estranged. The threat comes mainly from mistrust or unbelief in which we love. Estrangement of loving relationship resulting into suffering is due to the lack of harmony. The Christian writers thus find out a new meaning in suffering, that is, they do not take it traditionally as an evil *per se*, rather having a deep significance. When we say that God's love towards others lulls God Himself to some kind of suffering or we conceive of a suffering God, which cannot be destroyed by evil forces of the world, we are conceiving an empathetic God. But the empathetic relationship of God and the world can be distorted or disturbed by the evil forces. It is not the power of our sin that distorts this relationship or the eternal harmony, rather it is the way God responds to our sin that does so. God's love has to be thus viewed both transcendentally and immanently, the former rejects us on account of our sins, whereas the latter accepts us on account of being his loving children. We may say that God's nature has an 'in-built disharmony' in the form of transcendental and immanent *agape*, and thus, it is a prototype of our relationship with God. Such an explanation of suffering focuses one more interesting use of "suffering". It may be used to signify the highest action in *inwardness.* It has to be understood as inward activity. God's suffering has to be taken also in this sense meaning, thereby, an 'inner-disharmony' within His own inner self. Divine passibility or empathy may be thus understood as the 'possibility of disharmony of transcendence and immanence in *agape*' by the empathy of God due to the sins of the world. Whereas, the impassability of God means 'the inner nature is undisturbed and He does in no way, participate in human suffering'. An interesting use of "suffering" emerges from this. When the notion applies to God, it is only vicarious and *redemptive* suffering whereas "suffering" detached from the motive of love loses this very significance. "Suffering" may be thus meant as an 'enduring strength of love'. The evidences of such suffering (empathetic) is written large and loud in Matthew 26:24, 54, 56, Acts 3:13, Deutero-Isaiah 52:13, 53:12, Isaiah 53:3, 53:8. The conception of "Servant of the Lord" who suffers for us, has been nicely projected and thus the suffering of Lord becomes a historical reality in the suffering of Jesus Christ.

But many Christian thinkers differ in opinion about such uses of the notion of "suffering", particularly, when applied to God. They would prefer to put aside the idea of God suffering for us, saying that, He has no participatory feeling as we have, but He may have some *sympathy.* Sympathy is, nevertheless, not empathy. God is thus said to be not involved or immanent in the world's sufferings, nor is the Self in tension; He is neither aloof; He is merely a Sympathiser distancing Himself from the human acts. Thus God is *impassible, not* passable;

is their conclusion. W.R. Mathews says that "the reasons which have led the Christian theologians, on the whole, to reject the idea that suffering can enter into the Divine experience ...... come partly from the tradition, inherited from the Platonic and Aristotelian philosophy, that the essential nature of the divine is to be immutable and self-sufficient."[19] So, the concept of "apatheia" is closely related to the Greek idea of "autarkia". This tendency among the Christians is an early one and could be traced in the over emphasis of the distinctions of "persons" in Trinity.

Avoiding the squabble regarding empathy and sympathy, we can still find out important Christian uses of "suffering" even when the term has no great significance in the context of God. One may notice the remarkable use of this notion by the "apathia' theorists 'that is to say' how they denounce the idea of passibility. First of all, these thinkers use "suffering" to mean, "intrinsically evil" and argue that it cannot be a part of Divine experience. In 20th century, Baron F. Von Hugel champions such a thought. Hugel's opinion amounts to the obvious relegation of "suffering" to "evil" because he asserts that suffering is a state of affairs comparable to *sin* and even, as he says, these terms may be interchangeably used. Now, God's nature being one of the perfect Joy and eternal Bliss, He can never be said to suffer from human follies. Randles supports this view and shows objection in saying that "suffering" should be understood as a "loss of inherent excellence". He insists that any attribution of suffering to God is objectionable on the ground of this basic *negative sense* of the notion, which turns God to a miserable object of our pity. If God is supposed to be a miserable sufferer, He cannot be a redeemer and thus the most crucial issue of salvation will be at stake immediately. Randles thus says that God is impassible. E.L. Mascall also supports Randles in saying that if God ever suffers, we can never be united with Him or that both of us will suffer forever. This basic meaning of "suffering" is obvious enough to these thinkers because they follow Greek anthropology; in which, passions take a lower place in human souls. Although, Plato and Aristotle did not make passion an 'evil', they made it a lesser good, and, therefore, cannot be a part of God, who is the Highest Good. The early Christian notion of making "suffering" an "evil" is nothing more than making Greek anthropology look more acute.

The supporters of divine impassability also take the notion of "suffering" in the sense of "inner frustration" and argue that it cannot be attributed to God, who is Infinite in Power and Freedom. This sense of "suffering" is, perhaps, an outcome of a 'common assumption that if suffering of human beings implies some kind of frustration, the divine experience of suffering also amounts to frustration which we experience in suffering. If participation implies limitation, God, who is infinite in power and freedom, cannot be frustrated, and if God is frustrated, He is limited and in no sense, great. We are not in a position to accept all these things, and, therefore, we are not in a position to accept the passability of God.

Another interesting use of the notion of "suffering" is that the supporters of divine impassability use the notion to imply "bound in time", therefore, it is against the notion of divine transcendence and a timelessness. Christian thinkers like Mascal, Mozley and Robinson hold that the notion of "suffering" if applied to Divine Being, acquires a special significance, viz. "hunted in time" or simply, it encourages an idea of temporal God because suffering should be understood as a state of affairs happening within a time frame, in the corporeal world. God is neither temporally existing nor existing corporeally as we do, because He is essentially transcendent and independent of the world. Hence, Divine suffering cannot be accepted. What is interesting, is to notice that this amounts to the mere acceptance of the fact that 'time" and "suffering" are interwoven concepts. This is reflected in A.N. Whitehead's conviction that suffering (*pathos*) induces a lapse of time. Putting these two notions together in this manner, may be serious enough as there is a tendency to limit the meaningful use of the term "suffering" only in those propositions, which make clear temporal reference.

Thus the supporters of the theory of empathetic God rejected these criticisms of passibility to tell us other interesting stories about the use of this notion. The first point is that it will be very difficult to accept "suffering" as "intrinsically evil" and thus difficult to accept that God's suffering amounts to the limitation of Blissful God. In fact, the supporters of the theory of Divine passibility holds that when we consider suffering as a state of affairs, it may be due to evil as well as due to vicarious sacrifice. These projects two kinds of suffering, "general" and "redemptive", the former being *effected* by evil whereas the latter is *occasioned* by evil. The former one is thus an evil in the 'penal sense', whereas the latter is not. "redemptive suffering" is thus 'non-evil' form of suffering because the purpose of such suffering is to overcome all evils, and not to succumb to it. Even "general" or "penal" suffering may or may not be called an "evil" because it depends on the attitude of the person to whom such suffering is given as a raw material to shape. Thus, "suffering" does not carry with the meaning of "evil", it is the people who suffer give it that meaning. This reminds us of the *instrumental* or *teleological* meaning of "pain", when suffering, like pain, becomes an instrument for good to enhance us in participating in the empathy of God. But, if we do not have the right attitude, it may become instrumental in moving away from God. Thus "suffering" in itself is not "evil" or to put it in another way, both notions are not interchangeable.

The supporters of Divine passibility also object to the implication that "suffering" amounts to "frustration" and thus, God is said to get frustrated as we do, and so, He is no great God. Robinson holds that 'this is an odd implication because the experience of frustration which is often a part of suffering, cannot be attributed to God, because such attribution is possible in case of physical bodies'. Since divine nature does not have a physical body, He is not frustrated as we are. This amount to the saying that "frustration" may have some obvious connection with the notion "pain" which has been taken as bodily sensation. Hence, God does not feel any pain, and thus, is not frustrated by it. So, the sense of "frustration" shifts from "suffering" to "pain" with the obvious shifts of non-physical experience to the physical experience. To say, in "suffering of God", the "suffering" should be understood bearing a special sense, that is non-physical experience of no frustration rather voluntary or paradoxical limitation of God owing to His empathy. "Suffering" when attributed to God, thus, signifies 'self-limitation' of God, which comes out of His pure love for His creatures. Divine suffering is thus not a limitation, rather, a strength of God.

We can further see that "suffering" need not mean "temporal limitation", and thus, not applicable to God who is transcendental and timeless. "Suffering" does not simply amount to "temporality" in case of God, because God is not in time, time is in Him. It is the reality of God that creates and controls time. Therefore, the question of temporal limitation of God does not arise at all. Again, we are confusing the use of the notion of "suffering" with God, in the manner we wish, we would use with "human beings" who is in time.

This way the supporters of empathetic theory try to project interesting message to us. They try to tell us that using "suffering" with "God" may seriously be jeopardised if we have a confusion of the same-level use of "suffering" with regard to "human being". Even if, we carefully skip the lengthy debate, we can still make a sense out of this debate and that is, that "suffering" of "God" may have more senses than one.

With this we come to an end to discuss the ethical and theological uses of the notions of "pain" and "suffering". But as we have seen, these notions, particularly the latter one, has close connection with the notion of "evil". We have seen that to call pain and suffering evils may not be too safe but that in theological literature, the problem of evil is unavoidable. We shall now consider the problem of evil in a very general manner with an eye to what offering does the problem have towards an understanding of the use of this notion. To initiate this discussion, I shall now heavily depend on no other theologies discussed so far except Christianity. The reason is that the problem of evil along with the notion of "pain" and "suffering" has appeared clearly and widely in Christian theological writings, and one has, by now, picked up the main tone of discussion, would know that rather than going into the details of the problem of evil, I should concentrate in unfolding the ways, in which the concept "evil" has been used along with "pain" and "suffering".

One sense in which "evil" turns out be a problem in theodicy is, what is the meaning of "evil" or what is the meaning of "evil exists"? The theologians generally avoid giving a clear cut strict definition of the notion because they feel that rather than defining, it is desirable to explain in which different senses of the term may be really used in theological literature. First of all, "evil" signifies *pain and suffering* of animals, children and adult human beings, that is, of some beings who are helpless and unable to lessen their suffering, and of others, who sometimes but more usually do not bring their suffering upon themselves. The evils involved include absence of disposition of sight, audition, thought, mobility etc. with the consequent pain and suffering these absence of powers bring with them. Related to this is the *degeneration and aging of sentient beings*, that is, senility and aging.

The term also includes *natural processes* of birth, aging, death, and each involving physical pain, deep agony and misery. Further, "evil", in a very general manner, signifies *essential limitations of existing beings,* also who either live or live by preying on others sin in order to survive. This is the basic nature of all animals, particularly carnivorous animals, and parasites and predators too. With this, is associated *disease,* which is also referred to by "evil". This has caused and shall cause great suffering in the ecological society. Not only this, but "evil" refers to the occurrence of *natural phenomena* which brings pain and suffering to men and animals. The phenomena of avalanches, landslides, earthquakes, floods, volcanoes, drought, and the like, are evils in this sense. We may coagulate all these references of "evil" to coin an expression, viz. "physical evil". "Physical evil" is, in fact, "evil suffered" which is as certain as the existence is, and carries with it, the basic sense of "limitation". It is "limitation" of human as well as natural perfection. In this sense, we may call it a "privation" rather than a "negation". This "privation" is a limitation that characterizes all created things and with the idea of limitation, the notion of "non-being" comes to our minds naturally. It is "non-being" that limits all created things. Only God, who is eternal, timeless and unlimited, is free from all taint of non-being, limitation and privation. Hence, only He is free from all evils. On the other hand, all creatures being bundles of being and non-being, are limited and merged into physical evils. Such an idea of limitation and non-being conveys the sense of "metaphysical evil". Thus physical and metaphysical evils go together.

In another sense, "evil" refers to the suffering caused by man to man and to animals. This is a deliberate act of man, who rationally chooses to inflict suffering and physical pain. With this go the senses of "guilt" and "punishment" because deliberation of cruel actions causing pain and suffering causes a sense of guilt in us, and for all that, we are punished and with punishment, we suffer. This is the sense of "evil committed" or "evil done". It conveys not only senses of cruelty and harm, but also means the limitation of human beings in order to gain perfection. Such evil causing impoverishment of human intention, character and perfection is said to be "moral evil". It is not that only irrational human beings are sources of such evil action, rather vast misery, fear, anxiety, grief are caused by conscientious and godly men. This is best reflected in religious wars, racist wars and sufferings caused in the name of God. Moral evil is deeply related to other evils just mentioned, because the moral evils cause intense physical evil and reflect immense limitation and imperfection of human beings. It appears that physical, metaphysical and moral evils are subspecies of "evil". This is exactly what Liebnitz and Otto wants to say. "Moral evil" is a very broad notion, it may mean an evil owing to the failure of doing something what we *ought* to do rather than, doing what is intrinsically wrong. It may also mean 'deliberative choice' of a principle of action which is, intrinsically, bad and it may mean, acting according to a false moral belief that such and such principle or principles of actions are true and worth following, whereas, they are not so and thus essentially evil.

In theodicy, "moral evil" is perhaps the most important reference of evil, and in more sense than one, covers physical and metaphysical evils. Theists often look at is as a rejection of God because the existence of the basic moral imperfection points towards the basic fact that such a creature cannot have been created by perfect God, particularly, He could not have created man in His own image. Moral evil is distinct from physical evil (pain and suffering) and it would be completely unfounded *to* hold that with the management of the physical evil, moral evil may be resolved. Many utilitarian theists prefer to pursue this line of argument. But, even if a solution could be found for the problem of physical evil, moral evil would still constitute a problem unless the solution to the former also encompasses the solution of the latter. The main idea behind such an argument is that since moral evil points towards human limitation and imperfection in thought and deed, no resolution of physical evil eradicates moral evil. But if "moral" is stretched too far, it may lead to moral pessimism because being inherently limited and imperfect being, man can never pursue good rather remains bad. This is to go to the pessimistic limit of Liebnitzian theodicy. However, most Christian thinkers argue that although finite beings can never attain their ideal or attain pure perfection, the ideal itself may continue to drag them through their moral journey. Man may be thus a bundle of being and non-being, still pursuing the moral path of becoming perfect.

"Evil" is also used to refer to "ugliness" and thus focuses the sense of "aesthetic evil" and the theists would still be faced with resolving such evil with claim, that the creator is all-powerful, all-wise, and all-good. Aesthetic evil with its basic tone of ugliness, *prima facie*, refers to imperfection, an imperfection that does not directly relate itself to human will rather to God's perfection.

Thus man is a subject to every kind of evil and in all times to come. "Evil" is thus a matter-of-fact in past, present and future. In this sense, it is real and not unreal. In a nutshell the whole existence nurtures evil in two fundamental forms: pain and suffering.

But all theologians do not use the concept of "evil" to refer to "real" evils. They say that "evil" is fictitious or unreal. Hence, the problem of evil is not a real problem. One reason for saying this, is to believe that the concept of "evil" is a 'pseudo-concept' and not real, and, therefore, evil is an illusion. To accept this means to accept that all evils are apparent and not real. It may also be argued that all the so-called evil phenomena are mere appearances and not realities. It is important to notice first of all that "evil" as a concept bears no internal incoherence, and to call it pseudo-concept is to forget the fact that in huge body of scientific and non-scientific literature, it does appear with varying forces of meaning and use. It is certainly wrong to think it something, but to call something an embodiment of evil, meaning thereby causing harm, loss, frustration, pain, suffering etc. is not prevented by any extension of reason. To call all so-called evils 'real' has some philosophical force at least, but from that we cannot conclude therefore, that "evil" is a concept having no use. Only, we get an idea that we can, following some reasons, speak of fictitious evils as well. To say that some evils appear to be like that, though are not, may be backed by some reason, but to say that, therefore, the concept of "evil" makes no sense, is pointless. Again, what it focuses is that, at times, we may refer to "evils wrongly so-called". There are two irresistible impulses about using "evil" in theological literature. One is that it has to be "real" in the sense that we can experience objects, facts, events, ideas called "evil" and the other is that real evils pose a threat to the conception of God for more reasons than one, and thus, it has to be resolved. In Christian theology, evil has been considered in these lights, which point to the practical interest in facing the reality of evil reflected mainly in pain and suffering. Thus, there is no way, but to take evil as something 'real' and thus face it. But the Christians also know that there may be errors of belief and thus, it is perfectly all right to imagine evils wrongly so-called. H.J. McCloskey says: "moral evil, suffering and pain, when seen for what they really are, and not simply as they might appear to be, are seen to be full realities."[20].

If "evil" makes any sense, particularly when we try to look into the sensible ways in which "evil" as a concept has been understood as used in theological literature, several questions arise and they are more confusing. These questions put together may be called the 'problem of evil'. The problem of evil may, thus at the outset, seem to be an amalgam or cluster of various theoretical and practical questions. In its theoretical aspect, theodicy is ostensibly concerned with questions like:

(1) Can evil itself be regarded intelligible? We have been thus far involved with this question to find that both physical and moral evils (as well as metaphysical and aesthetic evil) make unique sense in theological literature and thus evil *per se* should be rendered intelligible.
(2) Is the existence of God logically compatible with the existence of evil? A variant of this question is "Is the existence of God logically compatible with the varieties and profusion of evil?" This logical form of question will be considered later on.
(3) Does the existence of evil constitute evidence that counts against theism? A theologian believes that theism has an explanatory function that will try to reply this question in the negative to assert the possibility of theism.
(4) What does God do to overcome evil and what do we do to overcome evil?

These questions are of practical interest which theologians certainly would like to answer. Hence, the problem of evil coagulates the problems of intelligibility of evil, logical compatibility of evil with the notion of existing God, evidence in favour of the possibility of theism in the face of evil and the practical concern about resolving evil. It is clear that, in theology, the notion of "evil" has been taken for signifying something real with a cause and that ought to be resolved.

The first three questions are theoretical in nature and if, we consider the questions of intelligibility and evidentiality, we find that "evil" is intelligible according to the theists only, in so far as we accept the truism that the notion refers necessarily to pain which is mainly physical, and to suffering, which is taken as agony, despair and frustration. To imagine a world without pain and suffering would be unwise enough and to think that we could overlook the reality and thus resolve it is equally irrational. Whereas to accept their realities means to accept the stark truth that they are, generally, speaking harm causing, noxious, disagreeable an so on, and thus has to be labelled by a name, and we use "evil" for that purpose. "Evil" is more mythical, however, to refer to many more things, but to the theists, if we just consider its two basic sense, i.e. it is imperfection at the existential and moral levels and it is physical noxious elements causing harm, it does make enough sense to consider it for further analysis. Naturally, we would ask, if God has created this world, why is there evil? Can we really justify why evil should be there at all? With that, we may add another question, in what sense can we still justify the basic theistic belief in all loving, all-powerful, good God, if there be evil? If one goes through the vast Christian literature, one may soon get lost at the face of range of excuses for why is there evil, even if, it is God's world and that this idea of having evil does not over-rule God's existence. I would not needlessly dwell into such excuses. What is, nonetheless, interesting for me is to notice that for the justification of existence of evil, one has to talk about God and pain and suffering. 'God-talk' comes naturally, as the main precondition for the explanation of thing and phenomena called evil, whereas 'pain-talk' and 'suffering-talk' are essential as far as facts and phenomena are called "evil" they are in fact, nothing but physical pain, and physical, mental and metaphysical suffering. Hence, evil-talk is God-talk, pain-talk and suffering-talk. This is the distinctive style in which Christian theology has progressed. It is interesting to find that the "problem of evil" is a logical construction of a set of theoretical and practical question, whereas the sub-questions are such that an answer of these projects the fact that "pain" and "suffering" are sub-species of "evil" and the fact that it will be very difficult for us to neglect the sub species to explain the genus concept. I would take the risk of saying that the Christian explanation is essentially *circular* in so far as it starts from the problem of evil to beg the notions of God and pain and suffering, and to explain pain and suffering along with God, it runs head on to find the problem of evil. It may be very interesting to notice that neither all theologies follow this circular path, nor do all non-theistic religions do that.

Another important thing to notice is that the very existence of the problem of evil fails to make any significance if God's existence, which is more problematic, is not dragged in the scenario. Also the problem would fail to make any significance if we do not refer to pain and suffering as kinds of evil. No doubt, a close circuit of concepts, each problematic in its own right, each having varying meanings and uses, is connected in theological household to illuminate the dark corner of the 'existence of evil'. It would be more interesting for us to know why should we conceive God at all, even if, we do have pain and suffering and why should we have to accept that these are evils? We may ask, why should we create a problem of evil by creating another problem of God being dragged to the scene simply by attributing Him creator, good, powerful and so on? To answer these questions is to go to the basis of theism, and, therefore, to resolve the problem of evil. We have to first decide whether or not, we would just accept God's existence and His attributes or we do not need them at all. If we do not need them, we may still argue for 'pain' and 'suffering' as important notions mingling in the genetic notion of "evil", but it will, then, let problem of evil fizzle out. "Evil" may still be understood as a problem in so far as its major allies, pain and suffering call for immediate management and any management demands etiology, but that is a different story, a non-theological one. If we thus come to what God ought to do and what we ought to do to overcome evil, a list of Christian suggestions shall surely fill our minds. We shall find that such suggestions are over-charged with morality. Human realization of the goodness of God and of the perfection of self along with the supremacy of the Loving God, who may be said to suffer for us, shall figure in naturally. We can pick out theistic management methods from such suggestions, which are mainly moral, but then, the God-intoxication in managing evil shall still govern supreme. Thus, the theological notions of God, evil and the problem of evil are essentially circular, pointing to each other. But the conception of a good God must be primary here.

Whatever I have said may be justified simply by going back to the *formal-logical* analysis of the problem of evil, which is most important in the modern Christian writings. The credit goes to many, but mainly to

Alvin Plantinga for its clear formulation and to H.D. Aiken, H.J. McCloskey and J. Mackie among others. Plantinga has pointed out that the problem of evil may be stated with the help of statements related to each other logically and such logical relationship among these statements poses a problem, called the problem of evil. These statements are:

(1) God exists;
(2) God is omnipotent;
(3) God is omniscient;
(4) God is wholly good;
(5) There is evil in the world.

What the theists have in mind is that if God's existence is beyond doubt, we have to accept, at least, three extremely important attributes of God, viz. He is omniscient, omnipotent and good, and thus, if the existence of evil in the world is beyond doubt (with pain and suffering lurking all around), it poses a problem—the problem of evil. Why is it a problem? Just because the assertion 1 is falsified along with 2, 3 and 4, because an all powerful, all knowing, good God cannot deliberately allow evil in the world. If he allows it, He is no good, not knowledgeable, not powerful and thus not existent either. The problem of evil is thus a problem for a Christian apologist and not for those who do not believe in 1, 2, 3 and 4 although one may believe in 5. This is a typically placed logical argument by the non-believer in particular and thus, it is a creation of non-believers seriously taken by the believers. The problem is really multifaceted problem in so far as all assertions need clarification, if not precise definition of God, existence, omnipotent, omniscient, good and evil. Each problematic statement thus begs clarification. Moreover, the meaning and significance of 5 cannot logically construct a problem by itself (I have said this) unless it is in conjunction of 1, 2, 3 and 4. Hence, the initiating of the so-called problem of evil begs several problematic statements to be clarified for its meaning and use. Once we delve into the statements 1, 2, 3 and 4, we would further find that it is not 2, 3 or 4 rather 1 which is basic or fundamental and any reference to 2, 3 or 4 without 1, loses all meaning. Hence, we have to go back to the meaning of 'god exists' and only have to go for all sorts of justifications that have enriched theological literature. I have said that the problem of evil is a making of believers and non-believers approaching it differently, only if, it is essentially circular, that is, goes back to the notion of God and His existence, whereas if we start with "God" and juxtapose His attributes with the belief in evil; which is nothing but pain and suffering in this world, we shall complete the making of the problem of evil. One should, however, be emphatic in declaring that the problem of evil is in fact "theological problem of human evil".

We can now drop this discussion. I shall move on to the important philosophical schools dealing with the notions of 'pain', 'suffering' and also 'evil'.

NOTES AND REFERENCES

1. Nowell-Smith, P.H., *Ethics*, Pelican, London, 1961, p. 132.
2. Baier, K., *The moral point of view*, Cornell Univ. Press, N.Y. 1964, p. 267.
3. Ryle, G., *The Concept of Mind*, Hutchinson Univ. Library, 1949, p. 109.
4. Bentham, J., *The Principles of Morals and Legislation*, Clarendon Press, Oxford, 1789, p. 1.
5. Mill, J.S. , *Utilitarianism*, H.B. Acton (ed), Everyman's Library, London, 1992, p. 40.
6. Moore, G.E., *Principia Ethica*, Cambridge Univ. Press, Cambridge, 1962, p. 212.
7. *Ibid.*, p. 212.
8. *Ibid.*, p. 212.
9. Hebbelthwaite, B., *Evil, Suffering and Religion*, Sheldon, London, 1952, p. 40.
10. Bowker, John, *Problem of Suffering in the Religions of the World*, Cambridge University Press, Cambridge, 1970, pp. 101-36.
11. Hebbelthwaite, B., *op cit.* p. 44.
12. Goerman, Ulf., *A Good God?* Verbum, Hakan, Ohlssons, 1977, p. 13.
13. Hebbelthwaite, B., *op. cit.*, p. 73.
14. Luke, 13, 1-5.
15. Hebrew, 12.7.
16. Hebbelthwaite, B., *op. cit.* p. 51.
17. Bowker, John., *op. cit.*, pp. 44-98.
18. Lee, J.Y., *Christian Concept of Man*, Philosophical Library. N.Y. 1971, p. 61.
19. Matthews, W. R., *God in Christian Thought and Experiences*, Nishet & Co., London, 1930, p. 247.
20. McCloskey, H. J., *God and Evil*, Martinus Nijhoff, The Hague, 1974, p. 42.

3

"Pain", "Suffering", "Evil" and Some Schools of Philosophy

"PAIN", "SUFFERING" AND MARXISM

It is extremely important to consider views of some of the schools of Philosophy, which deserve special mention for their distinguished contribution to resolve the *problems* of pain and suffering. Without extrapolating too much the way these philosophical schools deal with these problems, we may concentrate on the different uses of these notions and the meaning acquired thereby. It will be too cumbersome if I try to jumble the views of all important thinkers belonging to a school. It will be sufficient to concentrate on the general view of a philosophical school along with a detailed analysis of the views of some philosophers, as and when, it is necessary to do so.

To start with, I prefer to give an account of the way these notions have been used in the 'Marxist school' of philosophy. It is desirable to see what Marxism has to say about the problems of pain and suffering. First of all, like many philosophical schools, The Marxist school of philosophy hardly lays any importance on the problem of pain, because, they find it comfortable to treat pain under the broader generic notion of "suffering". Hence, Marxism considers the problem of suffering and tries to resolve it in an extremely distinguished manner. It is clear that the problem of suffering is basic in Marxism, and the so-called problem makes sense in the context of 'human suffering'. It has little or nothing to do with that of animal or any other suffering. Human suffering becomes a *problem* because it is something that deserves management by conscious, civilised human beings. To do so, one has to take into account the *genesis* of such problem. The causal explanation of suffering is written large in Marxism and so is its management. But within this body of explanation, we find the use of the notion of "suffering" and distinct meaning the term acquires thereby.

One has to be careful at the outset by knowing, that the Marxist view of suffering is not the one which has been advocated alone by Marx and not by others, and that whatever has been said about suffering could be found in one or two philosophical works of Marx. In fact, when we undertake this task, we are facing a peculiar situation. It is extremely difficult to find out one chapter written exclusively on this matter in the works of Marx and in the works of those who by far follow Marx's philosophy. One has to really collect from the vast Marxist literature (which is fortunately extremely rich) to discover what the Marxists think about pain and suffering. I must accept that my collection is scrappy and, therefore, the account may leave out many things, but I am sure, not the important ones.

We must understand that with regard to suffering, Marx showed a great practical interest because he did *not* consider it to be a theoretical problem, which can be resolved by mental gymnastics. Suffering is an acute practical human problem and, therefore, demands practical interest. It may be due to this that suffering has not been considered by Marx as something abstract; rather, as an actual fact or existential phenomenon about which the human being including the human societies are concerned. But the existential phenomenon of suffering does *not* beg either metaphysical or idealistic theoretical explanation. Rather, it has to be viewed in the actual contexts of 'those who suffer' and 'those who inflict suffering'. Marx's passionate and revolutionary observations of human society compelled him to think that human suffering could be discussed in the real appalling situations under which the working masses lived and died. This takes us, naturally, to the careful consideration of the uncontrolled industrial development and the exploitation of man by man. The horrific conditions, which are, in fact, the natural outcome of the exploitative industrialised economy at the hands of a group of people, who have silently set down the facts of human suffering. Marx has portrayed the basis of suffering in *Das Kapital* which was an outcome of studies based on virtual bondage of human beings in exploitative industrial economy and the study of slavery, which emerges from the same. On the whole, these resulted into wanton human suffering. Engels, who in turn, showed how class struggle has emerged in England from human suffering owing to industrial exploitation by the bourgeois. This projects a key notion in the Marxist understanding of human suffering, i.e. "alienation". Immediately, we are at hand a philosophical view which puts human suffering unequivocally for main consideration, and further, holds that any discussion like this has to be done in the real context of the evaluating society. There is, no doubt, that "suffering" is a generic notion covering 'misery' and the 'pangs of the masses' and as such is a *matter of fact.*

If "suffering" has to be notionally considered it cannot be done without a reference to facts and then, what is expected is to go for the *causes* of such facts. Hence, to consider the genesis of suffering is but natural because unless we discover the real causes of human suffering, we cannot manage them. It is obviously clear that Marx and Engels had no regard for the metaphysical or other sufferings when they considered the problem of suffering. Clearly, they had in mind the actual physical suffering of exploited people in a society. This reminds us of unexplainable miseries, worries, tensions, sorrows etc. It will be out of point not to cover mental suffering as well because suffering engulfs the whole man. There is no doubt then that the notion of "suffering" has been broadly used as a generic notion covering human 'miseries and agonies' resulting out of the exploitative conditions being faced.

Suffering, according to Marx and Engels, is so clearly related to human exploitation that they wonder how the problem could be viewed from any other angle. According to them, human suffering and human alienation are due to the relentless pursuit of "profit". Hence, it is the profit motive that becomes basic to human suffering. The profit motive engulfs the capitalists of those societies, which thrive on them, for the simple fact, that they own the production units, the capital and competitiveness. Competitiveness is not verbal; it is so acute and so ugly that it becomes the only condition for human survival. The people who have no power and no capital other than their physical capacities, are most likely to fizzle out in the tension of survival. The natural result, therefore is alienation. Hence, the possibility of a free and integrated life is not possible in capitalist societies because profit motive would ever enliven ruthless competition, exploitation and alienation.

It is natural that Marx had no single cut and dried solution to the problem of all suffering because most of the human suffering is caused by the biological and other accidental causes generally. What Marx hopes to have advocated is that why, in fact, *general* human suffering could be seen in the human societies. Marx and Engels thought that in an capitalist economy and in a society governed by the capitalists, the workers can never own the product of all of their efforts and labour. Hence, solely a person or a group of persons owns the product of the efforts of the labourers. The profit which they accumulate is for their betterment and not for workers' welfare or general welfare. The result is that the workers suffer physically and mentally because they have been completely robbed economically. The outcome is class struggle. Whatever Marx and Engels have postulated about the genesis of human suffering, is not mere theoretical abstraction, something flowing out of pure thought; rather, based on the empirical observation of the social, economic and the political facts in an ever evolving society. There is no doubt that when Marx went on further to construct a general theory of economics on the basis of such observations, he was involved in abstraction and generalization, but there was no role of intuition or idealism in it. The theory of suffering heavily based on empiricism reminds us of the existence of human suffering, to which, a mere theoretical construction can never do justice. The result of such an explanation of the concept of suffering enabled Marx to become the only exception in entire western philosophical tradition to produce an abstract *equation* which, however, is empirically based to explain what "suffering" is. It is difficult to restrain the desire to rely on the clarification advanced by John Bowker in the *Problems of suffering in religions of the world* (1970). Bowker's analysis of Marx enabled him to say that according to Marx the constant capital (C) and the variable capital (V) control the value of a commodity. In a straightforward society (that is, not capitalist rule governed), the value of an article is 'C + V'. However, the combination may lead to a *value* over and above the 'definite costs' of production. This is the 'surplus value' (S). In a capitalist society, the basic disposition of surplus value to distort value itself could be easily brought into reality by polarizing the surplus value which is, in fact, produced by an act of production. The polarization of surplus value, at the hands of the capitalists, who do not directly share in the act of production, is the reason behind much suffering.

But the capitalist has to find the surplus value from somewhere, it is not the same as profit; rather, an additional cost. The capitalists, by virtue of their power and capital, enjoy the legacy of reducing labour to a commodity by not extending even the half of what the labourers produce. This exploitation deprives the workers of purchasing power, of basic facilities and thus, alienates them from the basic product of their own effort and labour. The sense of non-belonging creeps in their minds and this causes the wanton misery—the suffering. Hence, in a capitalist society, value is nothing but C+ V + S, where 'S' is in-built in the process of exploitation of labourers. Thus, in a capitalist society, "suffering" is owing to alienation, i.e. owing to a simple equation C + V + S. It is but natural that Marx's explanation, first of all, clarifies the meaning of "suffering" in terms of an equation and the equation, in turn, holds out the key or the causes of suffering and indicates how it may be stopped. Marx visualized that a socialist economy, where 'C + V = Value' is strictly maintained and labour is not reduced to a commodity; could be the only answer to the stated problem.

Marx's view of suffering thus projects the use of the notion in unique *economic* terms. Although, it is in the form of an equation in a wholly *depersonalized* manner. The depersonalized use of the notion focuses that the meaning, which the term acquires, may be easily translatable in concrete factual terms. "Suffering" is a notion signifying "alienation caused by the exploitation of the labourers in the process of production". However, this is not the Marxist definition of "suffering"; rather a linguistic expression to clarify the meaning of an equation: 'C + V + S', which is basic to an understanding of the *fact* of suffering.

The Marxist management of suffering is simple if we have understood the meaning of the expression and the causes of the fact. Marx demanded that the true socialists know the actual *facts* of suffering. They should try to analyze its causes scientifically, and then, take action to remove those causes. For one thing, metaphysical and idealistic thinking or revolutions following idealism cannot remove the causes. Marx thought that all misguided reactionary thinkers hope to *reduce* suffering (and not eradicate it) in many ways. One is to give some relief within the prevailing conditions without changing the condition themselves. Second, by maintaining a *status quo* by consoling the sufferers that all is due to the misdeeds of past life and good actions shall put everything all right in another life, helps the masses suffer till the last breath. Marx was extremely against all religious and ideal solutions of the problem of suffering because they obscure the reality of suffering. The basic principle of the Marxist attitude to suffering is to face the stark truth pertaining to human suffering and to change the alienating and exploitative conditions by means of a complete mass *revolution*, which may in itself involve great suffering, but that suffering is not the real one; it is necessary for the eradication of a greater evil almost like an antidote! Marx calls this revolution 'proletarian revolution' expecting a self-change. He also calls it a communist action. Hence, Marxist revolution implies self-change, self-sacrifice and suffering (meaning "physical and other miseries for a total change"). Marx visualised further suffering in the course of total revolution because not only the proletariats have to impoverish by self-sacrificing all they have (and Marx said, "all they have are chains"), they have to *inflict* suffering on those who are the worst enemies in the class struggle (the bourgeois). Hence, strife, leading to suffering, is another natural outcome of the complete alleviation of real suffering. This focuses that, in Marxism, there are three distinct uses and meanings of suffering. First is the primary use of "suffering" to signify "alienation" (speaking briefly): the second is the secondary use of the notion to mean "*self-sacrifice* for a better cause" viz. "eradicating alienation" and finally, another use is to convey the sense of "strife in order to restore the basic harmony and balance in society". It is interesting to notice that although the first use of the notion carries a complete negative sense with it, the other two tend to be negative but they are really *not* so because they ultimately point towards a brighter side of reality. In all three cases, however, the use of the notion clearly indicate that it will be extremely impractical to divorce it from actual state of affairs in the society. But one wonders, why the basic meaning of "suffering" (C + V + S) gave way to other uses? There is every possibility that a not-so-careful-reader may confuse the primary with the secondary uses of the notion and not understand what really these thinkers have intended. However, if Marx's views are taken to be literally true, then it will be really difficult to conceive of a situation prone to remain ever in harmony, because going by the dialectical materialistic belief, the most harmonious society will tend to show the signs of cleavage within its structure for the reactionary forces would try to revert the situation. Then, one has to say that the secondary forms of suffering shall ever continue in human societies even if the basic suffering has been eradicated. Thus suffering in some sense has to be there in the human societies. The *teleological* or the *instrumental* sense of suffering is thus lingering in the Marxist faith. Mao is also no exception in this regard. He wilfully accepts that in order to maintain social harmony, the communist action never ceases to exist. Hence, acceptance of self-suffering as well as inflicting suffering on the counter-revolutionaries shall be always existent. Thus, human suffering has to exist in some form for its instrumental value. However, Mao has tried to put this under some limit by saying that in a communist society, suffering may be needed *only* if it becomes unavoidable for defense of the evolution. Mao could say this because the power of unity of people in a harmonious society is more than the destruction of the counter-revolutionaries. Hence, we have a way to think that, at least, suffering may not be as nagging as believed Marx. The result is that Marx's self-change in the process of revolution has been replaced by 'thought process' advocated by Mao, which may be very effective to change the basic notions of men and thus change their minds, and then, fortify it with some external deterrence, if needed. Suffering in secondary forms may be checked according to Mao if human thought process may be greatly influenced so that their full capacity of conscious moral actions may be effectively channelled in revolutionary path. It is clear that apart from knowing what suffering *really* is and how it is *caused*, one has to direct one's attitude potentially to plug the areas of suffering, primary or secondary. Hence, controlling the minds of men is an irresistible step for the Marxists to take.

It is time now that we further consider the general view of the existentialist school of philosophy, which champions in dealing with the problem of "suffering" (and putting pain within its broad field). It will be extremely interesting to consider these views because on the one hand, it may provide a range of the uses and meanings of the notion, on the other hand, it may provide a radically opposite view to the Marxists.

"PAIN", "SUFFERING" AND EXISTENTIALISM

The Existentialists are well known for their scholarly zeal to face the most bewildering problem of life, i.e. the sustenance of essential dualism lurking in nature between good and evil, pleasure and pain, suffering and bliss. The greatest merit in their approach lies in the fact that they do not try to brush aside or neglect the stark truth that permeates the nature, man and society; the truth is that the whole existence is permeated with suffering and it will be extremely unwise if we either neglect it or pretend to be fatalistic and providentialistic. The existential school thus starts with a realistic view and thinks that it is not the hell or the heaven or any ideal and which is man's destiny, rather, man is an end unto himself. It is very clear that in placing human existence at the focus, existentialism tries to descriptively analyze the structure, condition, potentialities and limitations of such existence. Its standpoint is basically subjective. Existentialism is protest against self-estrangement, dehumanization, mechanisation and objectification of experience. It is a voice against metaphysics referring to the abstract, the absolute and the supernatural. As man is the destiny unto himself, he is always in the making and the actual concrete lived personal reality is prior and basic to his conceptual and ideal essence. The essential freedom of man to choose and act shapes his personal existence. Existentialism is thus an attempt to delve into the subjective, minor depths of human personality for philosophical reflection. As such, it is natural that the existentialists attempt at entering into the subjective and personal realm with regard to analyzing the reality of suffering. Existentialism thus starts as an exception in the philosophical circle by treating the problem of suffering *not* objectively rather *subjectively*, i.e. as something, which has its footage in the subjective existence of man. It becomes clear that like may traditional and modern western thinkers as well as religious thinkers, existentialism would not prefer to pay any attention to what forms of suffering are there in this universe and how they affect us, rather, they would like to know how we confront, through our direct experience with the suffering that permeates the whole existence. Existentialism tries to break away from the shackles of objectively systematic world of facts and tries to enter into the immediacy of personal experience of an existence full of 'anguish'. In doing so, existentialism reminds us that we have been too long living an *inauthentic* life, a life which is objectively governed or standardised or given to us by others and the result is that we fail to forget ourselves in the fabricated chaos. It is due to such fabrication that even our understanding of suffering is blurred because it is inauthentic. We have been trying to understand suffering in the way it has been given to us by others and in terms of social customs but not authentically in terms of self-examination, self-criticism, self-exploration and self-judgment. It is, therefore, clear that the existentialist approach to suffering is markedly different in terms of the way the problem has to be encountered. The approach, being subjective, is the key to an understanding of the existentialist view of "suffering".

Keeping this in mind, we notice that the notion of "suffering" need not be taken as merely theoretical, to be used to denote such and such things or to signify such and such conditions, rather, "suffering" is the *mark of man.* To quote Sartre, "man is anguish". As such, "suffering" signifies man's nature itself because human life is an embodiment of misery and of anguish. It is remarkable, therefore, to find that the notion of "suffering" is not used to denote a 'state of affairs' or 'state of affairs' utterly painful or disagreeable, rather, "suffering" signifies "human existence as such". We can understand this, if and only if, we reflect upon our own nature i.e. if we delve inwardly. This is natural because "suffering" being not a physical state of affair, it is essentially mental, and, therefore, a matter of personal experience. To be precise, "suffering" is *personal.* But to call it personal is not the same as statement of a personal feeling, rather, signifies a specific statement about the notion "suffering". This is so because the sense of "suffering" cannot be understood without referring to the whole experience of a person. Hence, the existentialists do not prefer to consider merely the feeling and the emotive aspects of a man while stating about suffering, they speak of the "total experience of a man" or the "total frame of mind". Suffering is thus capable of presenting the human reality, which is far different from the illusory world of pleasures. In this sense, "suffering" is a notion used to refer to the channel of human consciousness enabling them to possess *self-consciousness.* Such self-consciousness is the consciousness of the 'inward frame' of mind and of the 'distinction' of minds. The knowledge of such distinction is further proclaimed through suffering because it is basically available to us through a conflict. Such an inward reference of "suffering" does not help us at all to speak of the suffering of animals because such talk is mere projection of our emotions, the super-imposition of our sentiments over and above the animal existence. Hence, following the existentialists in totality, it will be extremely difficult to use "suffering" to ascribe the state of affair of animals or otherselves. But, if we are left free for pain-talk and suffering-talk and then extrapolate suffering to other creatures by experiencing our own, we would hardly be able to know the inward realm of other creatures and fail to know their suffering. We may, however, imagine that animals lack the awareness of pain and suffering and for that reason alone there is *no* problem of suffering for them, though for a man it is a serious *problem.*

The existentialist use of "suffering" thus reminds us that it is not fragmentally biological, psychological, ethical etc. it is, in fact, a talk of an existence itself, an existence of unhappy consciousness, which, however, is impossible to avoid. This is the real problem which man has to face. A basic question may be, "why should self-consciousness reflect suffering in the least?" The question is basically genetic in nature. The existentialists do not avoid it either. But, then to answer it in our own ways may be unsatisfactory, particularly, if we literally believe them to be generally true. It is falling in the trap of objectification. Hence, one has to be very personal of his reporting or rather knowing why did his consciousness reflect him suffering. The kingdom of mind itself is a kingdom of ill at ease—a kingdom of want, craving and insatiable seeking. Sense organs, intention and awareness always feed this mental structure of man. Bikkhu Saddhajiva explains: "This ceaseless *want* is the irritant that motivates man, it goads him into agitation, the burning and subtle pain of pleasure to lead only to the cold sorrow of its fading; or if this burning is kept aflame, it leads to that worst state, the featureless desert of boredom."[1] And to refer to Schopenhaeur, "life swings like a pendulum backwards and forwards between pain and boredom."[2] It is very clear that suffering does not depend upon an external environment but is in-built in our being. It is, in reality, the basic *mode of existence*. J.T. Frazer clarifies. "Misery is an essential part of the human landscape and dread the fundamental mood of existence, the only mood uncontaminated by direction to outside object".[3] Heidegger's ontology reflected this in the form of 'angst' of 'dread'. He said that the human existence is bluntly humiliated. The only reality is 'anxiety' in the cycle of Beings. Man is a bubble in this cycle, fleeting, brief and embodiment of fear. Consciousness of fear is dangerous; it become anguish the cloak that covers man's whole existence. This fundamental dread or anguish manifests through a number of model, basic is "nausea" (Sartre 1947). One becomes aware of the fact that the existentialist mode of analyzing the genesis of "suffering" is not like analyzing the causes of a fact or a phenomenon, rather, analyzing the basic nature of the structure of human mind or human existence. This is possible only through *introspection* and not through any objectification. Thus "suffering" ought to be introspectively analyzed. When we do that, it turns out to be a referent of "anguish", of "dread" or so to say, of "nausea". In fact, whatever human feeling we may refer to, in whatever mode it exists, it is in essence, "nausea".

"Suffering" thus refers to that which is fundamental to existence because it is an awareness of the *incompleteness* of the existence. This is another meaning the term requires in the existentialist literature. Sartre aptly points out that human reality is a *lack* because that is reflected through his endless *wants* and his *desire* to be completed. Further, human will to *choose* (whatever degree of rationality may be involved) implies 'lack' and our anguish is reflected in the face of choice. Sartre thinks that if "suffering" refers to choice as well, then it implies that our being is essentially *contingent* because our existence was not our choice, it is unjustifiable. Hence, the lack of choice in the face of our own existence is further anguish. What we get is the range of the use of the notion of "suffering". To be precise, one may put it as simply as "existence experienced" but together with it, we get the sense of the possibility of the negation of that which has been experienced because existence is not necessary, it is contingent. "Suffering" may thus reminds us of the "absurd" because 'experienced existence' is superfluous, it is no necessity; it may be, nevertheless, a 'useless passion'.

Now, if "suffering" refers to the "superfluousness", the "senselessness" and the "emptiness", it is, nevertheless directing to "tragedy". But the sense of "tragedy" which goes along with "suffering" may have a double face in so far as we compare the tragedy of ours vis-ā-vis those great suffering endured by the great heroes.

Many great people have endured suffering. For them, it has a meaning because they find a reason in enduring great sufferings. But for us, it turns out to be a grim tragedy *without* a reason because we do not like to endure it. Such suffering is a mere tragedy hopelessly fleeting without teaching. Nietzche said that as compared to the 'overman', the 'underground man' (of Dostoevsky) does not joyously grasp a recurring majestic suffering, the defining of his existence. We, the underground men, are trapped in an eternal recurrence of suffering without any sense of majesty associated to it. Our suffering is non-teleological. "Suffering" may be thus a "tragedy" which crushes but still is negated by defying the fate and the heaven by the overman; whereas "suffering" may be a "tragedy" which does not tend to crush us, neither do we scornfully try to give it a drubbing, we are turned timid and feel petty in the fleeting existence. We thus turn out to be court jokers in the comedy of life, which is stale and yet, repeated naggingly. To quote Kikegaard, we are "mocked by existence".

If we accept this double faced use of "suffering" as "tragedy", we are immediately reminded of the futility of the conceptions of "suffering" as the one that trains us, as the one that is beneficial for us, as the one that disciplines us etc. The reason is that "suffering" is a "tragedy" for ordinary people. However, it may *not* be so for an extraordinary man.

Once we move deeper to discuss whether or not "suffering" should be taken as *problem*, we are facing a question from the point of view of a self-conscious person because we have seen that "suffering" turns out to be a problem for self-conscious beings and not for animals. But it is not merely a problem, it is a *mystery* as well. Gabriel Marcel's treatment of the issue focuses another interesting use of the notion in his book *The mystery of Being* (Cf. "On the ontological mystery"). First of all, we ought to understand that Marcel's treatment of "suffering" as a problem and a mystery could be understood on the basis of the stipulative uses of the terms "problem" and "mystery". This is needed for both these terms which have many uses and if all are wide open, we can hardly make any sense out of them in the context of "suffering". The first stipulation is that a 'problem' is so-called when some *disorder* could be clearly noticed with respect to the *natural* and it could be noticed also when the individual being is trapped in a mesh of functions, which depersonalize him. One notices that there is a dysfunction somewhere. Hence, a "problem" turns out to be a dysfunction somewhere in the nature, which is taken to be essentially *mechanical.* If this is the case, the problem turns out to be "evil". Next, stipulation is with regard to "mystery". Marcel thinks that evil, which is a problem, is also a suffering. Now, this poses a peculiar question to us, "why should there be such things in the nature?" This question is not a mere question, it is an unsolved puzzle or a "mystery". Thus, an evil due to which a person suffers, remains before us as living, unsolved puzzle. Evil is thus not a problem, it transcends it and becomes a "mystery". "Suffering", refers to an evil, which is not merely a problem, it is a mystery. As suffering is an existence itself, our whole existence remains dipped in evil and becomes a puzzle. I may experience the evil, the eternal puzzle, as long as I live. Hence, existential use of "suffering" now covers "evil", "problem" and "mystery" as well, needless to say, it covers "existence". We may be careful by not calling them synonymous, but we have the feeling that in the Existentialist literature once we step in to consider the key notion of "suffering", a gamut of notions suddenly spreads all around it like a cobweb, each having a different but closely-knit connotation. It is like moving from an individual's consciousness to discover a vocabulary that desperately tries to unfold the stark truth of existence. In existential literature, "suffering-talk" is thus related to many 'talks' and one has to refer to them if a complete view has to be obtained. One peculiar "suffering-talk" is what Marcel presents us. The presentation is a departure from many theological views which weave suffering with evil in an objective fashion, as if, our consciousness gets it from the external nature; whereas, Marcel tries to weave them into a cobweb out of the saliva of personal experience and introspection. Moreover, I think that the existential way of raising the 'why' question with regard to suffering or evil, which turns out to be mysterious, is not the same as raising a genetic question of the origin of suffering and evil, rather, to inquire how suffering fits into the whole scheme of reality. To be precise, it is a question of 'fittingness' of evil in a world system, which we painstakingly try to establish. It may be a vital question about the system itself. It may be a scientific question about the validity of absolutism in conceiving a system, when the reality may be chaotic. In fact, the hackneyed theological question about the genesis and management of evil is so heavily governed by objectification that it hardly satisfies the existentialists because an answer to this question would not lead to the mystery of suffering. The only way is thus to suffer personally and inwardly and then, reflect the fittingness of suffering in the objectified world order. Kierkegaard has tried to project it in his existential writings.

Kierkegaard says that the existential experience we have in times of social and personal catastrophe is the experience of disorder that evokes a sense of 'anxiety', the 'anxiety' of death and fate, and also the 'anxiety' of meaninglessness and emptiness. Kierkegaard imagines that in this 'sickness unto death' we suffer and to suffer is to be in "despair", which is *twofold*, it is "despair of despair". We are thus at hand another peculiar existential use of the notion. In analysing the sense of "suffering" as despair, Kierkegaard refers to an introspective discovery (no less a hypothesis) that man is a synthesis of the *temporal* and the *eternal*, the *finite* and the *infinite*. Unknowingly, (or may be knowingly) he allows spirituality to enter in the analysis. If this discovery is allowed, Kierkegaard imagines, despair is due to a basic tension owing to the sense of self-eternal being reduced to a meaningless-entity with all finiteness that is within its nature. This feeling of meaninglessness and death, our conscious introspection leads us to realize suffering like a double trouble. It turns out to be the "despair of despair". However, suffering balances the ever-changing deaths and the meaning moment. Kierkegaard carefully differentiates the ordinary meaning of "I suffer from such and such a thing" from the essential meaning. Ordinarily, the suffering-self (I) is taken to be a being but when we understand "suffering" as the "despair of despair", it is taken as the "whole of our being". "Suffering" does not merely refer to the ego it is "self-consciousness in complete form". The Kierkegaardian use of "suffering" as the "despair of despair" brings out the utterly dark side of the truth but there is no way out of it if we rely on our consciousness. But really speaking, the brighter truth, the essentially eternal and the infinite being of man is not lost. However, there is no doubt that out of a tension and despair it gets suppressed and what is projected then is utter suffering. The projection of suffering through consciousness brings out the crux of existential thinking. One is again reminded of the fact that it will be very difficult to find any positive aspect hidden in suffering as "despair of despair" because it is essentially dysteleological.

Kierkegaard and Dostoevsky may not think alike, the element of the ideal and the spiritual which they have carefully embedded in their view unfolds fully in their *theistic* conclusions. What is interesting for us is to see that these theistic existentialists breathe a new life to the teleological aspect of pain and suffering. We are also at hand another sense in which the notion of "suffering" may be used. "Suffering" refers to the human way of delving to the focal point of existence as well as 'the way in which God, through his compassionate love, enters the finite self'. There is no doubt that dread or anxiety and despair-evoked self-awareness but the surmounting faith of infinite and eternal leads us to an education that the self is free and may liberate it. Hence, according to Kierkegaard, men are spiritual beings, that they are before God and their dissatisfied finite selves shall liberate them from despair. The same tone of teleology of suffering and theological overtones in existentialism could be noticed in Bubber's writings as well as in the writings of the Russian thinker Berdayev. These existentialists reminded us that whatever is the revelation of the self to himself, it is about suffering as 'despair of despair'. In whatever sense be it a mystery, it may be, nevertheless, changed into redemption through Christ entering our selves. A new dimension is thus added to "suffering" as "mystery" because we now believe that although, suffering may be a tough-unresolved question of fittingness into reality, it is, at the same time, possible to transcend it altogether. Berdayev brings this optimum to the front and he changed the existential cry of a "dead God" to the "restoration of values".

However, existentialists like Sartre, could not accept such an interpretation of the notion of "suffering". Sartre like many other existentialists had no doubt that "suffering", obviously, refers to death and dissolution but such an *awareness* need *not* lull us into a sense of despair, because it is through our awareness we know that the nausea of existence could be eradicated through *free will* and *responsibility.* Sartre thinks that whatever we are, is due to our *choice* and we are free to choose either despair or relief; and if we choose the latter, a self-making process comes into operation. Further, through self-awareness one could realize that he has some responsibilities for those endowed with the same freedom. Sartre thus tries to clarify the sense of 'despair' more *logically* and holds that despair is not owing to an alien cause, it has not been providentially allotted or fated; it is perfectly within our choice to transcend. Here Sartrean existentialism seems to bear a clear non-spiritual and non-theistic as well as the non-theological existential analysis of 'suffering'. These forms of existentialism shares a common platform in so far as they speak of the self-awareness of the dread, of anxiety, of despair and yet show signs of dissatisfaction to transcend such state. Hence, they are optimistic in their own ways. But how such optimism takes shape has been not so clear to us. The 'angst' is so powerful that it smears pessimism all too much.

The scene appears to be a little changed while we analyze Schopenhauer's treatment of "suffering". Schopenhauer is best known exponent of 'empirical pessimism' as well as 'metaphysical pessimism'. He thinks that not only is human life an embodiment of suffering, the *suffering* must be there as the most important principle, the principle of will or the objectification of a blind will. As such, suffering first appears to us as a *tragedy* because it is the nearest example that comes close to clarify the nature of existence itself. But Schopenhauer maintains that if human life is compared to a drama played on earth, 'tragedy' is not the highest art. It is *music,* which is the highest. Hence, *not* suffering but the power to break out the shackles of 'objectified will' to exhibit will-itself is, what is the most crucial. First of all, the one who denies suffering, denies will and who denies will welcomes suffering; therefore, to know about the tragedy and then to objectify will is, what is crucial. Clearly if one does not go through the realization of suffering, one *cannot* pursue the path of purification of will. Then "suffering" is a notion, which conveys the sense that the human urge to 'purify the self' has to be there. The outspoken teleology of suffering is presented to us. Schopenhauer's use of the notion of "suffering" bears with Hartmannian *endaemonological pessimism* (which is a trace of German idealism) because human suffering is owing to a 'quest for happiness' which is always a losing venture. It also carries with it the Leibnitzian legacy to hold that suffering despite being 'irrationality of the will' is still the mother of teleology and progress because this world is the best possible world. Amalgamation of pessimism with an antidote of voluntarism leads Schopenhauer to prescribe clearly the way out of objectification of will. He clearly mentions for this purpose *aesthetic contemplation, altruistic act* and *ascetic attitude*. Schopenhauer thus comes closer to the Indian existential mind.

Not equally acceptable to the Indian existential mind may be the views advocated by Nietzche. He, too, puts "suffering" in extremely pessimistic color because the notion he holds, is one of "fallen state of existence" and thus 'terrible' and 'tragic'. He, too, adds that human outcry for redemption and salvation is what is the consequence of utter tragedy, but not in the way Schopenhauer prescribes. Nietzche may be clear in the teleology of pain and suffering but he departs from a number of existentialists in *not* using the notion of suffering to signify something essentially *evil*. He also does not think that suffering could mean the 'deobjectification of will' and 'human will to liberate'. It is unique to notice that "suffering" need not be taken as an evil because the main objective of Nietzchean existentialism is *not* negation rather affirmation. If "suffering" is deemed to be inherently and forever a negative conception (nothing but a mere evil), its basic purposefulness is lost under the curse that the term "evil" bears in this context. Hence, to portray the value of suffering, one has to first understand that it is not an ill-fated "evil"; "suffering", which is a tragedy, is a conception covering the sense of a 'human realization that drags him to transmute existence'. This transmutation of life itself is made possible by drawing an *aesthetic veil* over reality creating an ideal world of form and beauty. Thus Nietzche is essentially Greek; to be precise, Appollonian, not Indian or Schpenhauerian. Nietzche thus uses "suffering" in a manner so that it is indubitably horrific yet vulnerable to the human will to get it banished. Nietzche's mood is outrageously angry.

It is an interesting experience to go through the existential cobweb of the use and meaning of the notion of "suffering". There are lot of convergences and divergences, and, yet, one gets the idea that one is centrally fixed to a point, existence itself, which is indubitably suffering, if and only if, you pass through personal experience and introspection. Once we lay so much stress on the mental, the subjective element of man, no one sense in which the notion has been used appears to be, either true or false, neither do they appear non-sensensical. But the greatest tragedy may be that if we reject their basic presupposition and go the physiological, the ethical or so to say, along any objective explanation, everything appears to be clumsy and non-sensical. But does the physiological, the ethical and the metaphysical line of analysis free themselves from the subjective explanation? No, perhaps. But they were equally not relying too much on the subjective explanation either. Hence, the existentialist use of the notion, despite all its mysteriousness, shall remain ever attractive for a student of philosophy of language. We may now leave it at this point to come to consider a vast philosophical literature dealing with pain and suffering viz. the Indian Philosophical literature. Once we consider Indian philosophy in this regard, we are at the brink of understanding many philosophical views, the views of the ancient and the contemporary schools of thought. Interestingly, if we go through the views of any philosophical school, the need for separating the philosophical from the physiological, and the ethical from the metaphysical, and the ideal, would not be felt. Moreover, while we go through a body of the Vedāntic and non-Vedāntic schools of philosophy (barring the Buddhists and the Jainists), we may not feel to analyze the Hindu view separately.

But there are problems. First, a school of thought has many exponents. So it is impossible to put them together and it may become boring for obvious repetitions. Secondly, it will be very difficult to isolate chapters on pain and suffering in Indian writings barring a few exceptions. We have to do a lot of reduction for our present purpose. Finally, it will be difficult to separate the metaphysical use from the ethical or the physical in the Indian writings. If we desire to get a glimpse of the different use, we have to further rely on the general views of different school.

This may rob off from the whole body of the discussion something, which may not be otherwise desirable. But we have to do this. Interestingly I have to do another thing which has been already done while considering existentialism i.e. to consider pain and suffering as philosophical problems occurring in extremely technical language. For instance, while going through the existentialist school, quite often we had to consider the *technical* language of existentialism and discover the way the existentialists have in their literature used the conceptions of "pain" and "suffering". This is clearer when we consider the writings of the non-English speaking writers. We have to *discover* in their technical language, the use of "pain" and "suffering'. It is a kind of knowing about the uses and meanings of "pain" and "suffering" in an *indirect* fashion, i.e. through a technical language, which is of course *not* English. We face the same while considering the Indian

Philosophical schools. We have to go through Sanskrit texts or other non-English texts to discover the ways in which the concepts of "pain" and "suffering" have been used. Hence, it will be a foolishness to expect "pain" and "suffering" in existentialist and Indian philosophical texts because they are not in English. But we have to *discover* form these texts, the uses of the notions of "pain" and "suffering' in their technical languages, which is unique to these literatures.

"PAIN", "SUFFERING" AND BUDDHISM

I would like to concentrate mainly on two heterodox and some orthodox schools of ancient Indian Philosophy for the present purpose. To start with, we have the Buddhist conception of "suffering'. The Buddhist views are perhaps extremely important for us to consider at the outset. Not merely because it is chronologically prior or because heterodox views should be explained first; rather, the school takes great interest in explaining the problem of suffering. However for all practical purpose, Buddhism serves a good contrast to the western existentialism. We must know at the outset that there is no need to discuss either the views of the four schools of Buddhism separately or to make a special mention that we are discussing the views of the Hinayāna or the Mahāyāna sect. The moment we delve into the basics of the Buddhist philosophy and start knowing the different uses and meanings of the notion of "suffering", we may feel that it is also redundant to mention that this is a religious view.

As one turns to Buddhism to consider the ways in which the notions of "pain" and "suffering" have been used, one enters an ethico-religious philosophy standing on the firm ground of logically oriented metaphysics. It is Soul-less and God-less however. According to Buddhism, the notion of "suffering" is central to a philosophical discussion because it does not merely characterize human existence, it is embedded in every condition of existence. It is very clear that in Buddhism the notion of "suffering" has been very broadly taken as the one that portrays the essential condition of 'existence as such'. It is due to this that the first task is to know about its *causes*, the possibility of the *cessation* of suffering and the *path* that leads towards the blowing off of suffering. This constitutes the Four Noble Truths of Buddhism, which together explain what it is to speak about suffering as a problem.

It is extremely important to notice that despite four divisions in Buddhism, the basic conception about suffering, which is covered within the Four Noble Truths, remain the same. All the four schools of Buddhism thus abide by the presupposition that *existence* is essentially *fleeting*, it is full of *suffering*, existential facts at every instance have definite properties they are thus types of themselves and thus *nothing* is *common* to them and existence is nihilistic but neither a void or *unreal*, it is *real* anyway. It will be thus important to quote a passage from *Sarvadarśanasaṅgraha* to see what exactly has been said in this regard, 'Te ça Bauddhāçaturvidhayā bhāvanayā paramapurūśārtha kathayanti. Te ça Mādhyamika-Yogāç āra-Sautrāntika-Vaibhāṣikasaṁjñābhiḥ pratissdhābaudhhā yathākramaṁ sarvaśūnyatva- bahyārthaśunyatva-bahyārthānumeyatva-bahyārthapratyakṣatvavādānatiṣthaṅte. Yadyapi bhagavānabuddha eka eva bodhaitātathāpi bodhhaçyānaṁ buddhibhedāççaturvidhyaṁ. Yathabhisaraṇaparasvaharaṅsadāç araṇādisamayaṁbudhyante. Sarvaṁ kṣanikaṁ kṣanikaṁ, dukkhaṁ dukkhaṁ, svalakṣanaṁ, svalakṣanaṁ, śūnyaṁ śūnyamiti bhāvanāçatuṣtayamūpadiṣtaṁ dṛṣtavyaṁ[4]. The passage, apart from making clear that according to all four schools, viz. Mādhymika, Yogāçāra, Sautrāṅtika and Vaibhāṣika are unanimous about the fact of existence being permeated wither suffering, also make it clear that existence is only momentary or fleeting, every moment bears an exclusive property and it is nihilistic but *not* a void or unreal.

Buddhism makes it clear that one cannot understand anything about suffering if one is not *aware* of it. To know suffering is to be 'aware' of it. This invitation is not to know the gloom and despondency because that is very important; rather, it is an offer to observe the condition of existence, which is fleeting unceasingly under the influence of change. Hence, "there is suffering" is closely related to life, but it is *not* the same as "there is an awareness of an *ever-living* gloom, which has to be accepted". Buddhism has little doubt about despondency and never rejects the gloom but it does not become aware of an ever-living gloom, rather, about the truth that the state may be blown off forever.

The basic meaning of "suffering" could be known if we know the actual term used in the Buddhist literature, it is "dukkḥa" because "dukkḥa" has far wider connotation than which has been commonly meant by "suffering" (even if one considers the western existentialist trends, one fails to completely understand what "dukkḥa" means). "Dukkḥa" is a notion combining two broad connotations. It connotes ordinary "pain" or "grief" or "misery", which is contrary to what we mean by "contentment". In this sense it may cover "discontentment". Whereas another reference is to "impermanence", "emptiness", "lack of wholeness", which is *contrary* to what we call "perfection". Hence, "dukkḥa" connotes "pain" as well as "imperfection". It is clear that Buddhism is conscious about what is not normally done, i.e. to clarify the meaning of "suffering" in the sense of "dukkḥa" in its broadest terms to cover physical, mental, metaphysical and ethical pain and suffering. Such "dukkḥa" is what is in every condition of existence as such. To be precise, "suffering" (henceforth "dukkḥa") is broadly (and fundamentally) *used* in Buddhist literature to signify "discontentment" as well as "imperfection". Once we understand this, it may not be difficult to grasp what it is to be aware of dukkḥa and what is the significance of "all is dukkḥa". Dukkḥa is thus something which is 'everywhere' meaning thereby, 'in all conditions of existence', and to say this is to accept that dukkḥa is present as discontentment and imperfection. It is very clear that the notion refers more to the general nature and conditions of the existence as a whole than to a particular instance of human bodily or mental pain. When we speak of dukkḥa in terms of filling up the whole existence, it characterizes the nature of existence as *not* merely gloomy; rather, the one which is essentially *impermanent* or 'kṣaṇika', portraying "imperfection" as well as the one which is essentially conditioned by constant craving or *discontentment* or tṛṣṇā. Interestingly, the notion is used to clarify the basic nature and condition of the phenomenal world and is not otherworldly and it is quite scientific to talk about the essential entropic nature of the phenomenal world as also to speak of its basic nature of change. On the other hand, the notion is used to clarify the human psyche in being constantly agitated in the world of becoming, unrest and death. It is due to this that "dukkḥa" is said to be understood and experienced on three levels, the level of *life process*, in birth, old age, sickness, accidents and deaths, which is what we commonly refer to the biological or the physiological level of interpreting suffering in terms of physical and accompanying psychological pain. This level of suffering may be plainly expressed as "sarvaṁ dukkḥaṁdukkḥaṁ".

The second level of under-standing suffering is the level of the *aggregates or existence*, i.e. the suffering arising from some of the mental elements inherent in the nature of human beings. Such suffering is neither sequential nor exclusive rather plainly *experiential*, for instance, the plain matter of experience is that the human nature is so constituted that it will certainly, like other fleeting things meet decay and face death. This is the sense of "saṁkhara dukkḥa". The third level of understanding 'suffering' is the level of *consciousness of beings* because all sentient, conscious creatures come to realize that there is an ever-growing gap between their desires and desire fulfilment and a realization that all existence being transitory, his happiness is also transient. This is the sense of "vipariṇāma dukkḥa". In all these levels of the understanding of the notion of "dukkḥa", one finds the basic principles of impermanence and imperfection as the governing principles. Hence, any sense in which we use "dukkḥa", one cannot forget that it is some existential condition guided by the principles of impermanence and imperfection. It will be thus correct to allow broader use of the notion both in the sense of impermanence and imperfection.

Lord Buddha says, "Idaṁ kho pan bhikkhave, dukkḥaṁ ariya saçças̈aṁ. Jāti pi dukkḥa, jarā pi dukkḥa, maraṇampi dukkḥaṁ, śoka—parideva—dormanssūpāyāsapi dukkḥā, appiyehi sampayogo dukkho, piyehi bippayogo dukkho, yampiççaṁ na labhati tampi dukkḥaṁ, saṅkkhidyena pançūpādānakhyandhyāpi dukkḥā".[5] Buddha is emphatic about the first 'Ārya Satya' (The Noble Truth) that it is indubitably or phenomenally true. This essential truth has to be accepted by all. He clarifies that to hold this is to believe that birth is suffering, aging is suffering, death is suffering, grief, repentance, indifference and labour is suffering. Suffering is to come in contact with undesirable objects (desiring the undesirable), it is a suffering to be defected with the beloved. Suffering is the lack of altering the desired thing. Hence, suffering is nothing but the *five* 'skandhas' (rūpa, vedanā, saṁjñā, saṁskāra and vijñāna) emerging out of some 'rāgas'. It is clear that the Buddhist use of the notion of "dukkḥa" (or suffering) is predominantly psychophysical, as well as ethical. Hence, he says, one wonders how we can make fun out of such a state of gloom? ("Ko me hāso kiṁānando niççaṁ pajjalite sati")[6].

In so far as Buddhism lays stress on the awareness of dukkḥa, it invites a question, 'who is aware of dukkḥa'? And who is the one participating in the process of change'? When the Buddhists refer to the individual aware of dukkḥa, the 'ego' or 'I' is not synonymous to 'myself' or 'my soul' which resides in me and is permanent. Buddhism thus categorically denies the existence of the separate essence like 'soul' which experience psychophysical phenomena and suffers owing to its consciousness and participation. This leads to the Buddhist theory of *no self* or *anātta* closely relating to the idea of essential change or flux, is the idea of absence of changeless self or anātta. In fact, Buddha refers to the physical element and energies flowed together in what we call complex human being; these element themselves are under constant cḥange. This focuses the fact that the second level of understanding 'dukkḥa', which is 'saṁkhara dukkḥa' stems out of the Buddhist theory of impermanence as well as anātta because the *realization* of the impermanence of the aggregates of existence or skaṅdhas which constitute a human being lead us to think that in him *no* permanent self is conceivable. Hence, no permanent observer of suffering or carrier of the results of suffering is conceivable. Buddha makes it possible to still explain the awareness of 'dukkḥa' with the help of a psychophysical explanation in terms of the constitution and conglomeration of the *five* types of 'skaṅdhas'. Hence, the third level of understanding, 'dukkḥa' is closely related to the existence of the 'skaṅdhas'. But 'skaṅdhas' being themselves momentary, the human life is constituted of individual moments, which, however, being so closely knit that an *appearance* of continuity and permanence emerge out of it and it becomes a *convenience* to imagine a being. Existence is thus entirely conditioned by an endless chain of *causation* which is otherwise an unbreakable chain of being and non-being. But one can break this chain of existence, of birth and death, of constant suffering by finding *within* the chain something, which is worth reflecting. Hence, in Buddhism enters the conception of *dependent origination* or 'pratiççasamūtapāda'. This conception of twelve-fold chain of the origin of 'dukkḥa' leads us to face that merely we can find out the causes of suffering as well the path to stop it. From this, it is clear that if we consider the notion of "suffering" in Buddhism in the context of particular instances of human suffering then it must be linked to a chain of causes. It appears therefore, that it would *not* be undesirable in Buddhism to speak of the *genesis* of suffering and then the notion has an obvious *factual* reference. It is clear when we keep in mind the levels of understanding of 'dukkḥa'. Buddhist use of the notion also reminds us of the fact that they may be ready to accept psycho-physical use of the notion no doubt, but in *no* way ready to accept the ideal and the metaphysical use of the notion by relating 'dukkḥa' either to Supra-mundane causes or to the metaphysical realities like soul and God. But one is not in a position to hurriedly accept the fact that in Buddhism 'dukkḥa' has no metaphysical links because one is reminded of the fact that the moment one steps in to consider 'dukkḥa', one steps into tracing the fundamental or the basics of 'dukkḥa. What one finds naturally is that the agglomeration of 'skaṅdhas' under the influence of twelve causes becomes the knower of suffering as well the participant of the same process. But the question is, 'do we find any reference to metaphysical and ethical suffering in Buddhism'?

When we keep in mind the three levels of understanding "dukkḥa", particularly the first one, we know that the notion of "dukkḥa" do not merely refer to what is painful (physically and mentally) and for that reason it would be difficult to say that 'dukkḥa' is the corollary of 'sukkḥa' or pleasure because 'dukkḥa' is not a 'feeling-term' or the one that has been used to convey a feeling state of mind. Rather, the notion has far wider ramification covering the conditions under which the whole existence is said to be there. To know this is to be aware of it, but the awareness of 'dukkḥa' is not synonymous to the awareness of displeasure, discomfort (or a range of use we have already found in other existentialist literature). 'Dukkḥa' is the awareness of *impermanence* and *imperfection*, broadly speaking. This brings us closer to an ethical understanding of the meaning of 'dukkḥa' as 'imperfection'. Nonetheless, I think it is closer to a metaphysical understanding of the meaning of 'dukkḥa' as an 'imperfection'.

In the *Aṅguttara-Nikāya* there is a reference of kinds of pleasures (sukhaṁ) comparable to the experiences of 'dukkḥa' and, therefore, it will be unwise to say that Buddhism gives no recognition to pleasures, but it says that following the principles of 'kṣṅika' even pleasures are impermanent. Thus the awareness of the momentariness of 'sukhaṁ' is basic to the awareness of not only the truth of 'kṣaṅika' rather the faith of the imperfection written large over the much craved 'sukhāni'. This, in turn, evokes the awareness of the imperfection of human nature in terms of nourishing 'tṛṣṇā' for what is essentially fleeting. It will be possible for us to derive from this the truth that the notion of 'dukkḥa' has ethical use in so far as broadly speaking it means basic imperfection laid in entire existence, including the human nature. The imperfection is really in the *intention* of man because a deliberate *choice* to constantly crave for being, for pleasure, i.e. for all that is impermanent as well as imperfect, is evidently clear. I cannot resist the idea that Buddhism reflects metaphysical use of the notion of 'dukkḥa' as well because in the twelve-fold links the truth has been focused clearly in terms of *ignorance* or ajñāna, which is the first among the twelve links of the origin of wholesome suffering. The question is, 'the ignorance of what'? Buddhism has an immediate answer. It says that the ignorance is with regard to the truths of the basic principle of kṣaṅika, anātta and pratiççasamūtpāda, which is so basic to an understanding of "sarvaṁ dukkḥaṁ-dukkḥaṁ". This projects the truth that metaphysically 'dukkḥa' has been used in Buddhism to signify the "ignorance of the basic principles governing the reality". It may be said that metaphysical suffering in Buddhism is the suffering owing to the ignorance of the basic principles of existence. It may be added that one, who is ignorant of the fact that is possible to be knowledgeable about these principles to break the shackles of birth and death to attain 'nibbāna', is also in 'dukkḥa'. Hence, "metaphysical suffering" also means the ignorance of the 'true knowledge' and the 'knowledge of the possibility of blowing off suffering'. This speaks of the truth that it is quite different to speak about the sukhas and about life and to speak about 'dukkḥa' and its cessation. Once you enter into the intricacies of 'dukkḥa' and its cessation, you are dealing with extremely important metaphysical and ethical issues. Hence, in Buddhism, the statement that 'life is dukkḥa' is secondary to the statement that 'there is a way out of dukkḥa'. Buddhism is essentially optimistic, which is glimmering in his eight-fold path to 'nibbāna. Thus in Buddhism it has been affirmed that, "Rāgādijñānasaṁtānavāsanoççedasaṁvabā. Çaturnāmapi bauddhānāṁ muktireṣā prakirtitā"[7]. These is thus an unanimity of views again with regard to the attainment of the *summum bonum* of life, which is "mokṣa" when the rāgas are destroyed by true knowledge of reality.

One who is concerned with the fact of suffering in Buddhism and carefully considers the twelve sequence of the origin of suffering cannot fail to see that generally speaking, despite the theory of "anātta", the result of craving for the *understanding* is to enter into the cycle of birth and death or the 'kārmic' cycle. Hence, Buddhist theory of "suffering" has close connection with the notions of craving, clinging, karma and rebirth. If we carefully look into these closely-knit notions, are entering another discourse, the discourse of "evil". Karma and rebirth reminds us that no amount of "good" deeds might have resulted into such a vicious trap. It is natural to conceive that the ignorant misdeeds of men trap them in the kārmic cycle. Certainly, 'dukkḥa' (suffering) is owing to something which, as if, *punishes* us and do not prize us any way. With this, the idea of 'dukkḥa' as something caused due to intrinsic evils creeps in our mind. "Suffering" is thus focused as a problem, which is essentially evil and not good. It is thus difficult to avoid the Buddhist theory of "evil" in terms of "suffering owing to ignorance and kārmic cycle". Buddhism takes interest in calling something essentially evil to remind us that something is essentially good (parinibutto or nibbāna). But here we are reminded of the "human evil" and "human liberation" because one who is not conscious about the fact of "dukkḥa-dukkḥa" cannot perhaps constitute for him or her problem, which is so grave. Thus "dukkḥa" turns out to be a *human* problem which is essentially evil and not good. The use of "dukkḥa" to mean "something essentially owing to misdeeds" or "something which is an embodiment of evil" naturally comes to our minds. There is no doubt that what Buddhism preaches is that "dukkḥa" may be realized at all existential levels because "dukkḥa" is wholesome; as if, it fills the whole nature because it is difficult to conceive anything beyond change and decay, death and birth, and rebirth. But when this turns out to be an *evil*, it is we who *realize* it to be like that because we have the disposition to reflect and discover what great misdeeds might have resulted into horrible state of affairs. Thus, "dukkḥa" as a problem is a human problem and that too, evil. it will be premature to think that in Buddhism "evil" is a broader notion covering "suffering" because the sense of "evil" lurking within the notion of "suffering" is something to be discovered or reflected upon. Hence it remains central to Buddhist thinking. Really, the "evilness" of "dukkḥa" is known through the sequential chain of dukkḥa. Thus the basic immorality involved in "dukkḥa", the essence of its "badness" is a matter of systematic reflection, and it is not obviously as clear as we think it to be. But once we know the truth, we are at hand an explanation for puzzles like, 'why is "suffering" inherently so bad and not well and why some men who, although seem to do a lot of good, suffer'? Really speaking, to *do good now* and *after* this moment, is so important that it *may* not lead to further suffering, provided we do all that after *ignorance* has been *permanently dispelled.* Hence, one may suffer if ignorance had *not* been fully dispelled.

So far I have carefully avoided the deviation of views among the different Buddhist sects and Buddhist schools regarding the explanation of clinging due to craving and the cycle of karma and rebirth because I feel, these deviations would hardly matter if one understands my basic aim. One who understands it, shall find in the broad maze of Buddhist use of "suffering" or "dukkḥa', something of his or her liking. Let us now see whether or not other existentialist thinkers find something of their interest in the Buddhist use of the notion of "suffering". I think this wonderful passage from Bhikkhu Saddhajiva shall reflect something about this matter, He writes: "dukkḥa does not depend an external environment but is a *built-in structure of one being*—in fact, the basic mode of existence—misery is an essential part of the human landscape and *dread* the fundamental mood of existence. This fundamental 'dread' or 'anguish' manifests through a number of modes the most basic of these is that termed *nausea*"[8] (italics mine). Avoiding needless dealing, let me now switch over to consider some of the orthodox views in Indian Philosophy regarding "pain" and "suffering" but before that a few words about the Jaina view of pain and suffering.

"PAIN", "SUFFERING" AND JAINISM

The Jaina school of philosophy is heterodox in so far as it does not recognize Vedas as the valid source of knowledge. However, unlike the Buddhist philosophy, it recognizes the fact that soul is the eternal substratum of human existence and it migrates owing to bondage until it is not free from all karmic flux. Jaina does not recognize the existence of God. In Jainism we have references of both 'pain' and 'suffering', mainly conveyed through the notions of 'dukkḥa' and 'vedanā'. Both these notions occur in the context of bondage or ''bandhana'. It has been said that false recognition or 'mithyā darśna', non-difference or 'avirah̤', carelessness or 'pramāda', sin or 'kaṣāya' and influx or 'yoga' are the chief causes of the bondage of soul, i.e. the chief causes of falling into the cycle of rebirth. False recognition is that of the Jaina wisdom; non-difference is with regard to desirable and undesirable actions; carelessness is with regard to the freedom to allow the sensibilities; sin is due to wrongful intentions and influx is due to the activity of the soul at the levels of space and time. The Jaina philosophy further clarifies that we may conceive at least eight kinds of actions or 'karma', which binds a man to the cycle of birth and death. Among these eight kinds of binding actions we find the reference to 'vedanā', which, however has a peculiar use in the Jaina Philosophy. It has been said, "saḍasdvedaniyasya sukhaduhkhotpadākatvaṁsidhārāmadhulehanvat"[9]. It has been maintained that *not* merely pleasure or 'sukha', which arouses suffering or 'vedanā'' rather, pleasure and pain or 'dukkḥa' *together* arouse suffering or together they lead towards actions leading to suffering. The knowable things both as real and unreal are capable of evoking the feelings of pleasure and pain, they are not isolated. It is like the tongue being capable of both the feeling pleasure and pain through licking honey or cutting it with a sword. Thus, 'suffering' amounts to the state of the self as and when it is engrossed in the double feelings of pleasure and pain. Interestingly the recognition of the notion of 'dukkḥa' as a *feeling term* (like 'pain') as distinct from a generic notion of "suffering" which covers broadly a state of affairs of individuals self when feeling like pleasure and pain fills it thoroughly, reminds us of the fact that the Jainas are careful about making distinctions in the use of these notions. The same thing has been repeatedly used in Jaina literatures like *Aṣtasāhasrī*, a commentary by Vidyānanda on Sāmantabhadra's Kārikā. For instance, the commentator clarifies that "suffering" which has to be understood as "sukha-dukhaphala", is *not* the determinant of righteousness (puṇya) and unrighteousness (pāpa); rather, intention or 'abhisandhi' determines these things. It is due to this that the Jainas could differentiate the non-sentient beings, (essentially not moral beings), the sentient beings (either moral or immoral beings) and the saints (neither moral nor immoral beings) on the basis of the fact that both the non-sentient beings and saints may *produce* pleasure and pain on sentient beings, who further act morally or immorally because they have *intentions* or 'abhisandhi' to do all that. Thus, the feelings either of pain or pleasure alone cannot be the basis of morality.

Going by this explanation, as these feelings go *together* and thus arouse 'suffering', is also not the basis of morality. Morality is essentially internal; it is mental. Clear reference to the use of "suffering" (vedanā) in terms of "sukkḥa-dukkḥa phala" focuses the fact that it is not the synonymous of "pain" (dukkḥa). *Aṣtasāhasrī* comes out with the same use further in the context of the nature of unrighteous state of intention or 'saṁkleśāṅga'. It has been mentioned that 'saṁkleśa' is either distressing or 'ārta' or aggressive or 'raūdra' in nature. Distress of intention is manifested in *four* main ways, viz. escaping the unpleasant or 'amanojña', to attain the pleasant or 'manojña', the experience of suffering or 'vedanā' and unattained desires to grab power or nidāna. It is clear that according to the Jainas, it is not merely the feelings of pleasure or pain taken separately but the state of suffering (vedanā), which covers both the feeling states, is the manifestation of the distress state of intention. But we are reminded of another fact in this context that the Jaina theory carefully avoids the synonimity of pleasure (sukḥa) and pain (dukkḥa) with the pleasantness (manojña) and unpleasantness (amanojña) respectively. This is to focus that the feelings of pleasure and pain and the states of pleasantness and unpleasantness are quite different. Moreover, the opposite of 'pleasantness' is not 'pain', rather 'unpleasantness'. This further makes clear that together the *feelings* of pleasure and pain (*not* pleasantness and unpleasantness) arouse suffering, which is a manifestation of distress intention. There is *no* chance whatever in Jainism to muddle the meaning of "pain" and "suffering" and also the meaning of "unpleasantness" and "suffering". Consequently, the confusion regarding the synonimity of "pain" and "unpleasantness" is also not there. "suffering" thus stands out as "sukḥa—dukkḥaphala".

We may be reminded here of the Çārvāka use of pleasure (sukḥa) and pain (dukkḥa) in a manner such that the conception of either 'sukḥa' or 'dukkḥa' combines both (saṁbhinna). There is hardly any 'sukkḥa' without 'dukkḥa' and the *vice versa*. But unlike the Jainas, the Çārvāka holds that when are speak of morality, the exclusive intention of the attainment of 'sukḥa' (of any kind) is good intention. Thus, 'sukḥa' may be divorced from 'dukkḥa' the sphere of practical ethics, as a goal of moral action. But in so far as we conceive them as feeling states, they could be hardly isolated. Despite basic difference in the ethical connotation of the notion of "pleasure" and "pain", both the Jaina and the Çārvāka appear to agree that the conception of "pleasure" and "pain" go together. Yet, the Çārvāka does not think *it* necessary to mention that taken together, pleasure and pain is what we call "suffering" or vedanā.

With this, we can now switch over to consider some of the orthodox schools of Indian Philosophy. I would like to consider the views of the Vedas, the Upaniṣads and the Gitā briefly because without this background it may not be wise to shift abruptly to either Vedānta or for that matter to any other orthodox system.

"PAIN", "SUFFERING" AND THE VEDAS

The study of the orthodox estimate of the notion of "suffering" is a testimony to the ways in which this basic *concept* along with other concepts like "pain" and "evil" have emerged and used in different areas of orthodox writings. To start with, we have the Vedas, which have a direct and straight forward use of the notion of suffering in terms of "dukkḥa".The use is direct in so far as "suffering" refers to the wanton '*human* suffering' in terms of 'personal activity of the Gods' in this world because the entire world where human thrives, the forces which govern it, the different laws which govern nature, have been *personified* as Gods. Basically, human suffering is the one, which comes naturally to those in due course of a relationship that they hold with different Gods. The whole world may be seen also in terms of a peculiar relationship that holds between the wrongdoer, the good agent and the Gods. It is clear that in this straightforward relationship, it is the wrongdoer who is punished and they perish, while the rightful thrive. *Satarūdriya*, a collection of prayers from various part of the Veda (which I have collected from John Bowker's *The suffering in the religious of the world*) reads: "O Rūdra ... who makest the evil does suffer... let not any one of them (the rightful) perish... O Rūdra that being aspect of yours... a benign remedy for terrible suffering".[10] This focuses the fact that "suffering", denoting "human suffering" is not synonymous to the arbitrary notions of gods, which has been forced by men on them to punish the evil-doers; rather, it is the omnipotent act of the all powerful god to maintain harmony and balance in the world so that evil-doers are punished through grave suffering which is due to them. It is here that the notion of the endless cycle of karma and rebirth comes in alliance with the ideals of prize and punishment.

The conception of "suffering" thus gets mingled with the notion of karma and saṁsāra and this become so well projected in the Vedas that it will be unwise to put "suffering" in an isolation to mean an infliction of misery in the world by gods. Thus, "suffering" was not used to denote an *external* activity on the state of human existence owing to their own misdeeds, particularly owing to desire and anger. "Suffering" thus has a broader connotation than 'physical evil', it covers the 'psychic' and the 'metaphysical' as well as 'ethical evil'. The degradation of man in terms of evil thoughts and actions to invite suffering by trapping themselves into the karmic cycle brings out the ethical dimension of "suffering", particularly evident in the Yajur-Vedic hymns. Hence, in the Vedas, the notion of "suffering" taken precisely in terms of "human suffering" has a close relation with the assertion of a moral order underlying the worldly existence and a tendency to either maintain this order or to disharmonise it. Ṛg Veda says: "O Varūna! ... Whatever moral orders of yours we have, in our ignorance violated, punish us not, O God, or account of that sin"[11]. This further brings into light the main cause behind human suffering and we should know the Vedic interest in using the notion of "suffering" to mean some such thing which has originated out of the *conflict* dipped in creation. The conflict is one of the order and the disorder, harmony and disharmony, change and permanence, and morality and immorality. The Vedas strictly maintaining its theistic *monism* could not however give their idea of essential duality personified as conflict between the gods and the demons. If we understand the message of Vedic mythology in its true sense, the demons or the anti-gods represents those forces and inclinations which trap men in the cycle of misdeeds, carrying the effects of those misdeeds to take birth again and again and go on suffering. The conception of "suffering" being closely connected to the conception of "evil forces" is very clear. The idea is best personified in the epic literature of *Mahābhārata* when it has been said about Nirriti that, "She is the embodinent of all sins... and all others kinds of trouble. She is the wife of lawlessness (adharma)."[12]

A peculiar aspect of Vedic use of "suffering" is that it portrays the *ways* is which we suffer and the ways in which they may be controlled because the personification of the evils in the form of anti-gods and the personification of the conflict in terms of either relating the anti-gods to gods or to humans, brings out the truth that humans suffer owing to different evils in different ways, but the other face of the truth is that gods may help fizzle out all evils if such and such steps are taken by humans as well. The apparently misleading polytheism of the Vedas is in fact one way to bring the complex abstraction of human suffering to ordinary minds as something very concrete and real so that they may face this real world suffering more efficiently. It appears that the direct use of "suffering" in Vedic literatures is far more complex than what we usually think about it. The fact becomes clear when we take the double aspect of gods more seriously. The duality may be apparent in even gods in the forms of evil and good, in the form of the one who is punished and who is benevolent. The best way is to understand the double aspects of Śiva and Kālī—the essentially good for the good and the essentially evil for the evil. Really speaking, the double aspect is only apparent. It depends on how we look into this affair. There is no essential duality in these gods, it is their relationship with the evil-doers (portrayed as anti-gods) and the good-agents that the duality is projected in our minds. "Suffering" is thus an *experience* in the world, it may not be flatly used as an evil inflicted on us by gods. "Suffering" is thus "getting suffering in perspective". Truly speaking, in the Vedas, "suffering" has been used to express only is term of the *whole* consisting of the individuals, their intention and deeds and their experiences of the ways in which divine interference occurs if the basic worldly harmony has been in disharmony.

"PAIN" AND "SUFFERING" IN THE UPANIṢADAS AND THE GITĀ

The *Upaniṣadas*, which is the end and consummation of the Vedas, appears to be more profound, in its dealing with the notion of "suffering" or "dukkḥa". Although "suffering' has been used to portray the consequences of the basic conflict between the good and the evil, the *Upaniṣadas* tend to clarify the truth that the crux of the issue is that the notion is meaningful in the whole context of the way *we understand* the result of the duality of good and evil. *Upaniṣadas* would first require us to understand that the duality is only apparent because it is really a projection of our minds; next, it would ask to understand that duality rules out any dualism in the Real, the Brahman. Now, one who understands the abheda or the essential oneness of the Reality, understands that He, by *Himself*, is nither good nor evil, but certain creations are either good or evil by ways of their intentions and deeds, and most tragically owing to this when they suffer, their mental projection of the entire fact takes the Reality to be harsh or punishing or evil or otherwise good and benevolent. The *Upaniṣadas* would convey a double sense of "suffering". One is to convey the sense of the "results of the human follies in terms of bad intention and misdeeds" and the other is to convey the sense of "results of human mental projection in terms of creating bheda or dualism based on the apparent duality of the evil and good or avivekitā". Interestingly, quite a quantum leap from the Vedas, the Upaniṣadas would now clearly tell us that "suffering" might mean, "to create suffering in terms of dualism". To project bheda in essential abheda is to suffer. This suffering is both metaphysical and ethical. The notion clarifies the metaphysical sense in so far as 'to suffer' is to suffer from the *ignorance* of essential abheda as also the notion clarifies the ethical sense in so far as 'to suffer' is 'to' face the result of human follies in terms of "intention and deeds". For instance, in *Mahopaniṣada* (sloka 4/111) and in *Itihāsopaniṣada* (sloka 12), it has been said that "āsthā aparigraha" or "mistrust" amounts to ethical suffering.

The clear and straightforward use of "suffering" in terms of "metaphysical" and "ethical" suffering projects the Philosophical use of the notion in a new light in the *Upaniṣadas*. This brings out the truth that "suffering" is a notion never used to denote some reality, which is ultimate. When we experience suffering in the context of ultimate reality, only one thing appears to be real, that is, it is we, not the ultimate reality, which is suffering or is the cause of suffering. Brahmajñāna thus finds suffering to be meaningless and one, who has it, shall never do the wrong to suffer owing to the saṁsāra.

The *Upaniṣadas* do not rob off the "agonizing" and the "distressing" connotation of "suffering" but says that it all depends on the way a person uses this notion. Hence, the term is not basically a 'feeling term' but it is often used like that and the use is highly *relative*. Even if "suffering" is taken as mental projections in terms of what humans experience in this world, the notion may be used in a highly relative manner to convey what one finds in his mind's eye.

But in so far as we say that the notion signifies the result of the essential ignorance of Reality, the use cannot be relative, it has a stipulation as if, which is fixed. This is due to the fact that the metaphysical use of "suffering" is quite different from the use of the notion in the sense of clarifying a few 'feeling' overtones it also possess. The psycho-physical sense of the notion is thus restored in the Upaniṣadic use of "suffering".

We have seen that "suffering" is a notion which essentially do *not* convey the sense that it is evil rather, the "evilness" lies much on the way we counter the facts related to our psycho-physical existence and experiences in this world. Nevertheless, in so far as this notion conveys the sense that "suffering" is basically an absence of true knowledge of indifference, the "evilness" is not present in the form of mental projections rather intellectual *disposition*. Now, the use of the notion in the Upaniṣadas tend to speak of the primacy of the latter because of our intellectual disposition to know the Reality seriously jeopardized to cause 'ignorance' and thus suffering of all sorts. It is due to this that "suffering" signifies a *problem* only in terms of the results of our intellectual pollution and moral degradation, and not merely as what we think or what appears to us or what we feel. It is due to this that in the Upaniṣadas much stress has been laid on the realization of Brahman to dispel all manifestations because only this can lead man to be detached from the Kārmic cycle and saṁsāra. In this sense then, like Buddhism, "suffering" has a clear connotation of result of "human attachment to the transience projected as real". This also leads us to find out the *teleological* use of the notion because rather than being essentially evil, the notion signifies some state of the intellect, which, however, may lead us *transcend* it through the knowledge of the Reality. Without reducing "suffering" to something conveying the "illusory", the Upaniṣadas hold that it is a problem in a very deep metaphysical and ethical sense, which we can overcome only relating human suffering and Brahmajañāna. Suffering is a problem in relation to the lack of the knowledge of the Brahman.

The Upaniṣadic view of suffering may be seen in the *Gitā* as well. *Gitā* also speaks of the irresistible duality hidden in human experience and it says that the only way to encounter duality is to rise above it through true knowledge. The knowledge that duality is only misguiding is extremely important. One who is truly knowledgeable is able to pursue the path of 'dharma', which ought to be the *summum bonum* of human life. But the Gitā theory of suffering has another interesting aspect, which reflects clearly the teleological use of the notion of "suffering". The *Gitā* allows the view that to follow the path of 'dharmas' even deliberate infliction of suffering on others may be essential, if others are in the real sense against 'dharma' or are the supporters of 'adharma' and thus against humanity at large. The *Gitā* theory of the teleology of suffering could be well understood in the context of the 'grief' and 'sorrow' felt by Arjuna at the face of the performance of dharma, the 'misery' which is naturally due to those who were up against dharma and the necessary bondage due to those who are 'ignorant' of Reality. The notion of "suffering" or "dukkḥa" thus covers the senses of "grief" and "sorrow", i.e. it has 'feeling connotation in so far as Arjuna's suffering conveyed nothing but a specific mental state in which Arjuna was. It was broadly speaking, a state of despondence or "viṣāda" which is reflected through the use of "suffering". But that may not project the first-level meaning of the notion. The second use of the notion in terms of "infliction of suffering" to those who deserve it, bring out the second-level meaning of the notion. The 'infliction' may be intentional but the purpose is good, and, therefore, may be said to be good-in-itself. More interesting is to notice that to spare those who deserve some physical suffering or 'kāyākleśa' is not good, but bad, and to do that is to suffer both ethically as well as metaphysically. This takes us to the 'first level' use of the notion in terms of 'ignorant' about why some such suffering is needed, i.e. ignorant about the *summum bonum* of life and the instrumental value of infliction of physical pains if needed. The second level use of the notion in some sense amount 'physical pain' due to others, whereas the first –level use is quite different from the other uses in so far as it brings out the crux of human suffering in terms of ignorance of the truth. In this sense, the first-level use is akin to the Upaniṣadic use but other uses may be a remnant of the Vedic use in terms of essential psycho-physical pains inflicted by the gods. The first level use of the notion of "suffering" is so delicate in the *Gitā* that it carefully distinguishes the agent of suffering. Truly speaking, when one is suffering from 'ignorance', it is his whole self which is suffering, the *self* which is immortal and get so infected by the kārmic matter that it is bound to the saṁsāra causing relentless suffering. The *Gitā* says, "Ye hi saṁsparśajā bhogā duḥkhayonya eva te ādyāntavantaḥ kaunteya na teṣū ramate budhaḥ"[13] i.e., whatever pleasures are born in contact with the physical or the corporeal are the sources of *sorrow* or *suffering*, no wise man ought to enjoy them.

This brings out the truth that when we suffer, our 'self' suffers, which is not taken as psycho-physical suffering, it is largely a metaphysical suffering and in some sense ethical as well. But when we are said to suffer in other senses, it is *believed* that it is agent's *body*, which suffers (psycho-physical suffering) and not the agent's self which suffers. Nevertheless, this 'belief' may be completely mistaken because when agent's body suffers owing to one reason or the other it is basically due to the 'ignorance' of the dharma. Such ignorance leads to a "suffering" in the first-level sense. Thus the 'bodily suffering' although real, turns out to be glibly reflected if we forget that basically it is the 'suffering of the self of the agents'. The question is, does the self suffer at all? Now that the *Gitā* being remnant of the Upaniṣadic theory of 'self', it is an aspect of the Brahman and not something else; thus the true 'self' cannot suffer. Here again we have two levels of an understanding of the suffering self. The real self is indestructible and aspect of Brahman and thus not the sufferer but the same self being infested with the affects of karma has to suffer in another way. It is through constant cycle of birth and death. It will be really speaking difficult to speak of the 'self' being a sufferer but that has to be allowed in the *Gitā* only if we remember that the 'suffering self' is in any way not synonymous to the 'damaged self' where 'damage' is an essential physical deformity. If we understand the essence of the *Gitā* theory of self and suffering, we could understand why a suffering self can still recover from its miserable state to attain its true nature through the knowledge of Brahman and performance of dharma. Worldly suffering in any form, whether or not deliberately infected by others, is only coincidental. It may be *felt* as an utterly real experience, but it is not the final truth about reality or about the self, which possesses the disposition to realize the oneness of Being-itself and the value of dharma. The *Gitā* holds, "mān upetya punarjanma duḥkhālayaṁ aśāśavataṁ nāpnuvanti mahātmānaḥ saṁsiddhiṁ paramāṁgataḥ"

Hence, one who has reached the abode of God by the performance of disinterested duty are those great souls who do not get back to rebirth, the place of impermanence and suffering, for they have achieved highest perfection. The perfection is truly metaphysical and not merely ethical. With this we find that in the *Gitā*, the basics of *there* levels of suffering, i.e. despondence, psycho-physical infatuation owing to changing to the fruits of actions and physical harm stemming out of either infliction of harm for a greater noble cause or out of efforts given by a man for an ethical objective has been clearly stated. This given us an account of the psychic, the physical, the ethical and the metaphysical use of the notion of suffering or "dukḥa" in the *Gitā*. The notion of suffering or "dukḥa" in the *Gitā*, finds a strong ethico-metaphysical use, which is unique to the sacred doctrine.

"PAIN", "SUFFERING", "EVIL" AND THE FIVE ORTHODOX SCHOOLS

As we consider the Sāṁkhya School of thought, we find that the psycho-physical as well as the metaphysical use of the notion of "suffering" in terms of "Kleśa" is very clear. With this the Sāṁkhya school values the psycho-physical and metaphysical *management* of the so-called "evil". However, in Sāṁkhya theory we find a clear distinction between the use and meanings of "pain" and "suffering" because with regard to living being, the Sāṁkaya speaks of "dukḥa" or pain as distinct from "kleśa" or "suffering". With this, the Sāṁkhya tends to bring out the distinction of pain conceived in the phenomenal world *vis-a-vis* suffering as an evil state of affairs permeating the human existence, which is the enduring reality having a definite cause and it needs management.

The opening passage of *Sāṁkhyakārikā* by Īśvarakrisṇa reads: "Dukhatrayābhighātajijñāsā tadapaghātake hetau dṛṣṭe sāyapārtha çermeykāntātyanyatvabhāvāt".[14] According to Vāçaspati, the Kārika present the truth that the corporeal existence is soaked in "pain", which could be expressed as "rajaḥparināma rūpa dukḥa", i.e. the one which is essentially due to the "rajaḥguṇa" or due to the property or element of Prakṛti, which initiates motion. Hence, Sāṁkhya accepts that the root cause of corporeal pain is inherent in the very nature of Prakṛti. The element of motion is thus the cause of all pain. It is due to this that pain is basically due to something, which is the very basis of existence, i.e. Prakṛti. It is thus 'antaḥkaraṇavarti'. If this were the case then pain or dukḥa may be either internally or externally caused (āntara upāyasādhya or bāhyaupāyasādhya). Hence Sāṁkhya conceives of "dukḥatrayabhighata" or to be clear, according to Vyāsavākya, "dukḥānāmatrayaṁ", i.e. pain may be of three kinds or caused at three levels—the ādhyatmika, the ādhibhautika and the ādhidaivika. Standing on its firm psycho-physics, Sāṁkhya thinks that mind and body being parallel, one could speak of "ādhyātmika dukḥa" as the one which is "dvividhaṁ" or *both* physical and mental (sāriraṁ mānasṁ ça). Those pains caused by the disharmony in vāyu, pitta and kafa; the elements of the physique, are physical pains, whereas those caused by the psychic states of kāma, krodha, lobha, moha, bhaya, īrṣyā and viṣāda are psychological pains. We can also speak of psychic pain owing to desire non-fulfilment. With this, Sāṁkhya provides us with an a extent of those pains which are conceivable at the physical and psychic levels and are mainly caused by internal as well as external factors present in this world. But one basic factor in that without motion no such painful states may be conceived Sāmkhya further speaks of "ādhibhautika dukḥa" or pains owing to *extra-organic* or other than the psycho-physical factors like, other persons, animals and static things like stones or trees etc. Hence, Sāṁkhya conceives of organic as well as extra-organic pains and in the latter category he puts together the effects of those agents who are, living as well as non-living through the senses of an individual. He also imagines about the intentional acts eliciting pain, particularly by human beings (for different reasons) and about *non-intentional* reflex actions or defensive acts of non-humans and the non-intentional effects of the trees, stones, hillocks and so on. Sāṁkhya thus covers almost all organic and inorganic things as causes of pains in human beings. In fact we may imagine about Sāṁkhya çonception of *all* organic and inorganic things in pain because it is we who have the disposition to conceive of a feeling state like pain and effectively use pain-language, and, therefore, imagine pain in all existent things in some sense or the other. It may be perfectly justifiable that the Ganges causes pain (may be when she inundates) or the Ganges herself suffers from pain owing to different reasons (like putting a huge barrage across her). But in such cases it is we who could speak about pains and use a pain-language. In addition to this, Sāṁkhya imagines "ādhidaivika dukḥa" or pains produced by supernatural powers of Yakṣa, rāksasas, grahas and vināyakas. This may be highly objectionable if one does not go by the Sāṁkhya imagination. But there is no doubt that in human language we do have such use because many among us do imagine such pains though it is not a matter a proving or justifying because human language—use is often beyond such justifications. It may be a matter of acceptating such beliefs about pain.

Sāṁkhya effort to give a due importance to the feeling-self or the self that has the pain feeling and the one who is conscious about pain in other objects. Such a consciousness belongs to the Jīva or the personal self. Sāṁkhya holds that "pain" establishes an aversive or "pratikūla" relationship with consciousness and, therefore, one may speak of a state of consciousness, i.e. adversity with regard to pain or precisely, abhisaṁbandha". This may be going too far with the correlative use of "pain" with "consciousness", because *not* always and *not* necessarily would the psychologists hold that the consciousness of pain is essentially aversive, otherwise we may *not* imagine "pleasant pain" and "non-painful pain". Sāṁkhya justification is pretty simple. As pain is basically harmful or hurtful, it elicits aversion in us and for that matter we try to get rid of it or manage it. Hence, the "abhibhāva" or the non-occurrence of pain needs careful pain management through medicine, right livelihood and so on. But Sāṁkhya is not impractical, with constantly dynamic life, it does think of ever emerging occurrence of pain. Hence pain is neither "ekānta" or final nor is it "ātyanta" or non-occurring.

Sāṁkhya would thus stick to the position that "pain" is essentially "pratikūla vedaniya" or "aversive" and ask a few basic questions about its knower or the subject of feeling, the reason behind some essentially aversively felt facts, why people do not desire pain, what are the grounds for making a tripartite division among pains, why corporeal management of pain is never final as well as repetitive and how the final and non-repetitive management is possible. Without essentially delving deeper into these trifles, we could see for the present purpose that according to Sāṁkhya the *knower* of pain is not the "nirguṇa Puruṣa" or the non-determined self, rather the bodily self or the "sopādhika purūṣa" or the "jīva" because it is an agglomeration, a body, external and internal organs and vital forces as well as life. Such bodily self is the actor or the one performing threefold functions eliciting pleasure, pain and attachment. In conjunction with the knowing self, if an action produces non-aversion, it is "sukhavedanā or pleasure-feeling or else if it produces a feeling of aversion, it is "dukḥavedanā" or "pain-feeling" or if it is unclear, it is "mohavedanā" or feeling of attachment. This makes clear that pain is a feeling state of individual consciousness in relation to objects, which are essentially aversive. Hence, we may think of such things in nature. But what is vital is that pain-feeling makes sense is relation to the "kāraṇaprakṛti' or dynamic conscious self and goes on to say that the dynamics being *limited*, when an individual crosses the limit to do some actions in relation to other things, one *feels* pain. Hence "pain-talk" in Sāṁkhya is possible only in relation to the unbalanced dynamics of the self, which is necessarily related to the physical body. Hence, the more the "kāraṇas" are hindered, the more it has to act to get the feeling of aversion or pain. Sāṁkhya holds that the feeling of pain and pleasure is thus heavily dependent on the intrinsic nature of man, not on instincts. Sāṁkhya's use of "pain" also makes it clear that the word (dukḥa) is in fact used as "dukḥakāraka hetū" or *causes* of pain-feelings, it is due to this that we do not get a straightforward explanation of the nature of the concept called "pain", rather an explanation of *phenomena* called "pain", and it is an intricate matter when, we consider this phenomena because it should be juxtaposed with conscious self. Once we do this, we are considering the possibility of various shades of pain feelings among individuals.

Sāṁkhya's psycho-physical use of "pain" clarifies the nature of the feeling self or jiva because if we do not take care of the *body, senses* and *mind,* the origin of pain in man cannot be understood. Pain feelings in an individual possessing a body cannot be imagined without sense contacts and this speaks of individual relation with external causes or factors producing pain. It may cover 'other forms of life' (as we have seen), where "other forms" come in contact through the senses. But the effects of these forms of life through ones body may not be taken as "ādhibhautika dukḥa". Thus the pain feeling owing to the individuals essence, i.e. possessing body is quite different. However, an individual is essentially possessor of mind, and, therefore, the assumption of "mental pain" is justified. But mind is an internal organ inseparably related to external organs, i.e. senses. Hence, both mind and senses are *causes* of pain because in mental pain, none but the mind is in-pain, not the body. The subtle use of the "physical" and the "mental pain" focuses their difference, which tells us about the state of pain, which is *purely* mental. Hence, there must be made a difference between pain owing to receiving a slap on face and the pain resulting from listening to an abusive language. With this the effects of the external-cum-internal organs in pain-feeling has been clearly brought out. But it is our intellect or "buddhi" which is in bondage (baṅdhana) while we are in pain and it is the liberation of the intellect in bondage, which calls for greater attention. Sāṁkhya also draws our attention towards the fact that the feeling of pain in comparison to the feeling of pleasure, is greater elicitor of dynamics, as well as it demands the knowledge of its origin and management. This may be different from the Bentham's conception of the aversion of pain and desire for pleasure being the motives of moral actions, Sāṁkhya tries to bring out the truth that it is basically a problem of *cognition* that we put "pain" at a more important level. Its primacy is also owing to the need for its management because its endurance may lead to yet another evil, perhaps the greater one, viz. "suffering" or "kleśa". Sāṁkhya tries to bring another truth that "dukḥa" or "pain" may be looked upon as "apṛīti", whereas "pleasure", which is often termed as "pṛīti" may *not* be treated as the corollary of pain. Also pain, pleasure and despondence are *not* the ab*sence* of one another rather, they have a common locus, namely, the conscious and dynamic individual self. All these belongs to "ātma" or they are "bhāvarūpa", and therefore, *used* as "I am in pain", "I feel pleasant", "I am despondent" and so on. The ego-locusness is a keynote in the use of "pain" but it may not rule out the possibility of statement about otherselves. Sāṁkhya also tries to convey the truth that it is myself, i.e. the determined corporeal jiva (not Purūṣa), who really suffers from pain and for that reason the "I-ness" goes with "pain".

Sāṁkhya is of the opinion that "Kleśa" or "suffering" is a *generic* notion covering feeling state of pain. Nevertheless, it covers the state of affair of a person who is in pain. Pain has really engulfed the being that is in such a state. Hence "Kleśa" refers to the state of a person in pain. As Sāṁkhya imagines dynamics in the world-cause or Prakṛiti, the guṇas are in constant change and motion. As such, there may be no respite from pain and suffering. Although Sāṁkhya has no hesitation in ascribing the "I-ness" to "pain", it has been made clear that "I-ness" is not the same as the Purūṣa or the pure self. Individuals are inherently Pure Purūṣa and not Prakṛiti (having gúṇas); hence, when one suffers, the natural and common assertions involving "I" and "myself" or intellect or mind, may *not* be taken as meaning Purūṣa. Sāṁkhya thinks that great suffering is due to this *ignorance* of the nature of the Pure self *vis-a-vis* determined self always under the influence of Prakṛiti, and the guṇas become the abode of pain-experiences. Sāṁkhya now refers to an interesting non-Vedāntic use of "suffering" or "kleśa", where the notion has been juxtaposed with Prakṛiti-Purūsa *difference* or "bheda" because a sense of non-difference leads to suffering and not any other thing. This is so because any amount of moral action would be futile as they all cling to the guṇas to lead to further pain and thus suffering. Hence, pain and suffering is there where not-Self has not be clearly distinguished from the Pure Self. Thus, the Sāṁkhya notion of "kleśa" is not directed toward the self because the Pure Self never suffers but is essentially Blissful or knower of the difference of the Pure Self and the not-Self. In any case we are at hand a view of the multifarious psycho-physical as well metaphysical use of the notion of pain and an unique metaphysical sense is which "kleśa" or "suffering" has been used in the Sāṁkhya literature.

Sāṁkhya theory of "dukḥa" (pain) and "Kleśa" (suffering) are important for its clear-cut distinction of the feeling and the generic notion through their psycho-physical and metaphysical uses. As we now turn to Yoga, we find that the treatment is quite akin to its precursor, the Sāṁkhya. But one gets a wider use of "kḷeśa" in the Yoga Philosophy revealing thereby clearer distinction between pain and suffering. Turning to "dukḥa" (pain) first, the Yoga would like to consider it after an explanation, of "çittavikṣepa" or projections. This is important in order to justify that 'pain' has a deep *association* with the internal-organs and their projection on human persona. Yoga mentions *eight* fundamental types or modes of projection of internal-organs, which are in true sense "bighnas" as hindrances towards Yogic practices leading to the *summum bonum* of life, viz. the state of oneness with the Ultimate Reality. These "Yogapratipakṣi" or "anti-yogic hindrances" resulting into the ignorance or ajñāna about the nature of Reality and the *summum bonum* of life. But in addition to the light modes of projection, viz. vyādhi (disease), stayana (inaction), saṁśaya (sluggishness), avirati (infatuation), bhrāntidarśana (false knowledge), alabhyabhūmikatva (non-fulfilment of yogic goal), pramāda (carelessness regarding yogic practices) and anavasthitaitva (lack of concentration), the yoga mention "dukḥa" (pain) and *four* other bighnas (hindrances), which, however, are different from the above-mentioned hindrances. These latter kind of hindrances are *associates* of the basic modes of projections of the internal-organs but they are *not* participants or *members* of the class of basic modes of internal-organs, and, therefore, may not be considered as those hindrances which are *within* the citta or the internal-organs, they are *external* and yet *associated* to the internal-organs. *Patañjali Sūtra* mentions, "dukḥaelaudormanasyaṇgamejayatvasvāsa prasvāsa vikṣepasaḥabhūvaḥ"[15]. It is clear that dukha or pain, daurmanasya or hopelessness due to non-fulfilment of desires, aṇgamejayatva or feebleness of body, svāsa or unnecessary inhalation hindering kumbhaka practice and prasvāsa or unnecessary exhalation during kumbhaka are those hindrances which are associated to the projection of internal-organs and are external to them, i.e. "vikṣepasaḥabhūḥ". The eight projections being "viksepantarāyāḥ" or *within* the internal-organs, the demarcation line between pain and other modes of hindrance towards Yogic practices is drawn clearly. Undoubtedly, dukḥa or pain has being certainly used as a hindering factor, in a clearly *negative* fashion to refer to some such things or phenomena or non-physical supernatural existence, which are against the yogic efforts. This is to make clear that "pain" has a physical as well as non-physical reference, which has far reaching ramifications, viz. negative effect on the whole being in so far as an association with the internal-organs and their projections are anti-yogic in essence. This further makes clear that "pain" bears a *non-mental* reference and is thus closer to the natural, the supernatural and the metaphysical factors. With this we also have an idea about the three *causes* of dukḥa, the ādhyātmika, the ādhibhautika and the ādhidaivika, which are exactly like those mentioned by the Sāṁkhya.

Further, the Yogic use of "pain" in the context of its different kinds makes it clear that this state of affair permeates in all human beings, greater or smaller. In Sādhanapāda II, śloka 15, it has been said, "Pariṇāmatāpasaṁskāradukḥayerguṇavṛttivirodhāçça dukḥameva sarvaṁ vivekināḥ"[16]. It has been said, that due to the presence of three kinds of pain, the result of human action end up in all pervading pain without any exception whatsoever. As such, following the existentialist fervor, pain is for the conscious human beings an all-pervading reality. "Pain" thus stands out as reference to those states which permeate human existence, and which have an indubitable derogatory effect on man. The so-called pleasures are painful because its enjoyment causes fatigue in senses and thus ends up in pain. As such pain is an outcome of sense-pleasures, the Yoga calls it "pariṇāma-dukḥa". Another pain, which the Yoga calls "tapa dukḥa" or pain owing to envy, is infecting an outcome of comparison of pleasure-enjoyment between two persons. If the first type reminds us of the effect of corporeal pleasure, the latter reminds us of the danger of falling prey to the hedonic paradox. The non-hedonic inclination of the Yoga is clear. The Yoga ends up with the far-reaching effect of such pains on a human çitta. It says that the çitta gets clouded with the "saṁskāras" or the affects of these pains owing to pleasure gratification and we have a tendency to recall from memory those affects to get more soaked in pain. This is "saṁskāra dukḥa". To elaborate it further, the Yoga says that the modes of sattva and other guṇas are pleasure, pain and attachment, which mingle up *without* any internal conflict among them and for that reason, pain shall accompany the mode of "rajoguṇa". The result is that the conscious being shall realize that pain is with every means of infatuation. The implication of "pain" being used in this way is that the Yoga has to accept the *association* of pain with the modes of projections of internal-organs. With this, "pain" does not merely refer to an object or a thing causing certain negative effects on the body, it rather covers the sense of a "feeling" which has far reaching negative effect on human persona and life. The Yoga thus comes up with a conclusion that it is due to the ignorance of reality that a person under the influence of infatuation takes it to be pleasure and not pain. Hence, we can conceive of two kinds of people in this world, those attached to the means of pleasures, who may be said to be at the state of "rāga", and the other, wants to get detached from it or may be said to be at the state of 'dveṣa'. The Yoga also warns us that therefore the one, who is still not attached to pain, ought to prevent it dawning upon the being. Clearly, "pain" is a notion referring to some state of affairs, which needs immediate management. The Yoga has a clear prescription for this, which I shall not discuss here. It is desirable to move on to the Yoga conception of suffering or Kleśa.

The *Yoga Sūtra* does not provide a straightforward synonymous or verbal or real definition of the notion of "Kleśa" or "suffering". Rather, speaks of the examples of Kleśa. This is not to odd to do because one, who does not know about the term, could be easily explained by providing a few examples. Hence, defining by examples may be accepted as one sound way of knowing about "kleśa". The sūtra mentions: "kleśaḥ punaḥ paṅçadhā prasiddhaḥ-avidyāsmita rāgadvesabhinivesaḥ klesaḥ"[17]. Suffering may be thus said to be a state of a human being who is under the influence of either one or more or all five state of affairs, viz, "avidyā" or not knowing the really Real; "asmitā" or confusing çitta or internal organs with the Puruṣa or Pure Self; rāga or desire for wordily objects; "dvesa" or anger and "abhinivesaḥ" or an attitude of not parting with the physical body. The Yoga makes it clear that there is no reason to think that "suffering" is merely a generic notion covering different "pains" because there is no reference to pain as such in association with suffering. Rather, earlier on it has been clarified that the various modes of projection of the internal organs and its associates like pain are the important obstacles towards attaining *summum bonum* of life. Hence, suffering which is distinct from these obstacles is a more pervading obstacle that transcends both the gross body and the internal organs to cling to the psychic or the mental level of man as well as to the intentional or the attitudinal level of human character. Once we know about these examples of suffering, we will know about the way in which suffering as a state of affair could grip the whole personality of a being and sustain its effects in this life or life hereafter. First, "suffering" may be used as a notion covering "deep ignorance" or "avidyā", which is not merely 'false knowledge' rather, not knowing the Reality and a lack of such knowledge would deprive a person to fix the moral goal in his life. He or she would thus find no interest in conjoining one's own self with the higher self or realizing the true nature of the self. This is so serious for the Yoga that without this, it would say, the whole human life is in vain. Hence, "suffering" is a state of ignorance, which may be deep, enduring and agonizing in life here and hereafter. Second, this notion may be used to signify the lack of differentiating the Pure Self and the internal organs. Again this goes beyond the merely physical and the internal hindrances. It delves deeper into the consciousness level of a personality (like the first one). One who is not conscious about the truth, i.e. the fact that the Pure Self in quite distinct from the corporeal self (who is the *real* suffer or one who is in pain or one who is under projections of internal organs), fails to realize the above-mentioned fact that it is the realization of the non-suffering Pure Self that matters in human life and nothing else. Hence, 'to suffer' is to be under an agonizing and enduring stupidity to understand that the self suffers. It may be thus extremely important to transcend the ego-locussness at the mental level to realize the Pure Self and to know that it is *eternal*. Third, "suffering" is a notion conveying the sense of desiring the worldly objects, more precisely, corporeal cravings. It is much different from "desiring the desirable". Hence, the Yoga makes it clear that we are said to be in a state of suffering when we do *not* desire the desirable (the oneness with the Pure Self) rather desire the *desired*. This difference of attitude in our life is really a difference of moral attitude *vis-a-vis* immoral attitude. One who has an immoral attitude to embrace all corporeal things that comes in his way and later on hanker after them, are those who suffer. "Suffering" thus has a clear moral significance in so far as it points towards the goal of human life. Fourth, we have suffering in so far as we nourish the psychic states of anger and hatred. This is again an indication how the Yoga prefers to use the notion to clarify a state of human mind, which is utterly *undesirable* because it may lead us to nurture a negative element that destroys our intentions and thus moral actions. Carrying on with the excellent psychic-ethical use of "suffering", the Yoga holds that the notion may be used to cover some such habitual state of mind or intention of a man who *desires* to cling to his *body*. This is a kind of deep infatuation resulting again from ignorance of the truth that the Pure Self is eternal, whereas the individuals corporeal existence may face an end. The I-ness is thus so deep that it permeates the mind to cling to the corporeal, the non-eternal. Again such an attitude is injurious for the whole person. Hence, he or she suffers.

But the Yoga, who is distinct to its precursor in recognizing Iśvara or God to become theistic, says that "kleśa" or "suffering" may be regarded as just one among the four factors to determine the nature of God through *negation*, i.e. to say that kleśa along with karma, vipāka and āśaya are those factors, which are *not* present in a Reality called God. Yet, the jiva or the human beings are all determined by the four factors and are thus *not* God. Clearly, it is the human beings that are in pain or are under projection of internal-organs or are sufferer. Although, inherently such beings are eternal, they are under such negative influences owing to ignorance of the Pure Self. Thus suffering is essentially determined through human nature under the influence of ignorance. Suffering is thus more binding on human nature in the sense of prevention of realizing the Self. With this come to know that in the Yoga Philosophy, "pain" and "suffering" have been carefully used to distinguish between two state of affairs binding human nature either extrinsically or intrinsically.

The Nyāya takes great interest in pain and suffering, for which they use "dukḥa" and "kleśa" respectively. Interesting uses of these notions may be seen in the Vātsayāna Bhāsya on *Nyāya Sūtra* of Gotama. In the Prameyaprakaranaṁ we find the Nyāya mentioning, "iççādveṣaprayātnasukḥadukhajñānyātmano lingam"[18]. It says that içça or desires, dveṣa or envy, prayatna or effort, sukha or pleasure, *dukha or pain*, jñāna or knowledge, these *six* are the connoting properties of the individual soul or liṅga. This is no conjecture or a baseless hypotheses says the Nyāya because for the knowledge of individual self, pain and other are the prameyas or are knowledge through different pramaṇas or valid sources of knowledge. Among these, ātmā or the individual self is said to be the locus (knower and enjoyer) of both pleasure and pain. Hence, self is the one which *experiences* the feelings called pleasure and pain. Pleasure and pain are those factors through which the individual self makes its clear recognition. The Nyāya is very logical and careful in its approach. At the outset it makes clear that pleasure and pain must be residing at a locus, otherwise its knowability is jeopardized. Rather than speaking of either mind or internal – organs, the Nyāya thinks that pleasure and pain are properties of self. However, one may raise some doubt regarding the self-being the locus because one may still speak of intellect. The Nayāya clarifies that ātmā *alone* can be the 'pratisaṅdhatā' or 'inferring authority' from the various empirical knowledge obtained; for instance, "X gives me pain again and again" may be sufficient ground to infer through memory that an experience of 'X now shall give me pain again'. Hence, the present inference about X is closely associated to the vyāptijñāna, smṛtijñāna and anumāna of the past and for this we need an authority who can do so. Mind or intellect may *not* possess such dispositions but self can; hence, self is the reality which possess the property of pleasure and pain because it can *only* know such things.

The Nyāya further asks, "dukhamitinedamanūkulavedaniyasya sukhasya pratiteḥ pratyṣkhyanaṁ kiṁ tamhi?"[19] This is to ask whether or not pleasure and pain are corollaries or whether or not pleasure negates pain and *vice versa* because in the common parlance pain or dukḥa is believed to be "pratikūlavedaniya" or unfavourable feeling whereas, pleasure or sukha is "anukūlavedaniya" or favourable-feeling. The Nyāya would not follow such superficial logic because it would say that in reality pleasure and pain are close *associates* and not antagonists for the simple reason that for a person in bondage, who aspires liberation, is constantly under the influence of determined-pleasures or pleasures which are mere means towards constant bondage and *not* liberation. Hence, pleasures run headlong to constant pains and there is no respite. Hence, pleasure and pain resemble each other in being vaṅdhanas or elements of bondage or deep-rooted suffering, therefore, are close allies and not antagonists. The Nyāya thus finds it wise to prescribe the wise to think deeply and constantly that "sarvaṁ khalvidaṁ dukhaṁ"[20] or "all is pain". Thus the existentialist fervor of worldly pain present in all form of pleasures and other things could be easily seen here. The Nyāya finds a teleological value in such thinking as it may encourage deep sense of repentance and thus lead us to liberation. This may further remind us of the fact that both pleasure and pain are the motives of moral actions but the only difference is that not only that the avoidance of pain and attainment of pleasure is what is desirable, rather both are to be avoided as both are undesirable. Hence the Nyāya does not speak like the Benthamite utilitarian. Yet, they are teleologists of a different type. It is very clear that for *the* Nyāya, every form of existence, in birth and death, in decay and despondence, we find pain. Hence, pain is the name to convey the sense of some such element in human soul, which in association with pleasure induce deep-rooted bondage. It is thus a factor for human-bondage or a factor causing pretyabhāva or the cycle of rebirth. The desirable and is to end up this cycle or to attain apavarga (liberation).

The Nyāya now clearly states that pleasure and pain are thus "saṁvedanam" or "sensations" which we go on feeling in this corporeal world, which result into bondage. Thus, "sukhadukḥasaṁvedanaṁ" are "pravṛttidoṣajanitaṁ" or are due to several contacts and infatuations, which could be precisely mentioned as "phalaṁ". The Nyāya has no hesitation is saying that "pleasure" and "pain" are the feeling-notions, closely attached to the pleasure and pain incitors. This brings the Nyāya account at the doorsteps of hackneyed psycho-physical account of pleasure and pain. Until the Nyāya transcends it completely to mention that "pleasure" and "pain" as feeling–terms make any sense if and only if we attach it to the self as its properties and the originators of human bondage. This tendency of transcendence in the psycho-physics of the Nyāya is perfectly matched to many metaphysical account of pain and pleasure which brings out *interesting* dimensions in the uses and meanings of these so-called feeling-terms. Or a notion connoting the "vaṅdhanas" thus precisely mentions dukḥa or elements that cause *existential* pain or "piḍā". More clearly, "dukḥa" has an existential significance in so far as it produces some such disturbances in our body, mind and intellect at various epochs of birth and death that it ends up in nothing but deep rooted suffering. Vandhanas *thus* being the existential pain, something that naturally follows from it is simply, "dukḥa" or pain. "Pain" is thus a notion which, when, used, generally carries with it a physiological *connotation.* But the Nyāya continues to say in "dukḥa parikṣā-prakaranaṁ" that "vividhovādhanāyogadā dukhameva janmotpatti"[21]. That is, it would be too narrow to use "pain" (dukḥa) as a term denoting physiological damages or harmful effects because "pain" is some such sensation which one has to go through at *various* conditions of the existence or at different *forms* of origination. "Pain" is thus more extensively being used in the Nyāya to cover those undesirable affects caused by several factors at *all* instances of *spatio-temporal* existence. Because, to be "born" is to "originate" and to originate is to "come into being in many spatio-temporal forms". At each forms of existence, different feeling of pain could be imagined. It is, therefore, possible for us to extensively use this term to speak of "utkṛsta" or severe pain, "madhyaṁ" or moderate pain and "hīna" or minimum pain, respectively at the existential levels in the "naraka" or hell, i.e. after death when we are due to be put to punishments at the animal existence, i.e. when we are due to live like animals and at the human existential level, i.e. when we are prized to live like man. It has been conceived that at the "deva" and the "vitarāga" levels of existence (the godly and the wisdom levels of existence), the pain is more mild. But there is pain indubitably at every levels of the mythical, the corporeal and the metaphysical existence. The Nyāya account thus makes it clear that the notion of "pain" could be easily used to speak of the spatio-temporal existential *state of affairs* in which a self in bondage could be imagined. This covers the sensible use of this notion beyond its most general human-locus-use. There should be thus no hesitation when we speak about animal-pain and other pains, which are often avoided by many. With this, the Nyāya is better placed in justifying the existentialist use of the notion to speak about 'all-permeating pain' and even 'pain permeating in our intellect'. This is the main cause for despondence and the ruthlessness to come out of this terrible state. Whatever degree of pleasure may be thus attained or are being constantly enjoyed, it does not reject pain, pain pervades pleasure. But the all-pervading pain does not engulf pleasure altogether. It has *not* been said, "birth is pain", or that intrinsically, it is painful. Rather, it is intrinsically a pleasure. Yet, we impose a feeling of pain in it (birth) in the sense that the *cessation* of the cycle of *rebirth* is needed, for it is *essentially painful.*

Further, the Nyāya maintains that the result of constant spatio-temporal-existential levels of pain is that the being is said to "suffer" or "kelśānubandha". Hence, the human bondage we have been mentioning is in fact, "suffering". Every being is thus under the conflict of suffering, which is not easy to shake off because one who is particularly dwelling in the influx of suffering often do not try to find out the real causes behind it. It is due to this that if sometimes the influx of suffering seems to fade off or normalize, the bondage of self or suffering does not shake-off. The truth is that worldly suffering is a natural course, it is *eternal* in that sense; therefore, to shake it off will be very difficult superficially. Clearly, the Nyāya maintains that it is not pain, which is more disturbing rather, enduring suffering is disturbing. "Suffering" is thus a notion which does not merely cover a species called "pain" rather a state of a person who is in bondage and such a state may be completely got rid off only if we get the true knowledge of the Absolute Self, which is never in either pain or suffering.

As Sāṁkhya is to Yoga, Vaiśeṣika or Alūkyadarśana is to Nyāya. The Vaiśeṣika is extremely clear in its treatment of "dukḥa" but relatively silent in using "suffering" or "kleśa". However, like the Nyāya, it takes great interest in treating "dukḥa" with "sukha" or pleasure. But unlike the Nyāya it does not prefer to call pleasure and pain as having a pervading associative relationship, rather, "pain" has been clearly mentioned as the corollary of "pleasure". We find Annāmbhatta defining "pleasure" or "sukha" as: "sarvesamānukūlatayā vedaninaṁ sukhaṁ" and "pratikūlataya vedaniyaṁ dukḥaṁ"[22]. This is to say that "pleasure" is a *sensation* of *favourableness* for all those who enjoy this sensation, whereas "pain" is the sensation of *unfavourableness* for all those who are cursed with such sensation. But these definition are not satisfactory because it would be an unwise and illogical generalization to speak of "*all* favourably consider pleasure" but not pain or *vice versa*. This would rule out possibility of "pleasant-pain", "unpleasant-pleasure" etc. Moreover, the saint does not favourably consider "pleasure" as valuable and the masochist may not unfavourably consider "pain" as valueless. The Nyāya being more logical did never go for such hasty generalization and definition. It is due to this that Praśastapāda proposes other definitions of "sukḥa" and "dukḥa". According to him, "anugrahalakṣanaṁ sukhaṁ" and "upaghātalakṣanaṁ dukḥaṁ". Praṣastapāda realized that it would be better to project prominently pleasure as a sensation. He holds that "pleasure" means a sensation, which is generally favourably accepted by men. It may be related to both our past and future, whereas, "pain" means a sensation which is *generally* unfavourably accepted by men. This may be related to our past and future. Although Praśastapāda has been careful, he could not avoid using these notions in the contexts of "sensation-talk" and "human psyche". He also did speak differently from the Nyāya in so far as the corollary characters of these notions have been clearly spelt out.

The Vaiśeṣika proceeds further to hold that the effects of pain are thus unfavourableness, aversion (dvesa) and paleness (dainya). Interesting is to notice that the Vaiṣeṣika also speaks of conditions inducing pain, viz. proximity to an aversive thing (anabhipretaviṣayasānnidhya), apprehensive of evil (anistopalabdhi), sense stimulation by external objects, inequilibrium in the organic structure and demerit. These clearly brings out the truth that the Vaiśeṣika found more interest in mentioning the underlying characteristics of pain in so far as being a sensation, it demands such an analysis. Further, Vaiśeṣika's interest in the origin of such sensation bring out its psycho-physics into limelight as it enters into the realm of a person in pain permealing body and mind.

We may now move on to see how the notion of "pain" and "suffering" has been used in the Advaita and Viśiṣtādvaita Vedānta. In Śaṅkara Vedānta, both "pain" (dukḥa) and "suffering" (Kleśa) have been unequivocally brought under a much broader notion of "evil" (aśubha) because there is no doubt that both pain and suffering are just forms of evil and these evils are there not without a reason as well as not without a far reaching effect. Hence, it will be more appropriate to look into "evil" first. To speak of evil is to ask for its cause. Śaṅkara has in mind, "adhyāsa" or superimposition of individual mind as over Reality *owing* to avidyā for lack of the knowledge of the Reality. Hence, Brahmajñāna or the ultimate knowledge of Reality or vidyā only eradicates the root cause of all evils and thus wipes out pains and sufferings. Vedānta in brief is thus management of evil (not merely pain and suffering) through the knowledge of the ultimate Reality. Hence, it starts the discourse pursing "athāto brahmajijñāsā" or "now let us know the Brahman".

According to Śaṅkara therefore, it will be pointless to discuss about pain and suffering without relating it to the natural and endless superimposition of individual self (jivātma) to distinguish "asmad" and "yusmad" to create a false knowledge of "I-ness". But the eternal Ātman or the real Self inherent in the individual gets superimposed and the basic knowledge of the indistinguishable entities (Thou and I) is lost, causing all sorts of evil. Management of evils is thus a matter of true cognition. This distinction of the individual Self and Self under the influence of false-knowledge results into a conception of the individual Self-acquiring three dispositions. One is that the superimposed Self becomes extremely inactive or subdued, i.e. its "antaḥkaraṇa" (internal organs) in a state of deep sleep. It appears that at such an inactive state, the internal-organs, which is said to be the abode of *feelings* like "pain" may avoid pain as such. Second is that the superimposed Self has the disposition to get associated to the subtle body, as if the internal organs are suddenly awake to receive all external influences eliciting pain-feeling and physical suffering. Yet, the Self has the disposition to get fully awake as if, to free itself from all ignorance through true knowledge of Reality, i.e. to attain mokṣa from the saṁsāra cycle (birth and death and other evils). Only at this state the distinction between the individual self and the Self vanishes and it is an evil-free state and thus free from suffering. Clearly, the feeling states of pain and psycho-physical suffering may be attributed to a self or jīva under the shackles of ignorance because the evil state of pain and suffering suggests that the Jīva have not regained its inherent capacity to attain mokṣa. This also suggests that according to Saṅkara, the notion of "pain" and "suffering" are used as feeling-terms and state of affairs respectively which may be called "evil" as well because they bind individual self *to* all pervading and eternal pangs of birth and death.

It is clear that the concepts of "pain" and "suffering" in Śaṅkara Vedānta has been meaningfully used in the context of *phenomenal self* under the influence of a few metaphysical principles. It will be thus wrong to believe that the "āndanamaya" state of the subdued self is a suffering free state because the self in the state of deep slumber may yet wake up to come in contact with gross elements. Hence, at this state, the self is *not* at refuge nor is it desirable that it remains in a permanent trance and tranquil. It would be thus wrong to think that Saṁkara's management of pain, as an undesirable feeling is to put one's self to permanent trance or best is to die. In fact "death" may *not* end pain and suffering, it may be a beginning as the phenomenal self is further born to live another dreaded life. Hence, any stage of the phenomenal self, which is forged into worldly affects to grace death and birth, is the "Virātapurūṣa" and it is the real sufferer. Even at the "taijasa" stage of this self, it is bound to saṅsāra or the cycle of rebirth. But "pain" and "suffering" looses all significance at the level of transcendence of phenomenal self. It is the stage of identify of "asmad" and "yusmad", the phenomenal self and the Absolute Self or Brahman. At such a state, one is not dead rather, here on earth it shines with its intrinsic glory. The freed self thus finishes the journey of saṅsāra without further bondage (because the reality has been realized) and all external affects and evils of actions fail to make any sense. Perhaps, he never comes to live a phenomenal life after freed from gross body-who knows? What is more important is to notice that when the self is at the stage of godhood or "Iśvaratva" and not "Brahmaatva", it may still suffer from worldly affects because at this stage, "māya" grabs the self in relation to gross elements, i.e. 'Virātapurūṣa" nor the self in relation to subtle elements, i.e. hiraṇyagarbha is free from suffering because in such a state the self is prevented from the realization of the real Self or Being itself.

There is no reason to think that according to Saṅkara the worldly pains and suffering are unreal and therefore, these are non-sensible conceptions. Śaṅkara holds that one can understand the sensible nature of these conceptions when one realizes the truth that many people deserve pain and suffering because they are ignorant. Thus pain and suffering are absolute projections of one's mind. But to imagine that therefore, the Self itself is absolutely under such projections is unreal because the Self in itself is beyond such evils. Hence, the "suffering Self" and the "liberated Self" are two distinct states of Self, only the latter is really Real, whereas the former us unreal in so far as for the liberated person it makes no sense. Pain and suffering is thus sensible in the context of phenomenal self's journey in this corporeal world.

The Sāṁkhya poses an interesting question. If individual self and the real Self are identical, can we ever make a practical distinction between a person who suffers (bodily or mentally) and the suffering self? If not, then Śaṅkara must accept the suffering of Brahman or pure Self as well, which will be self-defeating. But Brahman being the only Reality, there can neither be the sufferer and the suffering as two distinct things, or any relation between them. What Śaṅkara tries to make us understand is that the notion of "suffering" has to be stipulatively used only in the context of the self which is under māya and avidyā, whereas, it bears no significance in relation to the transcendental Self, which is pure and unblemished. The body of a person for all practical purpose may be said to suffer owing to the pain it feels caused by scorching sun, but if this body-in-pain is the true self then Sāṁkhya would have to admit that Purūṣa is body and thus the sufferer. Then, it has to be admitted as did Çārvāka that with the end of the body, pain and suffering ends. But neither Sāṁkhya nor Śaṅkara would admit it. Hence, it is better to have assumed a permanent unblemished Self, which is beyond all suffering and the blemished Self, which suffers, in the true sense. Interestingly, when the sense of identity prevails with the dawn of knowledge (vidyā), the identity of a suffering-self vanishes. With this explanation, *an* extremely technical use of "pain" and "suffering" in the Śaṅkara Vedānta has to be accepted. The technical use brings out a clear distinction between the "bodily or corporeal suffering" or the "body-in-pain" and the "metaphysical suffering" or the suffering properly so-called owing to deep rooted ignorance about the identity of the Jivātama and Ātman". The "suffering self" is thus *not* merely someone in-pain or someone receiving sensation which are painful, rather, the reality which when garbed in ignorance believes that it is "myself" who is suffering. Hence, if we fail to free ourselves from the "suffering properly so-called" there is no respite. Śaṅkara have a pertinent answer for a question asked by many. "Is the body in pain when the self has attained mokṣa?" The answer is simple. The body may be receiving noxious stimuli *called* painful but the Self is *not* in-pain because the Self has liberated itself from the suffering-properly so-called. Hence, in Śaṅkara Vedānta we have to distinguish the metaphysical and psycho-physical uses and meaning of "pain" and "suffering". We may for the sake of understanding speak of the *first order use* of these notions, which may be stipulated as, "suffering due to ignorance" and the *second order* use of these notions, which may be stipulated as, "suffering due to Kārmic affects". Both these uses are closely knit, the former paving a way to understand the latter.

Nevertheless, Rāmānuja would not completely agree with these stipulations. He has something different to propagate in Viśiṣṭādvaita. Rāmānuja clarifies that the cit or the *individual soul* is the real sufferer, and the world and the souls being as *real* as Brahman themselves (because all are *transformations* of the Supreme Self), are co-eternal entities. Despite this, the Brahman is *not* the sufferer because when it transforms into various existential modes, it is the Lilā or sport, which is effective. Hence, He allows His infinite will to transform this Self to corporeal self. Once this is allowed, the law of Lilā necessitates creation enabling the subtle element Prakaṛti to evolve gross elements and materially enveloped souls. Such souls are then subject to incessant suffering or kleśa because it is subjected to all sorts of misdeeds. Hence, "suffering" is a notion used to convey the sense of individual soul trapped in karmic influx owing to the natural consequence of evolution. God is neither the cause of suffering nor is *He* deemed to be the sufferer or empathizer, He is rather at His Will, initiating evolution, which, however, has its own consequences. This may be a kind of test or the individual intelligence, who is endowed with the dissolution to realize the Truth, that dawns, and one may be free from all sufferings. Bodily suffering or corporal suffering may be thus a result of ignorance of the Reality. Hence, through jñāna and bhakti one may attain libation at His life, here, in this world. It is needless to say that Rāmānuja's theory is different from Saṅkara on many grounds. The basic difference lies in the nature of Brahman, in the nature of creation and the status of creation. Let, us avoid the intriguing analysis of these distinctions and the relative merits and the demerits of these theories. There is no doubt that with Saṅkara, Rāmānuja distinguishes the individual self as the real sufferer at the supramundane, metaphysical sense (the first sense or suffering-properly so-called) and the phenomenal sufferer at the psycho-physical level (the second sense or suffering improperly so-called). The former sense of "suffering" is more theoretically and practically prominent because without the knowledge of this sense of suffering, one is really unable to see why the latter, although relatively unimportant in the sense of mere management, is nevertheless extremely unimportant in so far as it may serve the empirical basis for the permanent management of suffering. The advantage of Rāmānuja over Śaṅkara appears to be that Rāmānuja is more capable of providing a realistic solution to the otherwise vagueness inherent in the status of the psycho-physical suffering one undergoes during this life (hopefully the one having enjoyed the realization of the Brahman and the soul). Rāmānuja's solution does not project illusoriness of psycho-physical suffering and thus does not rob off that sense in which the notion may be meaningfully used even if one accepts the truth that one has attained the true knowledge. The reason is that Rāmānuja clearly asserts the *real* nature of the world and the soul by allowing God's 'lilā' with the Law of karma to start creation and destruction along with saṅsāra. Rāmānuja realistically argues that the bodily and the mental sufferings are real no doubt (even to the liberated) but it is only *temporary, not* final. Moreover, through constant psycho-physical training and devotion, one can manage 'suffering' at *both levels.* In fact the truth is simple. One has to really counter psycho-physical suffering *now* to attain true knowledge because it is an arduous process involving the whole person. Hence, "suffering", sustains a clear dual meaning in Rāmānuja's writings.

"PAIN", "SUFFERING" AND A CONTEMPORARY INDIAN THINKER

One may not find too pressing to consider the contemporary Indian thinkers in this regard because their views may be remnants of their precursors, especially the Advaitins. But for a change and for novelty one may consider J. Krishnamūrthi's treatment of "suffering". So far we have been heavily depending on transliteration of "pain", "suffering" and so on, but for now, we may consider the views of someone who uses the English terms in his book, *Truth and Actuality* (1995). For this reason we may have considered Aurobindo's views and other writers of Indian Philosophy who write in English (Radhākrishnan may be the other person) but I do not think that it would be vastly different from what has been already said. Krishṇamūrthi thinks that suffering, pain and anxiety are all *contents* of the *consciousness,* and, therefore, it is needed that radical *imitation* in consciousness takes place to stop the influx of these things. As soon as the notion of "suffering" has been placed in the context of "human consciousness", the question of physical pain, the endurance of such pain resulting into suffering and the psychic state of affair to cope with it or to get rid of it, gets juxtaposed. For instance, Krishnamūrthi is very clear in his assertion about "physical suffering", which, he thinks, is owing to an endurance of physical pain. But physical pain is naturally incumbent on our psyche, that it tends to break up our consciousness into several bits and we go neurotic. The level of disharmony in consciousness distorts our thought process and prevents objective thinking to break up the human persona. Thus "suffering" in one sense is "physical suffering", meaning thereby body-in-pain and its enduring effect on consciousness. But when we speak of the psyche of a person, we are at the brink of using the expression "psychological suffering" as well. "Psychological suffering", says Krishnamūrthi, an *attachment* to ideas, to conclusions, to ideologies, which are believed to be the securities of human thought process and when this false security is at danger, "psychological suffering" creeps in. Hence, Krishnamūrthi makes it clear that "suffering" could be sensibly used in the contexts of bodily suffering and its psychological accompaniment and psychological suffering owing to *attachments*.

Attachments are *not* only, to our ideas or ideologies rather, they may be *personal*, mainly owing to *relationships* in this ecological community. Relationships are mainly dependent, but one may be free in a relationship, whereas the other person may not be free. This evokes a conflict and thus suffering. Hence, "suffering" may be notionally used to convey the sense of "conflicts in a dependant relation". But suffering may be also due to loss or detachment owing to death and due to an attachment with somebody or something in the past (as in memory), which we have lost at present, such a loss, although mental, it may have a corporeal attachment. Yet, says Krishnamūrthi that we may conceive of a situation wherein the mind may *not* be at apparent conflict in a relationship situation, may be owing to impositions like self-interest or tolerance bat what is needed is love and compassion to end a conflict. Whatever it may be, Krishnamūrthi's treatment of the *genesis* of suffering that reflects its kinds as well, projects the different meaning the term may acquire.

To stress further the role of human consciousness in suffering, Krishnamūrthi says, that in a state of suffering, the *observer* of suffering and the *observed*, which is suffering, may *not* be said to be dissociated. Hence, "suffering" is a state of affair, in which the observer and the observed are not different. Krishnamūrthi writes, "... observer is the past, the accumulated memory, experience and knowledge. And with that knowledge, one dissociates oneself from suffering; one is different from suffering and therefore one can do something about it. Whereas the observer is the observed".[24] Hence, suffering is not the same as the one who suffers but when we speak of the *experience* of suffering, it is certainly identical with the experiencing being, otherwise the experience turns out to be nonsensical. He says, "so we are saying that when there is suffering, either, momentary, or a continuous endless series of causes that bring about suffering, to look at it without the observer. You are that suffering, not, you are separate from suffering".[25] It is in this context that we get an idea of the *holistic* sense in which the notion of "suffering" may be used. The use thus covers the self and a specific temporal experience.

Krishṇamūrthi further stresses that "suffering" may be sensibly used in the context of "love" because love, he thinks is inseparably related to "pleasure". Be it sexual or love for a country or an idea, all gives us pleasure and when we deny such pleasure, we are at violence causing tremendous suffering. Moreover, even if we are feeling compassion for someone or many people or nature or animals, we are at love and if we *deny* it or are deprived of it, we are suffering. But a number of religious organizations in this world are deprived of such compassion as they fight for their ideologies, causing harm and thus suffering. But if we neither accept nor put up with suffering rather *live with* suffering, a great compassion evolves, which is the mother of a new generation. Hence, "suffering" may be conceived as a notion having a negative bearing in so far it is a *denial* of pleasures as well denial of compassion. This sense is well projected when we use "suffering" in the context of "death", which is a complete *denial* of life. Life is so important for us and its denial so painful because intellectually and emotionally we desire immortality, i.e. survival at the physical and the psychological level. In fact, both "suffering" and "death" are related inseparably to "time", *not* the measurable moments but the very process of movement in thought and deeds. But this "time" has created in "us" a sense of attachment to the world, to the objects, to the memory and the past. It is this sense, which allow us to aspire in further time to remain attached to such things, and, therefore, try to avoid death because we believe, that may be an *end* to "our attachments" in time-frame. This is the cause of great suffering. Hence, "suffering" as "death" is essentially a *denial* of attachment in time-frame. However, Krishnamūrthi would *not* like to go along with the ideas of kārmic cycle and suffering of the individual self until the true knowledge has dawned. Rather, he thinks that even when a corporeal body dies, physiologically speaking, and the *movement* of time for other *ego* goes on forever because the totality of experience of life and death in time, produces great suffering. Hence, "suffering" is basically a "*crises* in the stream of consciousness, which is a movement in time". To stop this is to understand that it is our consciousness level from which suffering has to be eradicated *now* and not that metaphysical knowledge of pure self would be of great help to us. This is an understanding of the consciousness, of oneself and of the world. This can prevail in us through pure intellectual reflection and *not* through organized teaching, religious or whatever it may be because the *Gurū* or the God or the Knower is *in* us.

At the end of this chapter we find, that the way the notions of "pain" and "suffering" have been used in different philosophical schools of the west and east, provide a wide maze of meanings depending on the real contexts of the use of these terms. In the Marxist literature, the capitalists have unequivocally caused "suffering", whereas the existentialists may not like this idea completely as they often remark that the Marxist society exploits human freedom and cause suffering. But the existentialist would use the notion in an extremely wide manner to cover mental and physical suffering at all levels of existence. One suffers, is really a matter of discovery in our consciousness and not extremely determined. Really speaking in the Marxist writings, the meaning of "suffering" has to be discovered and we get an idea that this discovery of meaning is not dependent on our consciousness but *outside* it, in the real world of production and exploitation, the existential use of the notions of "pain" and "suffering" returns with Buddhism and Krishnamūrthi. Nevertheless, the difference is clear as well. Buddhism starts with suffering as a fact and through the genesis of pain goes on to manage it in non-theistic manner. Whereas Krishnamūrthi speaks of the consciousness anchor to suffering, but does *not* provide a similar genetic account. The scenario changes with the orthodox schools of Indian Philosophy, which are heavily metaphysically charged. There is no doubt however that both the psycho-physical and the metaphysical use of the notions could be clearly seen, the latter being more prominent.

With this we now move on to the penultimate chapter in which the most important task will be undertaken, which is the task of evaluation.

NOTES AND REFERENCES

1. Saddhajiva, Bhikkhu, *Anguish the mark of man* in Three Facts of existence, III, Buddhist Publications, p. 30.
2. *Ibid.*, p. 30.
3. *Ibid.*, p. 31.
4. Mādhvāçārya, *Sarvadarsanasaṁgraha*, Hindi Translation and commentary by Umāśaṇkara Śarmā, Chowkhamba, Varanasi, 1994, p. 36.
5. *Ibid.*, p. 61.
6. *Ibid*, p. 61.
7. *Ibid*, p. 103.
8. Saddhajiva, Bhikkhu, *op. cit.*, p. 31.
9. Mādhavāçārya, *op. cit.*, p. 36.
10. Bowker, John, *The problem of suffering in the religions of the world*, Cambridge University Press, Cambridge, 1970.

11. *Ibid,* p. 202.
12. *Ibid,* p. 204.
13. Rādhākrishnan, S., *Bhāgavadgitā* (Eng. Trans. and Commentary), Blackie and Son (India) Ltd., 1976, p. 183.
14. Bhattāchārya, Rāmśaṅkar (Ed.) *"Sāṁkhyatattvakaumūdi"*, Motilal Banarasidass, Delhi, 1989, p. 2.
15. Goyandakā, Harikṛṣṇadāsa (Translated and Explained), *Pātanjalayogadṛśana*, Gitā Press, Gorakhpur, 2025, Saṁvat, p. 40.
16. *Ibid,* p. 69.
17. Mādhvāçārya, *op. cit,* p. 691.
18. Saṭhaśastri, Dvārkānātha (ed)., *Vātsāyana Bhāṣya on Nyāya Sūtra* by Gotama, Bauddha Bhārati, Vārānasi, p. 27.
19. *Ibid,* p. 26.
20. *Ibid,* p. 34.
21. *Ibid,* p. 302.
22. Jhā, Harimohan, *Bhāratiya Darśana Pariçaya* (VII), Pustak Bhandar, Laheriyāsarāi, p. 83.
23. *Ibid,* p. 83.
24. Krishnamūrthi, J., *Truth and Actuality*, Krishṇamūrthi Foundation India, Pondichery, 1995, pp. 132-33.
25. *Ibid,* p. 133.

4

"Pain", "Suffering" and "Evil"

An Inquiry into their Definitions, Uses, Meanings and References

THE NEED FOR EVALUATION AND THE SEARCH OF CRITERIA

Our inquiry so far has revealed clearly that the scientists and the philosophers indubitably have the concepts of "pain", "suffering" and "evil". It may not be very important to know whether or not those who have these concepts also have the feeling of pain, whether or not they really encounter evil at some point of time. More interesting may be to know about what it really means when one says that he has the concepts of "pain", "suffering" and "evil" and when one says that he wishes to *use* these concepts to convey some *sense* (meaning) and possibly to *refer* as well. One may not doubt that to have these concepts also needs to be expressed in language. For that matter, to have the concepts "pain" "suffering" and "evil" is to have for our use the English words "pain", "suffering" and "evil" (we may have other equivalent words as well). Nevertheless, to fix some words or signs is not preceded by having their concepts; rather, when we have these concepts, we need to express them in language. Interesting things happen when we start using these words in different contexts. We have seen in details the different use of these words in scientific and philosophical contexts. This has been an interesting and important philosophical venture in so far as ambiguity, vagueness and clumsiness regarding the use, sense and reference of these words could be dispelled. This is really speaking a linguistic task not undertaken in this manner by either the lexicographers or the grammarians. More interesting is to notice that more often than not we are not careful about making clear distinction among "pain", "suffering" and "evil". If we really have in our mind a clear conception of such distinction as well, we may refrain from different confusions owing to the overlapping, synonymous, vague and ambiguous use of these words in scientific and philosophical contexts. Moreover, many people would not care too much to consider whether or not the scientific and the non-scientific *definitions* of these concepts serve any purpose. If they do, what they are and if they don't, why should we define at all? It is, therefore, important (philosophically speaking), to analyze the different definitions of these concepts, which is basically a *critical* inquiry and to *evaluate* these concepts, which is *curative* as well as *suggestive* in nature. So we have now for us three important tasks (a) to put together the scientific and the non-scientific use of "pain", "suffering" and "evil" to *probe* into the different sense and reference which they convey; (b) to analyze the different definitions of "pain", "suffering" and "evil" and (c) most importantly, to evaluate "pain", "suffering" and "evil". I shall begin with the second task first for all practical purpose because I think that to perform the last task, we have to perform the first task as well. The reason for such belief shall be explained at a proper place. I also think that if we address to these three tasks properly, some such findings may be filtered out which may be the basis of knowing the sense in which we say that we *have the concepts* of "pain", "suffering" and "evil". The reason is that having definitions of these concepts may *not* be the basis of *having these concepts*. Similarly, knowing the proper use of these words may *not* be the basis of having these concepts. But evaluation of "pain" from "non-pains" or evaluation of "suffering" from "non-suffering" or evaluation of "evil" from "non-evils" may provide us a basis (a criterion) for *having these concepts*. Nevertheless, *evaluation* itself begs a criterion or criteria, which we have to discover. I believe that this is possible if we look into the different use, sense and reference of these words. Thus evaluation is related to the first task mentioned by me but this is *not* the same as saying that evaluation, which may be basis of having these concepts, depends on the findings of the first task.

The second question shall be attended first but before that we should understand at the outset the meaning and significance of *evaluation* in this context. First, we should know that in this context, evaluation is *not* like evaluating social justice as good or dishonesty as bad or John as good or gold as precious. Nevertheless, evaluation of the notion of "pain", "suffering" and "evil" is like an evaluation of "pleasure", "happiness" and "bliss". This is so because evaluating "pain", "suffering" and "evil" in this context is neither a factual evaluation nor a moral evaluation but it is a conceptual evaluation to cure the oft ambiguously, vaguely and even clumsily used notions in scientific and philosophical contexts. Thus the use of inverted commas with regard to "pleasure", "happiness" and "bliss" reminds us that there is sometime a problem of evaluation of concepts in use or an evaluation of concepts in force. We should remember that the above parallel is only superficial and no exact parallel could be conceived between "pleasure", "happiness" and "bliss" on the one hand and "pain", "suffering" and "evil' on the other hand because they have different use, sense and *reference*. It is thus very important philosophically to "*make a clear distinction*" among different notions, which is often not done (and that is not proper), and to do so is to "evaluate" these notions. Evaluation of these notions is thus an important linguistic task *qua* philosopher (not *qua* grammarian and/ or lexicographer).

But why call it 'an evaluation'? In this context, evaluation is neither subscribing to generic value nor subscription to a value or making an evaluation on the one hand, and on the other his or her ascription of a value. Or, an evaluation of someone or, to evaluate an ethical action or, a thing or state of affairs. Evaluation in this context has a different meaning. i.e. "making clear distinction among some notions in use" because 'e-value-ation' suggests 'a distinction making activity', for which we need a criterion or criteria. Evaluation taken in this sense is not an abstract exercise without a value. It is purposive and valuable in so far as it aims at linguistic clarity and bears a philosophical value. It may be said according to Nicolai Rescher that evaluation like this is generally a 'specific–purpose resort'. Moreover, such an evaluation begs no scale, either monopolar or bipolar because the former conceives of a spectrum of negative-to-positive (uninteresting to interesting), whereas the latter conceives a movement from negative-neutral-positive (dishonest-indifferent-honest). In fact, in evaluating "pain", "suffering" and "evil", we cannot conceive of any movement in either the monopolar or the bipolar scales. But there is no doubt that even if 'evaluation' is 'distinction making', we ought to have a criterion or a criterion at least, otherwise 'distinction making' would not be possible. Another point is that evaluation is possible only in the context of actual language-use, which need not be understood as merely English language use because we have freely entered the other language uses through *transliteration* (as in the cases of Sanskrit and Palī languages) which is by far dependable. The same is the case when we entered other oriental language (in the case of existential writings). The best thing is to remember that we have been constantly referring to different scientific and philosophical writings) to analyze the use, sense and reference of "pain", 'suffering" and "evil". To be precise, our inquiry hinges on *technical languages*. It is in the context of these technical languages that the force of the notion of "pain", "suffering" and "evil" becomes meaningful and this may provide us the basis of evaluation. But this is a matter of discovery. It is also interesting to notice that we do *not* give meaning to these terms, they acquire meaning while they are in force and while they are used to refer. Another point, which is worth mentioning, is that the inquiry does not merely involve notions, rather language containing some sentences in which these notions figure prominently with force. Thus, we may speak of inquiry of sentences containing "pain", "suffering" and "evil" as well. It is also important to notice that the force or use of these words and sentences are governed by the pragmatic rules or conventions of technical languages and relates *not* merely to reality but to the real contexts of their utterance and commits the user in many ways. Clearly, if we care to consider the meaning of these terms and sentences in a broad sense, we have to consider the force or the use of these notions and then we may come to know that these words are not synonymous but they are really *different* from one another. This is to stand at the doorsteps of evaluation to avoid carelessness in language use. If philosophical enterprise like this one is *curative* in nature, it is *suggestive* as well because from all this we may discover how some words should be distinguished from a group of words bearing a family resemblance.

It is important now to start with the *critique* of the definitions of the notions of "pain" and "suffering", definitions which are scientific and philosophical. One may wonder about such a philosophical criticism because the purpose of such criticism may not be clear. In fact, if the definitions of these notions are so important, we must ask, why at all are these definitions so important? Or are they important at all? Or do we need these definitions?

DEFINITIONS

The problem of the definition of "pain" and "suffering" is not so simple because we may be extremely simplistic in saying that a scientific definition of "pain" and "suffering" is *possible*. The reason is that some sort of definition or the other of "pain" and "suffering" is no doubt possible and it will be too much to think that "pain" and "suffering" should be defined in a particular way and not in another way. But we may still ask, if we define "pain" and "suffering" in one way or the other, what is the *purpose* in providing such definitions and what purpose *should* definitions serve in general? In this context, we may thus ask, what is the purpose of scientific and philosophical definitions and what should these definitions aim at? To find pertinent answers to these questions, a critique of scientific definitions is needed at the outset and then we may proceed for a critique of philosophical definitions. To start with, we may consider some of the *physiological* definitions of "pain" in particular. Our inquiry reveals the following definitions provided in Physiology:

(*a*) *Causal* or *genetic* definition which aim at *referring* to "injurious stimulus causing damage to tissues, such as mechanical or chemical or thermal or diseases";
(*b*) *Denotative* definition aiming at clearly mentioning the sense in which "pain" as a general name is used in Physiology, as in the expression, "it (pain) is a disagreeable sensation";
(*c*) *Connotative* definition aiming at conveying the sense that such and such properties are needed to conceive of "pain", as in the expression, "it (pain) is an experience of unpleasantness which permeates a person at a given point of time";
(*d*) *Ostensive* definition, which aims at *pointing* out those "sources capable of stimulating nerve endings beyond limit, viz. stabs, burns etc.";
(*e*) *Behavioural* or *operational* definitions which aim at making a statement about "class of behaviour operative in protecting and/or managing noxious stimulus" and

(*f*) *Real* definition aiming at stating which thing or set of things (as distinct from others) "affect the whole personality of a being in an extremely adverse manner, as in 'gout-pain'".

Physiological definitions of "pain" is a testimony to a range of definitions having clear purpose, clearly not to find out the exact synonym of "pain" but to do other things. These definitions are thus *not* comparable to those given in a dictionary. But how far are these definitions satisfactory and what if none of these definitions have been provided? A careful inquiry shall reveal the truth that the denotative, the connotative and the behavioural definitions of "pain" aim at the clarification of the *sense* of the concept in Physiological language. Let us try to find out what sense has been clearly focused. We find "pain" means (a) "a disagreeable sensation", (b) "an unpleasant experience" and (c) "protective and/or management behaviours in the face of noxious stimulus". The problem is that taken separately, none of the *sense* conveyed to us in Physiology may be satisfactory. We know that definition should *not* be too narrow or too wide or unsatisfactory. All these definitions are unsatisfactory for calling a sensation 'disagreeable' may be precise (not vague) but it has certain *ambiguity* nevertheless because even if the *type*, viz. "sensation" may be clear enough, conjoined with "disagreeable", the *token* becomes extremely confusing. Moreover, "sensation" itself is a concept, which needs further clarification, and one may understand it in Physiological context in technical terms but that may be too cumbersome for laymen; the definition it provides of "sensation" and "pain" is in no way a satisfactory and generally acceptable definition. To argue that Physiology does not attempt at providing a generally acceptable definition, it must at lest satisfy a few people trained in Physiology but the introduction of "disagreeable" creates a lot of problem for the basic fact that it creates a *linguistic* trifle and not a Physiological confusion. The token called 'disagreeable sensation' is extremely unclear because "disagreeable" to *whom, when* "disagreeable", *why* at all disagreeable, in *what degree* disagreeable, remain cloaked. Things become more complex when we consider peculiar examples in Physiology itself, namely, masochists for whom pain is agreeable and for Yogis and students and athletes, physical pains are agreeable.

Definition by connotation is more ambiguous because the type "experience" and the token "unpleasant experience" create several linguistic trifles and perhaps not a Physiological one. But the definition for the ambiguity involved in both type and token, poses greatest confusion for the Physiologists because neither "experience" nor "unpleasant" are widely used and understood very restrictively because any attempt at clarification of the sense of "experience" (by the Physiologists) expectedly will be along scientific stipulation and "unpleasantness" treads into a realm which transcends Physiology in many respects to await unnecessary stipulation. Moreover, the exact demarcation of "unpleasant experience" begs further Physiological criteria, which may *not* be generally acceptable and there may be high degree of disagreement in fixing what exactly should be called "unpleasant experiences".

Behavioural or Operational definition of "pain" in terms of protection/management of noxious stimulus is highly dissatisfactory because rather than clarifying the sense of the term, it clarifies what behaviours or operations do we normally find when someone is facing noxious stimulus. In fact, there is great degree of ambiguity again with regard to "noxious stimulus" and "protection/management". To find a stimulus "noxious" is highly subjective and so is the behaviour pattern. Hence, we may say "what someone is doing now or what steps taken now" in the face of some stimulus *called* "noxious" (may not be really noxious) is *not* the dependable basis of framing a generally acceptable definition even in Physiology. There may be cases of overt or covert behaviours, which may be so misleading that hardly one gets a clear idea about what "pain" means by simply witnessing such behaviours.

As we come to the causal or the Genetic definition of "pain" in Physiology, we find that the definition aims at clarifying why at all do we have a feeling called "pain", a feeling which is generally speaking, disagreeable to us. In this direction causal definitions often *refer* to those agents or state of affairs, which elicits the disagreeable feeling. Interestingly, a long list of such causes (included in the definition) which is often believed to be exhaustive, may *not* be a good attempt at defining "pain" because "pain" as a technical term in medicine does not include its causes in the definition of the term. But, technical terms in medicine may be satisfactorily defined causally because the term includes the definition. It may be very difficult to find the sole criterion of the presence or absence of a virus that *cause* "influenza" and thus have a definition. It is very interesting *about* pain feeling that it often accompanies, 'stimulation of nerve endings' owing to such and such factors but it is *not* included in the term itself as its definition. Hence, causal definition of "pain" may help us in unfolding a few factual discoveries about pain but that is not the definition of "pain". Therefore, to know pain is *not* to know about its definition.

Quite akin to the causal definition of "pain" is the possibility of having a *real* definition of "pain". There is a possibility if and only if "pain" is a *thing*, which may be clearly explained, in equivalent *factual* terms. But there is *no* such chance as "pain" is *not* a thing but a concept. In Physiological terms, it is a concept, which does *not point towards* anything. If definition is restricted to words and/or phrases, then definitions of *things* are ruled out. Even if one asks for the *essence* of a thing called pain, there is not a single thing whose essence could be clarified. Therefore, "gout pain" cannot constitute the definition of "pain" in terms of a thing called "gout" or a state of affair called "gout" and if at all it can, there are so many things like this that we would be soon dismayed by such things.

Ostensive definition of "pain" is *not* defining by equivalent terms or verbal in nature rather *non-verbal* in nature. In one way it is defining through *pointing out* to make the meaning of a word clear. This definition essentially does *not* beg other words but does need an object or objects in the world to *show* what the name stands for. Is this the case with "pain"? To answer this, we should first say that so far we have seen that several verbal definitions of "pain" turn out to be defective, limited and even unsatisfactory. Definitions by denotation and connotation fall short of expectation. But it may be too hurried to conclude that, therefore, no definition of "pain" is possible because we may provide a stipulative definition and even an ostensive definition. More interesting fact is that if definition demands some way to clarify the meaning of the term, "pain" stands a good chance but the question is about the *need* for some way to define even if they are clearly limited, defective and even unsatisfactory. Thus the question is whether or not "pain" should be defined at all. The problem starts here. No doubt there are many terms which may not be verbally defined but they may be ostensibly defined, as is the case with "yellow", "love", "hatred" and so on. Does it mean that "pain" may be ostensibly defined as well? Or should we ask why should we define at all? In fact the chances of ostensive definition of "pain" does not seem to be good because there is hardly anything or any phenomena which we can point out clearly or show clearly to mean, "this is pain". We may point out a limping man, a crying baby, a bleeding boy and yet cannot point out the feeling called pain or the experience of pain. Yet, we may *not* point out a man on bed of thorns and say, "this is pain". What do we point out or show when we refer to Yogi in 'samādhi'? One way is to slap on a boy's face or to kick him to say 'you see, this is pain' and still we may fail to convey the meaning of the term because we did not perform many other activities and uttered "this is pain". Thus, ostensive definition of "pain" is not possible. Stipulative definition of "pain" is possible in physiology, but that hardly carries a pragmatic value in so far as we fail to understand why the same stipulation should be accepted in other sciences for all practical purpose. Moreover a stipulative definition of "pain" (in Physiology) fails to distinguish a relatively clear and precise stipulation from one which is not so.

With this, we come to know that Physiological definitions, which fall under the broad categories of verbal, denotative, connotative and non-verbal definitions, are *unsatisfactory* as they fail to serve the *purpose* of definition itself, the purpose being the *effective use* of the term "pain" in the proper context so that one *knows* clearly about what the word *means* in a particular context, or in a situation and one *knows* about *rules* governing the use of the word in a discursive situation. But the question is, 'Should we define "pain" at all? This is a broad question, a reply to which should be given only when we have considered other definitions (scientific and non-scientific). Before considering Psychological, Sociological and other forms of definition. I would like to inform the readers about two things. One is that the Physiological definitions hardly inform about the *usage* of "pain", i.e. how the physiologists often habitually use them because that is of little or no value because we hardly have an idea of the uses, meaning and rules of definitions of "pain". It is thus a mere information about what scientists prefer to do and thus not definition properly so called. Another point is that the range of Physiological definitions may be easily classified under *linguistic type* of definition in so far as these definitions are *empirical reports of linguistic behaviour* and may be said to report some empirical generalizations often used by the scientists. Thus on both fronts, the empirical and the stipulative usage, Physiological definitions become vague and ambiguous and uninformative about uses and meaning of "pain" as well.

We may clarify the psychological definitions of "pain" as: (i) *denotative,* i.e. to denote or clearly mention the sense in which the terms "pain" is generally used in Psychology, viz. "an experience including an unique sensation" and (ii) *Causal* or *genetic*, i.e. to *refer* clearly to "common origin of pain sensation through noxious stimuli acting on nerve endings or through individual and intellectual function of the thalamus and cerebral cortex".

If we consider the main purpose of definition, we find that the denotative definition is a desperate attempt to mention the genus and the diferentia in order to formulate a definition of "pain". The genus is being "an experience" and the differentiating property being "unique sensations". The denotative definition thus appears to be not merely a report of Psychological usage of "pain" rather, clarification of the use of "pain" in the discursive context of Psychology. But the appearance need not be taken to seriously because Psychologically speaking, the genus is "a conscious state of mind" and *not* "an experience". In fact "an experience including unique sensation" may be the diferentia and not the genus. Moreover, the aim of the definition is not clear. Does it aim at reporting how Psychologists use "pain" or take "pain" to be like? If the definition is a report of mere psychological usage, the meaning in this context is not clear to us. What really do we understand from "pain" "being an experience including an unique sensation"? In fact, if one does not go through such an experience or is not in a state of consciousness like this one, do not really follow what is an experience of "pain". Finally, this definition is also ambiguous in so far as the *type* called "an experience including an unique sensation" is wrongly so understood or to be clear, a token has been confused as a type or that a token has been used as a type.

The causal definition sounds more sensible because rather than pretending to be a definition *per genus et diferentia*, it attempts at clarifying the reference of "pain" as an unique sensation. Pain is a sensation, is beyond doubt but rather than remaining vague, the *origin* of such sensation has been mentioned in elaborate terms, tracing the physical and the mental pathways and then relating them in terms of complex activity. One wonders how carefully the kind or the token of "sensation" has been left out, and for that reason, the ambiguity (about the sensation) remains there in this definition. Had it been clearer regarding this matter, the definition could have entered the realm of connotative definition (which would have raised different set of problems no doubt). The origin is always probable and thus dubitable and, therefore, one would be wise not to take the definition to be literally true. It may be an account *about* pain through such and such factual reports but it is hardly a definition of "pain" which aim at clarifying the use of the notion in Psychological context to unfold its meaning and to know about the rules underlying such a definition. Thus, the so-called "definition" does not serve the purpose of definition and is unsatisfactory. One may again ask, why should then the scientists be so worried about a definition of "pain"? But that is different question. We may easily notice that the definitions provided in Psychology are either denotative or verbal in nature but essentially we may put them under the *Linguistic type* for the obvious reason that these definitions tend to supply informative empirical reports of the usage of "pain" which is *uninformative* about the uses of pain and its meanings in the context of Psychology.

Although the Sociologists do not take great interest in defining "pain" in so many words, the definitions are nevertheless emphatic in stating that (i) "the term 'pain' lose all significance if we do not relate it to an 'averse feeling' or eliciting an averse feeling in a person" and (ii) "more explicitly, 'pain' is a pure physical experience of negation evoking a sensation of 'against' or aversion, which ought to be got rid off'.

Without intending to be either causal or ostensive in their intent to define "pain", Sociologists often tend to be precise about *the meaning* of "pain" in terms of "averse feeling". As such, the definition aim at expressing what the user of the term wants to convey. Clearly the user intends to convey the property without which the term shall lose all significance, and, therefore, it is a definition by *connotation*. Whereas the other definition is wider in so far as "averse feeling" (or a negative feeling) has a pure *physical* accompaniment and has an *operative* dimension to encounter such sensation arising out of physical conditions. The definition thus comes closer to both the *real* (non-verbal) as well as *operational* (verbal) definitions or is perhaps an amalgam. The definition tends to unfold the hidden *rule* of clarifying the genus, viz. "an experience of sensation" and the diferentia, viz. "having a physical accompaniment, which is aversive". However, the definition is ambiguous in so far as it is very difficult to follow what "an experience of sensation" is if one does not have such an experience and in so far as one does not have a complete satisfactory list of aversive physical accompanying factors even if one says that these are those needing proper management. Thus the main purpose of definition to clarify the use in sociological context and its meaning is defeated. These definitions again may be classified under *linguistic* type of definition, which turns out to be report of mere sociological use of "pain", which is uninformative about use and sense of "pain" and about the rules of definition.

USES, MEANINGS, AND REFERENCES

We may now consider the scientific definitions of "suffering" for a thorough critique. We have seen that Physiology does not show much interest in defining "suffering" for it does not include it within its first or second order tasks. Yet stray definition of "suffering" (like the one given by Beompard) holds that "it is an experience of organism involving physical and mental pain, which is accompanied by some feelings of loss, frustration and so on". To be precise, the definition is fundamentally *denotative* in nature, showing the signs of a technically correct definition *per genus et diferentia*, and, therefore, may be further classified as *linguistic* type definition. We could now see easily that the genus and the diferentia are both ambiguous and the aim is just reporting a usage of "suffering" *along with* "pain" but *not* the definition of "pain" or clarification of its meaning. However, the only idea one gets from this empirically informative definition is that if we analyze the meaning of "suffering", it would be very difficult to avoid using "pain" (physical and/or mental) along with it because "suffering" may be understood at least as a generic notion covering "pain". This clearly projects the empirical information intent of the definition of "suffering" in so far as the concept is usually taken as or used to signify a 'state of affair' of a person owing to a sensation called "pain". This definition produces a blurring image of a *causal* definition as well because "pain" stands out as a definite *cause*, of suffering, which is a state of affair. Interestingly, the cause itself remains unclear to us at both its physical and mental levels because one has to be at such levels to know what exactly is the meaning of "in pain". Moreover, the empirical generalization about "suffering" that it is owing to pain, is an empirically valuable discovery but not so valuable for a satisfactory definition that either clarifies the meaning or unfolds the rules of definition. Thus, we may carefully sidestep physiological definition of "suffering".

Psychologists are relatively more interested in "suffering". We may still have this one for our consideration: "suffering are complex and high level modes of consciousness as regret, anxiety and despair". What does this definition aim at? It appears that "suffering" has been used in the context of Psychology to mean an unique mode of consciousness but this unique mode simply stated is complex and of high level but does it make clear what it really is? Even if "suffering" is notionally defined in terms of "mode of consciousness" (genus), how is it different from other modes is *not* clear because 'being complex and high level' does not constitute the proper differentiating property. It is too precise and thus *vague*. But there are examples to make us think that what the diferentia could be. The examples are anxiety, regret and despair. It is not too odd to define by giving examples, particularly when one is not able to follow the meaning of the term clearly, and if one is not previously acquainted with the definable concept or thing for example, it is not odd to define "justice" by citing an example of "helping friends" or "helping the poor" but that does not solve the problem, because if you define 'X' giving the examples, viz. 'a', then any instance of 'X' being *not* 'a' or 'a' being not-X, destroys the attempt at giving such a definition. Similarly, if the psychological definition aims at clarifying the meaning of "suffering" by first spelling out the genus and then some examples (which may not be the same as the diferentia), the problem is that the meaning is still not clear for even those who did not know what "suffering" means (like an African not knowing what is "snowfall") for the simple reason that the cited examples may be such that they remain vague or unclear to many and thus need a series of definitions (if possible by examples) and so on. Yet, after all that, one may still ask, 'Is suffering, always regret'? Or 'Is regret, always suffering'? Thus, any attempt at defining "suffering" by *identity* invites criticism, they are normally unsatisfactory. The definition may be thus not stipulative in

Psychological context but it is still *linguistic* in nature because the information obtained are *discoveries about* suffering but not definition of the term "suffering". It may nevertheless, inform an interesting *use* of the notion in Psychology.

Sociologists often do not care to define "suffering" but like the psychologists, they tend to *use* "suffering" in different ways, mainly keeping in mind that it is a broad generic notion covering "pain". It appears that refraining from providing a definition of "suffering" is owing to greater care in using the notion to clarify its sense. Should we not do it in case of "pain" as well? We shall consider it after considering the non-scientific definitions of "pain" and "suffering".

A tendency to refrain from giving definition of "pain" (also "suffering") could be seen among the ethicists as well because they would rather prefer to tell us about the different *uses* of these terms in ethical contexts to clarify meaning and reference. The same is the case if we go through the views of the living theologies of the world because the theologians are mainly interested in unfolding the sense in which they use this concept rather then telling us how they wish to fix a meaning for these terms. But the position is not the same as we consider the different philosophical writings.

Marxist use of "suffering" is extremely interesting but it is difficult to find any definition of the same. The reason is that the Marxist conception of "suffering" could be *explained* only along highly technical terms, in terms of economics. On the other hand, the existentialist conception of "suffering" could be *explained* along another extremely abstract line, which is unique to it. It is the line of 'discovering from within the consciousness of man'. Hence, there would be hardly any need of definition again. Like the Marxists, the Existentialists would feel no urge to explain or to define "pain" as well. Following the same line of the Existentialist thinking, Buddhist conception of "suffering" has been better *explained* on the basis of deep philosophical understanding of the matter, and, therefore, no definition were needed. Jaina also followed the path of philosophical *explanation* of "pain" and "suffering" and like the Marxists, the Existentialists and the Buddhists they prefer to explain "pain" and "suffering" by calling them some state of affairs having a definite cause and having a definite course of management.

The tripartite line of explaining the notions of "pain" and "suffering" could be clearly seen in the Vedas, the Upaniṣadas, the Gitā and in the Sāṁkhya doctrine as well until we reach the Yoga philosophical school. It is here that we find "suffering" or "kleśa" being *defined* by citing certain *examples*, the examples are of those "state of affairs of human beings which is either one of Ignorance or one of confusing the Real Self with the corporeal organs or desire for worldly objects or anger or clinging to the physical body". What we find from this type of definition is that the proponents of such definition, are pretty sure about those examples of "suffering" which are sufficient as well as necessary, so that we get a clear idea about what it really is. How one can be so sure, is the crux of the question? It *appears* that the Yoga may be so sure for it refers to not merely reflection or contem-plation but intuition, which holds the key to such knowledge. It is not that empirical observation and/or reflection has no role to play in this matter but what is crucial is an internal capacity to know that such and such examples complete the list towards knowing what it is *to be in suffering*. Here lies the problem. The examples clarify the sense in which we are said 'to be in suffering', i.e. the examples unravel something *about* suffering and this need *not* be either necessary or sufficient condition to *define* "suffering". The definition of "suffering" needs rules to follow, which is not clear to us. Moreover, as I have said, defining by examples appears to be effective and pragmatic but they invite certain problems, too. There is every chance to have a 'sixth' example or to find one example, which may *not* be a case of suffering. Hence, the Yoga effort to define "suffering", although apparently *essentialist*, is really *linguistic* for it confines itself to empirical observation and reports and tells us *about* a state of affair called "suffering", which, however, should not be taken to be literally true as we often do.

The Vaiśeṣika's attempt to define "pain" or "dukḥa" marks a transition from its predecessor, the Nyāya, in so far as the Nyāya do not take much interest in defining "pain". The Vaiśeṣika definition of "pain" is very close to the psychological way of defining "pain". First, the Vaiśeṣika defines "dukḥa" as "sensation" and then clarifies the nature of such sensation as "unfavourable". As expected, the Vaiśeṣika further takes interest in the *causes* of such unfavourable sensation, which affect us, and that is a simple scientific report. Needless to say that defining "pain" in term of "sensation" and the mark of "unfavourableness" reminds us of one of the vague and unsatisfactory attempt at defining by *per genus et diferentia*. In fact the rule is *not* so clear as it appears to be because even in "sensation", "unfavourableness" is a *mark* of man who has that sensation, and, therefore *not* either the property or the species of sensation. "Unfavourableness" is rather a psychic or an emotive state of man, which may be clear to us through behaviour or gesture but it is certainly *not* the property of sensation. Thus "unfavourbleaness" cannot be the unique or the differentiating property which may be used to define "pain". Moreover, if "unfavourableness" is taken to be a property of the sensation called "pain", it may be generally speaking, quite sensible to accept but *not* necessarily true (at the factual level in particular). "Unfavourableness" is too precise to qualify sensation called "pain". The result is that "pain" remains vague and the so-called definition, too narrow. This *linguistic* type of definition is a discovery about "pain", which does not constitute the definition of "pain".

Leaving aside the Saṅkara and Rāmānuja Vedānta for they provide no definition of either "pain" or "suffering", we may now come to the question we have been avoiding so far. *Should* we define "pain" and "suffering" at all? When I raise this question, I do not have in mind the Physiological or the Sociological or the Philosophical definitions in particular rather, I have in mind the very *purpose of definition* itself. We may say that the definitions discussed so far being of predominantly *linguistic type*, had the purpose of telling us as clearly as possible in ordinary language *about* what the definable term is in *factual* or *empirically observable* terms. Precisely, such definitions are empirical information about the definiens. But as I have said that such definitions *are not* definitions in the real sense of the term in so far as the definiens remains vague as well as ambiguous to us. We do *not* really understand the *meaning* and what *rules* underlie the attempted definitions. It is due to this that I prefer to hold that the Physiological, Sociological, Psychological and Philosophical definitions all alike, being predominantly linguistic in nature, are empirically informative but uninformative technically, i.e. uninformative with regard to definitions properly so-called. To this I should add that even if one painstakingly attempt at the *contextual* or the *pragmatic* definition of "pain" and "suffering", which aim at clarifying both the sense and the reference along with the rules of defining, one wonders whether this may be done successfully! In fact we have to accept that there are many terms which may *not* be defined even in this way because they are *primal terms,* not complex or simple, the properties of which may not be conceived. "Pain" and "suffering" are such terms. Even if "suffering" is taken to be a wider notion, covering "pain" and in some sense a generic notion, it may not be contextually defined because the rules of definition does *not* allow us do so. "Pain" is never the *diferentia* of "suffering", pain may be the cause of a state called "suffering". Most crucial thing to notice is that even if we avoid the definitions of "pain" and "suffering" by any extension of the term, it may still be meaningfully used in several contexts. Thus, what is crucial is to mark out clearly the contextual uses of "pain" and "suffering" (and not merely its usage, which generally people do) to clearly know about their *sense* and their *reference*. We shall therefore, proceed to perform this crucial task, i.e. to unfold the different *use*, *sense* and *reference* of "pain", "suffering" and "evil," not without a purpose but having clearly the purpose of *evaluating* "pain" and "suffering".

On the basis of the foregoing discussion about the possibility of definition of "pain" and "suffering" we concluded that there is hardly any doubt that the physiologists, psychologists, sociologists and some of the philosophers did care to define these terms, which, however, turned out to be futile keeping in mind the purpose of definition. We concluded that it is wise to refrain from providing some definition or the other of these terms because they may create a lot of confusion rather than turn out to be useful enough for all practical purpose. We also came to know that often definitions of these terms are provided habitually, i.e. some people (scientists and the non-scientists) habitually does that for they think it to be of great worth. Hence, we come to know about a lot of the *usage* of "pain" and "suffering" through these definitions, which neither tell us about the *uses* of these terms nor about the rules of definitions. It is not so important to know about what people habitually do with words like "pain" and "suffering" rather, what should be done with these words in the real contexts of different sciences and philosophy (we have left out English literature and many others), because in doing so we may come to know not only about the different uses of these terms in different language contexts, we shall know about the different meanings of these words and about what they refer to or how these words are *related* to their referents. Only in this way, we may be able to know *about what to do with these concepts* in scientific and non-scientific literature to thus *discover criteria* of evaluation of "pain", "suffering" (also "evil").

Once we have fixed two definite objectives for us now, i.e. to inquire about the uses, meanings and references of the words "pain", "suffering" and "evil" and to evaluate these concepts on the basis of definite criteria, we find that indubitably "pain, "suffering" and "evil" are concepts and not things, and we are at hand some words or verbal signs for these concepts. Hence, we are at hand tasks involving some 'words in use': Several points have to make clear before I proceed to perform these tasks. First, it has to be made clear what I mean by words and sentences (containing some words). Second, it has to be classified what is 'words in use' (and also sentences in use) and meanings of words and sentences. Third, it is important to see what it is to speak about words and their referents. Finally, it is important to know why is it so important to consider the uses, meanings and references of "pain", "suffering" and "evil" in the present context.

To be precise, words, phrases and sentences are bearers of meaning. They are *abstract* entities and not spatio-temporally located things. It is too odd to think that "pain", "suffering" and "evil" as words (and as words occurring in sentences) are spatio-temporal entities or things. We may say that these *words* are at best a pattern of temporary arrangement of sound types having particular soundings. But these sound types have certain *force* or *use,* which is evident when *we* consider their occurrences in different sentences at different contexts. Hence, it is most likely that these words do *not* have considerable force or clear use when taken isolatedly, unless we perform a lexicographer's job to give an equivalent meaning of these words. But that is a different effort, which has nothing to do with the meaning these 'words in force or in use'. Clearly, we are not interested in either defining these words or stipulate a use and meaning or give them a meaning. To think that when we use these words with a certain intention on certain occasion we give them meanings or that these words lose all meaning when we misuse them, is completely unfounded. We have seen that these words have been in habitual *use* or have been misused but they have not lost their meanings.

Next, *sentences* are some such expression composed of sound types or words or phrases put together in a sensible fashion bearing meanings. Word-meanings does not culminate necessarily into sentence-meaning, rather, the meanings of sentences (having the three sound types we are considering) has to do with the *use* to which certain group of words are put together. One such use is to *assert* but we shall soon see that there are many. But we need not think that sentences containing these three words in consideration are necessarily propositions because we are *not* considering *true* or *false* sentences here. Philosophers are interested in such sentences only in so far as they are carriers of meaning and when we know the meaning, we can know whether or not the proposition it expresses is true or false. Hence, every sentence cannot be a proposition; we shall find that sentences containing "pain", "suffering" and "evil" are often *not* assertions, which is either true or false. Clearly, to know this we have look into the force of these words in the sentences and also the force of these sentences in different contexts.

Like ambiguous definitions, sentences containing "pain", "suffering" and "evil" may be ambiguous as well because most of the time owing to the *order* of these words or owing to the *use* of these words, sentences may bear more than one *meaning*. In addition to this, like vagueness in definitions, sentences containing "pain", "suffering" and "evil" may be vague, too. The reason is that the *meaning* may not be precise or the meaning conveyed by the grouping of words may not have precise meaning. There is no doubt however that the sentences are far more suggestive and have far more secondary meaning than words; the sentences containing "pain", "suffering" and "evil" may be far more suggestive and have secondary meaning than these words taken in isolation. One has to keep in mind that all sentences containing "pain", "suffering" and "evil" are *not* propositions, which may be true or false. But some sentences are assertive of truth and falsity, and, are therefore, propositions. Some such propositions could be easily identified in Physiology in particular. Nevertheless, the proven falsity of any of such propositions do *not* amount to the meaninglessness of such assertions. Hardly can we say that sentences containing "pain', "suffering" and "evil" are meaningless. But how do we claim their meaningfulness?

This is a difficult question. Sentences containing "pain", "suffering" and "evil" are *not* meaningful merely if (a) such sentences have effect on the hearer; (b) such sentences may be explained in different terms so that the explanation clarifies the meanings of "pain" or "suffering" or "evil", and (c) these words in the sentences express what things we are taking about. Nevertheless we must keep in mind that (a) "pain", "suffering" and "evil" being abstractions should not be used in sentences as temporally located entities; (b) these words need not be vaguely and metaphorically used and (c) the uses, meanings and references of these words should be located in different language contexts and should be located in the context of what users do with these words. Thus, meaningfulness of these words largely depends on identifying their *force*. I would like to argue later on that such forces are mainly *descriptive* and *evocative*. Although such forces are *not* tied down by either *de facto* regularity or fixed set of rules, we have to consider the *context* in which these sentences have been used. But one may wonder, why consider referents of "pain", "suffering" and "evil" when there are none because they are not spatio-temporally located things?

We speak about the reference of a word when a word refers to an *extralinguistic* thing out there in the world or when a clear *relation* could be seen between a word and its referent. Further, we know that whenever we speak about words and their referents, we relate them to the meanings of words. Quite often, meanings of words vary *without* a corresponding variation in referents, and, therefore, having a certain meaning may *not* be the same as having a reference to a certain object. This is the case with "pain", "suffering" and "evil", which we have already seen. Then, why at all should we consider the reference of these words in order to consider the meaningfulness of these words? It is pretty clear that these words are neither conjunctions nor propositions not categorical terms so that they have meanings without being *related* to referents; rather, they may have meanings *in relation* to referents or *in relation to* what they denote. Most interesting fact is that 'a relation' which we may find between these words and their reference (in a sentence, within a technical language context) is neither automatic nor tied down by *de facto* regularity, rather, it is owing to "an activity of the language user". It is due to this that there is no *reason* to believe that sentences bearing these words make them "declarative" in nature, and, are therefore, either true or false in so far as they refer to "something". Rather, such sentences may be meaningful if we try to locate what *it is* that *relates* these words with their referents (if there is any such reference). This takes us to discover further that it is the 'activity of the language users' which enable us to locate meanings of these words as used in sentences. Without knowing what users of the technical languages (of sciences and philosophy) do with words, one *cannot* know meaning or reference or any other *semantic* status. It is language-use and not extralingustic discovery, which gives these words *different* meanings. We have to remember that in the context of sentences bearing "pain", "suffering" and "evil", the logical grammar of "means" does *not* imply "specifying an entity in the world" but what language user purports to do with these words in a given context. It is largely due to this that in the definitions of "pain" and "suffering" in particular, the logical grammar of "means" has been wrongly taken as "something out there in the world" and for that reason it would be desirable to avoid such definitions and to concentrate more on language use. It is now clear why we ought to consider use, meaning and reference of these words in technical language contexts not merely to look into what they mean but to see what we do with these words. This effort, I believe, may be the basis of "evaluation" of these words as well. But we must be careful in remembering that to look into language-use is *not* to look into usage.

If we go through what has been already explained in Physiology about pain, we find that "pain" is an abstract concept, which these scientists have clearly in their minds to serve useful purpose. Let us find out how "pain" has been *used* as an *abstraction*. First, the abstraction is not through intuition or is not there *a priorily* in our minds but obtained through *complex experiences*, the *meaning* of which is clear to us in the Physiological context when we *relate* it to a great variety of feelings, particularly physical hurt. Second, the meaning of such an abstraction is clear to us when it is *related* to "noxious sensations", which has the disposition to induce or evoke distress and may end up in great suffering (in the physical sense). Third, the abstraction is also meaningful to us when the Physiologists use it in relation to unique psycho-physical states of a person which call for immediate management. Fourth, "pain" as an abstraction is meaningfully used in relation to noxious experiences, which themselves are extremely distressful and end up in more prolonged suffering (mental). Fifth, it has been used in relation to a special class of sensations as distinct from others to mean that throbs, itches etc. are not pains.

It is very clear that if we care to consider the meaning of "pain" in the context of Physiology, we have to state clearly that it is an abstraction and *not* a spatio-temporal entity. It is also clear that the meaning of "pain" as an abstraction should be understood on the basis of how it has been used in relation to some of its referents but we may now analyze such relational uses of "pain" to find that in Physiology in particular, the word becomes a unique vehicle to convey the *sense* (meaning) that 'it is a unique state of affair pervading body as well as mind of human beings, which is owing to a unique class of noxious sensations emanating feeling of distress, the experience of which could be lasting and which may end up in suffering of great degree'. The readers need not think that this is putting together earlier findings to shape up a physiological definition of "pain". But what I have tried to shape up from earlier findings is what the word means in physiological context when it has been used in relation to so-called referents. Nevertheless, those who think that this way we may formulate a *normative definition* of "pain", which may be generally agreed, I believe, they may face a lot of challenge. So let us avoid it now.

Physiology does not merely take the abstraction called "pain" to speak about unique state of affairs in which human beings are. It shows interest in using the notion to speak about unique state of affairs of animals as well but in a slightly different fashion. In case of animals, the abstraction has been used in relation to referents like 'some such sensations' with either *warning signals* or *counterproductive signals* needing subsequent *management*. Such a use is not completely alien in the context of human-pain but in this context, pain is in relation to some 'sensation' which stands out as those 'signals' which are *bodily,* with definite *psychological accompaniments*. We may say that it is the *communicative* or *pragmatic* use of "pain", meaning thereby, 'sensations acting as signals demanding management'. We may now add to the above sense of "pain", this one, and if we wish, we could elaborate our so-called normative definition now (only if it is so important).

Closely connected to this use of the word "pain" in Psychology, is another one, which, I think, is extremely important to notice because the sentence in which "pain" has been so used are clearly *assertive* in nature. In Physiology, definite truth-value (true) is often assigned to these assertions or *propositions* because Physiologists think of it mostly drawn from factual observations and experiments. But there is no reason to think that if in due course of constant verification, these propositions turn out to be 'false', they become 'meaningless'. Hence, propositions containing descriptions of 'pain-phenomena' is always meaningful irrespective of their truth-values derived from factual evidences. But meaningfulness is *not* context-free or even use-free. The *descriptive force* of "pain" in Physiology does suggest clear meaning of "pain" in terms of 'a state of affairs pervading human beings and animals *owing to* such and such external and/or internal sources'. The description of this 'owing to' is vivid and multifarious in Physiology and equally vivid is methodical description of 'what happens owing to' and how we finally come to 'feel pain'. The description of pain as a *feeling*, its *psychophysical pathways* from terminal noxious *sources* is the crux in Physiology. In the midst of it, "pain" gets its meaning, clearly within the body of physiological use. Physiologists do not give it the meaning that it now acquires.

It will be worthwhile to remember in this context that using the concept "pain" in Physiology and knowing its meaning depends on *experiences* of unpleasant sensations which ought to be called "pain", it cannot be taught or demonstrated or shown to us but it is *not* at all important to learn "pain imageries" first and then through experiences of unpleasant sensations express what ought to be called "pain". Hence, 'pain-imageries', although drawn from the external word (shooting, bursting etc.) are neither necessary for pain experiences nor, is it necessary for learning the meaning of "pain" in real life situation but it may be one way of 'pain avowal', may be of some pragmatic value for the doctors. "Pain" with "imageries" when used together might convey meanings mostly vaguely understood but practically needed. How these are in use in real life situation by even a person gifted with no education is astonishing. But *why* people use such imageries with "pain" may be interesting to know, we are at the brink of unfolding another use of "pain" (which is also very important) if we try to resolve the problem mentioned just now.

Most of the time people use "pain" with "imageries" in a *pictorial, poetic* and *symbolic* fashion for "pain" has definite *emotive* use in Physiological contexts. This emotive force of "pain" is clear from the fact that more often than not such use amounts to drawing attention of others, expressing deep distress and grief, drawing attention for care and cure. To be precise, to 'evoke' our emotions or to 'persuade' us to do something (management, as mentioned early on). "Pain avowals" in Physiology, which are the resources of knowing about emotive use of "pain" may be nevertheless, extremely confusing. It may *not* tell us anything about pain at all or it may not tell us where the pain is or in what degree it is felt really or what is its severity. Yet, we need them and people do use "pain" with imageries etc. to evoke emotions or to express emotions. It may thus mean, a deeply distressing or agonizing state of affair in which a man is; thus saying, '(please) do care him or (kindly) manage it'. However, how to manage, may not be clear to us.

"Pain avowal" and knowing about "pain" through those 'avowals' (not about the feeling itself but about the word "pain") is extremely intricate because we have to take into consideration several factors, the psycho-physiological factors and the socio-cultural and anthropological contexts in which the word has been in evocative force. This is particularly interesting in the case of the avowal of pain (in human language involving the word "pain") through an *inhibition* of pain feelings. Such avowal may be as vague in their meanings as are imagery involving avowals because little or no clear idea could be obtained from why someone has used "pain" when, suppose, he was laughing while hot water was poured on his head and he was saying, "where is pain, not on my head at least!" Here too, the evocative use of "pain" should be clearly seen because the activity along with the avowal is of greatest importance. The activity of inhibition expressed in a tone of exclamation with the accompanying gestures (laughing etc.) ought to be seen (and unless someone's sees it, the avowal has no sense) and then one suddenly understands the word "pain" has been acting on his emotions in this context. May be, to enjoy it more and more or to stop it at once or to run off from such sight. The speaker or the user of "pain" does clearly understand what "pain" is but not that he fails to use it properly, rather, he would not use it in its usual intension now.

A different contextual evocative use of "pain", with which Physiology is interested, is 'causalgic pain' but we shall cover it elsewhere. The predominance of the evocative use of "pain" in Physiology could be seen when (a) the word has been used as a noun along with adjectives in Physiology, such as, "painful pain", "non-painful pain" and "pleasant pain" or to be precise, in the context of "pain threshold" and (b) when the word has been used as a noun with an adjective "chronic" conveying a dysteleological or non-purposive sense. In the case of "threshold pain", the word "pain" raises a few eyebrows because it is highly debatable whether or not one *should* use "pain" with regard to some such cases which may not be called by that name at all. In order to make a clear distinction between what should be 'pain properly so-called' and 'pain not properly so-called'; we often use "pain" with "painful" *vis-a-vis* "pain" with "non-painful" and with "pleasant" as well. It appears that at the cost of clarity, "painful pain" has become a redundant coinage in Physiology, for "pain" is but "painful" and nothing but "painful". It is so obvious that one wonders what it is to speak of "painful pain". But "painful" cannot be the connotation of "pain" and, therefore, nothing much could be known from that expression until we juxtapose in a queer psycho-physical context of the possibility of some cases of "pain" which are nevertheless, not *felt* to be so "painful" as normally people do in normal conditions. These may be distinguished as "non-painful pain". Whereas, there is another possibility of cases of "pain" which are not *felt* in that manner, rather, are "pleasant" to people of different kind, who are clearly distinguishable. Hence, these expressions involving "pain" are meaningfully used in Physiology only in the context of the possibility of some queer cases of people who are under the influence of feelings called "pain". What is interesting is to notice that in the above mentioned context, with every expression, a "pain" has a clear evocative force in so far as "painful pain" amounts to "really in pain" (and need management). Whereas "non-painful pain" amounts to "not really so agonizing" (and does not demand much care) and "pleasant pain" amounts to "pain is really not hurtful at all, it is enjoyable nevertheless", (no management please). The case of "chronic pain" is different. In Physiology it is comparable to the pragmatic or the communicative use of "pain" because in this context "pain" has been so used that a state of despair could be imagined which has no answer (or management). It conveys the sense of 'meaninglessness', 'helplessness' and 'hopelessness'. In other words, the other name for "worries" or an embodiment of "evil" having no answer. It is here that more appropriately we use "pain" with "suffering" and say, "I suffer from chronic pain". Whatever the case may be, the "evocative" force of "pain" when used with "chronic pain" is evident because in medicine in particular, such expression carries a dysteleological significance in so far as it is difficult or nearly impossible to manage such cases but it certainly calls for great attraction and care if not cure.

The emotive or the evocative force of "suffering" is evident in the context of Physiology because in Physiology, "suffering" has been used predominantly in the sense of not explaining any state in which a person (sufferer) is owing to prolonged or deep feeling of pain. In Physiology, the meaning of "suffering" is particularly not clear by providing a definition, rather, with the help of evocative use of the term. The abstraction called "suffering" in Physiology at best bears a meaning in relation to its referent "unpleasant sensation" only if we keep in mind the fact that such sensation are not merely experienced, they affect the *whole being* in a far more wider perspective. It is very clear that "suffering" has a *descriptive* use as well because we do speak of "suffering due to" but it is quite possible that suffering may be due to pain itself. The *semantic* behaviour of "pain" is independent from "suffering". "Suffering" is often used to cover the sense of the state in which the 'whole man is'. It needs no qualification of pain-qualities either. We do feel that "suffering" has a broader evocative force covering the senses of "distress", "agony", "anguish" and "helplessness".

We should notice something interesting with regard to our normative definition. It is almost lost in the maze of the uses, meanings and reference of a "pain" and "suffering". Perhaps we do not feel to construct such a definition now in so many words which will expectedly clarify the sense of "pain" and "suffering". The sense is clear to us as we go on explaining the different use of these terms in the physiological context. It is, therefore, important to see what physiologists do with these notions. Let us now leave the task of more inquiry into this matter to the readers to delve into the realm of Psychology. This is of great importance because we have seen that quite frequently physiology of pain go hand in hand in hand with the psychology of pain. Moreover a shift from physical to the psychological explanation of pain may open new vistas of the uses of "pain" as well.

In Psychology, "pain" has been often used in *relation* to referents like unique "physical and mental sensations". But the meaning is not clear owing to the fact the expression becomes too wide and thus vague. In fact such use projects the fact that despite such a relation with the above-mentioned referent, "pain" remains a "mind-word", the ostension of which is impossible, and, it is very difficult to tell publicly what this word stands for unless one has such sensations. But there may be divergence in opinion in so far as the Behaviourists think that private feeling of pain does not tell us about the connotation of the term "pain" but it tells us about the relation of the word to a referent only known through a *piece of behaviour*. Several problems arise from this. One with which we are directly involved now is whether or not a piece of behaviour and a comparison with a feeling (of pain) I now have may be good enough to clarify the meaning of "pain". Behaviourists would agree that although "pain" may have a sense and a reference, it may not have well defined intension for it is ever growing with the growth of human knowledge about this matter (for this reason, a strict definition may not be possible). Nevertheless, a whole cluster of criteria that are synthetic should control the use of "pain". Thus *no* satisfactory way of clarifying the sense (meaning) of "pain" could be found. This commitment to essential vagueness of "pain" is unique to the Behaviourists. However, we may say that according to them if "pain" is meaningful only when it is used in relation to a *cluster phenomena* or *overt behaviour* then we have to accept that the meaning of "pain" is tied down by such and such behavioural patterns (which is factual), and, wholly unsatisfactory. Moreover, in case of suppression of so called behaviours which are referents of "pain", can we really know the meaning of "pain"? No, perhaps. But this is a horrific statement to make because whether or not someone has suppressed a feeling called "pain", the word "pain" does not lose its meaning content. "Pain" may be still meaningful to us. With this, we come to conclude that the Behavioural use of "pain" in terms of behavioural references or as symbol of passive-aggressive behaviour pattern fails to clarify the meaning of the term in the context of Psychology.

The *descriptive* use of "pain" in Psychology could be seen clearly when the *materialists* use "pain" with some such physical entities and states that the "mind-word" of psychology is completely translated or described in terms of "physics words" or we may say, the meaning of "pain" is clear when used along the line of physics, depending heavily on factual informations gathered by scientist, viz. 'the excitation of C-fibers owing to certain noxious stimuli'. This means that "pain" and "the feeling elicited owing to the excitation of C-fibres by noxious stimulus" are *identity* statements. Hence, such statements *de facto* govern the meaning of "pain". We have seen in the context of Physiology that why this cannot be accepted satisfactorily. The problem is that all such physics statements, are contingent and bear a truth-value, which, when turns out to be false or else they are modified, the identity may be destroyed to have another meaning, which is further not dependable. Then why we have to accept that the meaning of "pain" is never clear to us, for it depends on factual discoveries. Is this a happy position? We do not say that "pain" *per se* must have a fixed meaning, what we say is that it need not have a fixed meaning because it need not be used in one way and not in other ways. The meaning of "pain" in thus never *de facto* factually governed. But there is no doubt that in Psychology, we do find such a descriptive use of the notion, which, however, may not be the only way in which the notion becomes meaningful to us. In fact, it may not be clear at all to us.

Rather than being used descriptively or even behaviourally in Psychology, "pain" has been widely used in an *evocative* fashion, which, I think is basic to an understanding of the Psychological use of the word. Modern functionalists for instance, would like to cover the descriptive as well as the behavioural use of the notion in one fold. But does it serve good purpose? It may not be so in so far as the emotional and the management aspects are completely overlooked. The functionalists may care for this as well and then what comes out is interesting. We are at hand the evocative use and meaning of "pain" in the context of psychology. In fact, psychology has been careful in using "pain" as a "mode of consciousness", which may be specified clearly as either "regret" or "anxiety" or "despair" which calls for immediate attention, for care, cure and prevention. Hence, "pain" does have the evocative force or is used as a "communicative noise pattern soliciting help". The evocative force of "pain" in psychology could be clearly noticed when "pain" has been used as a "symptom", particularly along with adjectives "phantom", "causalgic" and "hyperalgesic". The sense it conveys may be briefly put as, 'this part of the body hurts like this' and with this it says, 'it needs management, please do so'. Interesting point is that in case of "phantom pain", "pain" has a peculiar *anti-thetical* use, i.e. it conveys the sense that 'this part of the body hurts as if it is *lost*' as well as 'this part of the body hurts and it is *present*'. Once we understand this anti-thetical use and meaning of "pain", we feel that it is a case of "neurosis", which needs serious attention. The same evocation of emotion is made possible by the use of "pain" in "pain inhibition" (as in masochism) and in cases of "painful pain", "non-painful pain", "pleasant pain" and "unpleasant pain". Most interesting to remember here is that the meaning of "pain" in these expressions in psychology appears to be clumsy only when we take these meanings literally or on the basis of physics. What is needed is the analysis of the meaning of these expressions along the line of psychology. This makes clear that the meaning of "pain" in psychology has to be analyzed in a proper context and not in any other context.

If we come to consider the use and meaning of "suffering" in psychology, we find that it may not be known along the definist and the behavioural line of thought. In fact the use of "suffering" in a sentence may not be known through reduction into either physics-talk or pain-talk. We have to analyze the meaning of "suffering" from the angle of psychology and from this we know that the basic totality of "suffering" is "distress". However, in the common parlance when we use "suffering" in *descriptive* manner to clarify that "suffering" is due to pain, pain as the genesis of suffering is revealed to us naturally. In this sense then the abstraction conveys the sense that 'suffering is a state of distress engulfing the whole man, mainly due to endurance of pain (physical, metaphysical, mental etc.), which evokes our emotions'.

The striking feature of Sociology in using "pain" is that it has been used as an *abstraction* and *not* a thing out there in the nature but it places the psycho-physical double mature of man at the heart of the discussion. The result is that the word has been used to *describe* what kind of an *experience* does human beings have when they are said to suffer. In the common parlance, the description of such an experience is in the 'negative', meaning thereby 'a pure physical experience of negation' or 'aversion' or 'against the human being'. "Pain" is thus used to make clear that when a person is in such a *state*, it is a state of experiencing a definite 'negative' accompanying physical factor and the experience is marked by "aversion", "negation" and "against the whole being". It is also clear that "pain" has been used to convey the sense of "disvalue which is but natural to be there in the existence." "Pain" in sociological context has been used to paint the existential situation of a person in dark. It conveys the sense that the existence of man in 'totality' is "grim" in so far as among many things the person's *inability* to do certain things, like, seeing, hearing and so on permeates the whole being or the personality as such. It is clear that the *evocative* force and sense of "pain" is very strong in sociology because the use of "pain" in this context is closely associated to call for different modes of treatment and/or prevention. More often than not "pain" in a sentence thus has a unique evocative function to mean thereby, 'please respond to this negative state'. Often the evocation is possible without uttering pain-words, with the help of groans and moans etc. but sociology takes interest is constructing a coherent group of "pain words" (adjectives with "pain", e.g. "severe pain") to enable the most likely influenced group of persons, the doctors, to encounter the terrible condition. It is interesting to notice that these "pain words" are capable of *describing* the "sensory content of pain" and even the "affective" and the "cognitive" contents of the pain-experienced.

"Suffering" has a clear *descriptive* use and meaning in sociology. It is used to describe a state of a person in prolonged pain. "Suffering" is often used as a noun to convey the sense that 'someone is distinguishable on social and cultural grounds'. Hence, it has been used to describe the existential nature of the self in society. It is clear that "suffering" in sociology has evocative use and meaning as well (urging for help etc.). Most interesting is that the most efficient description with the help of "suffering" is marked by "as if" type objectification, which need fertile imagination. Hence, whatever description we obtain about a person's state called "suffering", it is mostly covered by such objectlessness that it will be very difficult to understand what the state is like unless we *are* in that state.

A brief remark before we move to consider the philosophical uses, meanings and references of "pain", "suffering" and "evil". We shall find in a short time that in most cases the evocative function of "pain" and "suffering" clarifies the meanings of "pain" and "suffering" in terms of more or less 'metaphorical-translations', which we better avoid because rather than clarity, it encourages ambiguity.

To know about the uses, meanings and references of "pain" and "suffering" (also "evil") in philosophy is of great importance because it is a branch of knowledge which takes unique interest in such things. Moreover, it is philosophy that takes exclusive interest in knowing about how these notions have been differently used. Another point is that it is philosophy, which makes a detailed inquiry about suffering and evil. It is not that sciences do not take interest in these things but philosophy devots greater attention. As we have done before, we shall first of all concentrate on the uses and meanings of "pain", "suffering" and "evil" in the context of some branches of philosophy, viz. ethics and theology and then move on to inquire into the uses and meanings of these notions in the context of some philosophical schools.

"Pain" has been often used in ethics in relation to its referents. For instance, it has been used as a generic expression in relation to those sensations and physical conditions (of man) towards which a 'con-attitude' (unfavourable) is shown. The result is that "pain" in relation to "human con-response" conveys the sense that 'there is something present in pain, which naturally deserve moral disapproval and thus demand its effective management'. The former 'referential' use of "pain" is akin to its physiological use as we have seen in case of Ryle, who uses "pain" in relation to "sensations we dislike having" to mean that there are certain things and/or facts which are really painful. "This is painful" is thus statement about an object, which carries with it a distinctive factual meaning. However, the latter 'referential' use of "pain" in ethics is quite different. It is reflected in Kurt Baier's account of using "pain" in relation to "something" to convey the sense that "I find something painful". This clarifies the fact that in ethics in particular, "pain" is often used to project our predilections. (con-altitudes or con-response). Hence, in ethical use proper, "pain" used, as "sensations" are not which are really painful but which we find painful. But there is no reason to think that therefore, "finding some sensations painful" constitutes the definition of "pain" or is a part of the definition of "pain".

Apart from the referential use of "pain", the word has been effectively used descriptively in ethics. Moore for instance, uses "pain" to describe "a kind of a positive evil". But he says that in the context of ethics, we do not lay much importance on speaking about such an evil in a factual manner, rather, we speak about the "consciousness of such an evil" (I am conscious of something painful). Although "pain" has been taken as a feeling-term and described in terms of something ugly we are conscious about, it bears the signs of proper ethical use. It is however peculiar to find that "pain" has been described not only to mean something evil but something intrinsically 'ugly'. Here, we have the synonymous use of 'evil' as 'ugly', which may be carried on with "pain" as well. It appears that Moore presupposes the feeling called "pain" to be a feeling of "hurt" (and not otherwise) and he takes "hurtful" to be "evil" and thus, "ugly". Moore's use of "pain" as "hurtful", "ugly" and so on has a merit and a demerit. It has a merit in so far as it explains why "non-painful pain" and "pleasant pain" are not "pain" properly so-called because 'non-painful pain' and 'pleasant pain' are such that we do not have the consciousness of 'hurt' or 'ugliness' or 'evil' as in the case of "pain" properly so-called. Thus, it is how we are conscious about a feeling called "pain" that we distinguish "pain" from "non-painful" and "pleasant pain". The demerit of Moore's use of "pain" is that it encourages an absolute stipulation of the notion to mean, 'a feeling which is hurtful or ugly or evil'. But such a stipulation may not be accepted in ethics at all and may not be useful as well. If we follow this stipulation, the teleological use of "pain" (as beneficial, in medical context) shall appear to be non-sensical, which it is not. It is also difficult to understand the sense in which "pleasant pain" or "enjoyment of pain" is not "ugly" or "evil". Masochists not finding "pain", painful or hurtful does not mean that it is not "ugly" or "evil". To borrow what Moore himself has said (in *Principia Ethica*), "enjoyment of cruelty" is a positive evil. Hence, only "pain" cannot be "ugly" or explained to be "ugly".

"Pain" in ethics has been used to not only describe "something hurtful" (I find this hurtful), rather, "something which is intrinsically undesirable". Hence, in ethics, "pain" has been used to describe some such thing, which can never be the 'desirable end' of human life, it may be nevertheless, a 'desired end' for some (masochists). Thus "pain" has been used to describe 'that which is ultimately undesirable' or 'that which I hate'. But "pain" is "that which I hate" conveys my predilection, it does not tell us about what pain is or why pain is like that. 'I hate pain' is empty and uninformative about pain (feeling). It is also difficult to tell people why the word "pain" should be used as something "hateful" and "undesirable". It may be a linguistic convention, we may like it or not. There is reason to think that "pain" when used with "pleasant", "enjoyment" and "non-painful" conveys the sense that for such and such reason "enjoyment of pain" is not a value and not desirable, whereas "non-painful pain" is a value and desirable. Thus the descriptive use of "pain" as "undesirable feeling" does not tell us why is pain "undesirable".

The descriptive use of "pain" could be seen in ethics in the hedonistic writings in particular. For instance, Bentham uses "pain" to describe "a prime mover" or "motive of actions" in the sense of "initiator of avoiding certain state of affairs *vis-a-vis* others" (viz. pleasure). Now "pain" in the sense of "something ought to be avoided" carries with it a hedonic criterion of ethical goodness and the seeking such goodness is ethical rightness. Thus "good" and "right" has any sense at all when related to "avoidance of pain" (and "acquiring pleasure"). The logical sense is that "good has any meaning at all when used with avoidance of pain". In this sense then in Benthamite hedonism, "avoidance of pain" being the only end is not an analytic statement but essentially evaluative or essentially meta-ethical statement which clarifies the correct uses and meaning of "good" and "right". This also clarifies the sense that "pain" with "avoidance" is an "advantage" or "benefit". The descriptive use of "pain" thus brings out the sense that in hedonic literature, "pain" may be described in terms of "motives" but its meaning is not merely "motives" or "a kind of motive", more than that it has to be conjoined with "avoidance" and "benefit" to bring out the full sense of the notion in hedonic literature. In hedonic literature, "pain" with "avoidance" and "beneficence" also makes clear that avoidance of pain is a intrinsic value *vis-a-vis* instrumental value because it is a desirable end but not desired end. Let us overlook the trifle regarding this matter to find that "pain" used in this way comes closer to the evocative use as well because "pain is the prime mover in so far as its avoidance is good and right" means "this hedonic prescription of action be accepted", do so as well. And if "pain" is used in relation with its referent a "hurt" to mean "disvalue" or "evil" (but not good), then "painful feelings are hurtful and non-beneficial" is to say that "prescription is to avoid it", do so. It is clear that the use of "pain" in such contexts is "evocative".

But "suffering" is not widely used notion in ethics. Even if it is sparingly used, it is neither used in relation to its referent viz. "feeling" or "sensation" not to describe a "prime mover". Clearly, "suffering" has a descriptive use to mean, "state of affairs gripping the whole being owing to external and internal influence". But "avoidance" of "suffering" has not been used as a goal or an end in western ethics. But it carries an evocative use and sense no doubt, which is better reflected when we come to Indian ethics, particularly Buddhist ethics. But for now, let us inquire into the theological uses and meanings of "suffering" and "evil" (not "pain because that is subdued in this context).

"Suffering" in theology has been widely used descriptively to speak about state of affairs transcending mere psycho-physical pain but covering the state of pain as well. Among other such states, we have, those of fear, anxiety, remorse, envy, humiliation, famine, flood, ignorance, injustice, death, love, personal loss, boredom, frustration, poverty etc. "Suffering" used descriptively as a noun with adjectives "emotional", and "metaphysical" conveys the sense that 'some state of affairs may be such that they are so enduring and inwardly gripping that the whole human personality is affected'. In theology, "suffering" has been generally taken as "human suffering" the causes of which should be known and the management of which should be undertaken because "suffering" refers to evil. But theology may not be accused of completely overlooking other than human suffering. In fact, "suffering" has been used descriptively to point to states of "misery" and "distress" pervading the whole existence. Existence as such may be an embodiment of suffering. Generally in theology, "suffering" has been used in relation to reference like the "sinful acts of human beings" and it is thought that "suffering" as "human sin" is best covered by the broader generic notion of "evil". Hence, "evil" has been generally used in theology in the sense of 'human and animal pain, phenomenal suffering and sinful acts'. It is clear that with the use of "evil" and "suffering" (like "pain") in theology, the description of such state of affairs in terms of 'having definite causes' is not ruled out. It is also interesting to notice that in theological context, the use of "suffering" often goes along with "evil".

As we come to consider the Zoroastrian theology, we find that "evil" as an abstraction has been referentially used in relation to "a metaphysical force against another one which is essentially good". But most astonishingly in Zoroastrianism, "evil" as a 'metaphysical principle' conveys the sense of 'a constructor of existence'. Moreover, "suffering" in Zoroastrianism has been used descriptively to tell us about 'an embodiment of evil' or 'an embodiment of a metaphysical principle against the good'. In Zoroastrian theology, we find that the concept of "suffering" has been also used to 'those states which grip man owing to wrong moral choice'. Hence, "suffering" in relation to 'wrong moral choice' conveys the sense that it is such a state, which is quite distinct from those of physical pain. It is in this context that "suffering" as a state of "wrong moral choice" need immediate management (theological perceptions), and, therefore, evokes our sentiments towards such states in a positive manner, i.e. to manage them.

Islām uses "suffering" more prominently in a referential manner in relation to an "omnipotent God" in the sense that God as the highest metaphysical reality has the attribute to create infinitely and as such, creates worldly suffering. Clearly, "suffering" with "God", does not raise doubts about why states called "suffering" are there but why is the highest principle called "God" like that. It is also clear that the reference of "suffering" in relation to "God" conveys the sense that with God, some such states are conceivable in the world created by him that there are "misery", "death", "anguish" etc. Such an unique referential use of "suffering" in Islām also conveys the sense that states called "suffering" have a purpose, which may be, "punishment for sin" or "trial of test" or "something to be endured by the name of God". It we consider "suffering" in relation to "immediate divine punishment", it conveys the sense that 'it is a warning signal from God to man, in its worst pain, portrayed in death'.

"Suffering" used to describe about a state portrayed in death, decay and immoral choice of man is seen in Judaism as well. In Judaism, "suffering" has been also used to describe that it is a sub-species of "evil". Judaism uses "suffering" to refer to those "states of human beings" which they do not deserve but there is no respite as well as those "states of human beings" which they do deserve. Hence, "suffering" with "immoral choice" and also with "pious choice" has been used differently to speak about "temporary state of a person (pious) and the sustaining state of a person (non-pious)". Now, "suffering" used to describe "state of affairs" gripping humans in this world and hereafter, is often associated with its genesis and management. In fact "suffering" in relation to "ignorance of man" (about right knowledge and right-path) on the one hand indicates the genesis of the state and calls for management. With this call, the evocative function of "suffering" may not be ruled out. "Suffering" has also been used to describe a state not without a purpose, rather it has the purpose to test human faith on God. Moreover, "suffering" used as a noun with adjective "redemptive" has a strong evocative force in so far as it brings out the value element (purposive as well) of the state called "suffering" in so far as it initiates us to attend a higher spiritual goal, called "liberation". The same is the case when "suffering" is used with "sacrificial" in the sense of "something morally and spiritually good". Similarly "suffering" in relation to "sacrificial death" evokes us positively to a 'life after death, which is more glorious'.

Christianity takes great interest in using "suffering" and "evil" and it is here that we find clear statement as to "pain" and "suffering" as those notions which are subsumable under broader generic notion of "evil". First, in the New Testament theology we have clear referential use of "suffering" in relation to referents like "punishment, agony, misery and death, i.e. to be precise, bodily conditions essentially against a man". Such suffering (bodily) refers to "physical pains" as well, which have definite physical causes and may be due to human follies, demonic activities and will to restore natural balance. "Suffering" in relation to its referent, the Son of God or "Jesus as servant" conveys the sense that physical suffering (in the above sense) is only an appearance for a pious or a symbol but not unreal. To clarify further, "suffering" used in relation to a symbol (crucified Jesus) carries the sense that 'leading a good life is essentially valuable because after bodily suffering awaits the prize for the pious'. Hence, "suffering" used in relation to its referent "God" reveals the image of the Divine, which the user has. Such an use of "suffering" in relation with "God" reminds us that in theistic context we do not relate "pain" with "God" as its referent because "pain" goes with a sensation which we have but not God. In this sense even "God" may "suffer" for us, wherein the sense is one of "distress" and not "pain". But in this context, "suffering" with "God" does not mean "frustration" because God's nature is never frustrated for his voluntary paradoxical limitation; this is rather strength of God. Further, "suffering" used in relation with its referent "God" in Christian theology means 'God, a Divine Being, is vicarious or redemptive or embodiment of Love'. There is however a basic controversy regarding the proper use of "suffering" with "God" as its referent because such a use reduced God as a Divine Being to one 'bound in time' whereas God has been conceived as transcendence and timelessness. Thus use of "suffering" in relation to God has a temporal reference, which is not a proper use in so far the meaning conveyed to us may be quite contrary to Christian theology. But many people do not agree. They think that such an use is perfectly sensible and goes along Christian theology which advocates God as both "sympathizer" and "empathizer". When "suffering" in relation to God conveys the sense that the Being is one who does not participate in human miseries and His inner nature is undisturbed', "Suffring" is used with God, the symp athizer. Whereas, "suffering" used with God as "empathizer" conveys the sense that 'His inner harmony is disturbed, and He participates in human misery'. The use of "suffering" with God as sympathizer carries with it the sense of "suffering as something intrinsically evil, and, therefore, God cannot participate in evil". This takes us to much deeper level of meaning of "suffering" in relation to God in Christianity. In one sense "suffering" has been used in a "general" sense that is, 'something affected by evil', whereas "suffering" in a "redemptive" sense is 'something occasioned by evil'. In the first sense what we get is that "suffering" is a "penalty" whereas in the second sense, it is "a force to overcome all evils". The referential use of "suffering" takes a few interesting turns in the Christian context. If we follow the use of "suffering" with 'empathizer God', we have to accept that at times "suffering" may not carry with the sense that it is a sub species of evil or that "evil" subsumes "suffering" because it is we who suffer give "suffering" that name. Hence, "suffering" without being marked as an "evil" may carry with it the sense that it is some state having great instrumental value in either becoming a party to be God's empathy or given the right attitude we may attain the Godhead.

Nevertheless, in Christian theology, the word "suffering" has been descriptively used as well, mainly to describe "a state of affair" which is although finite, i.e. may come to an end or destroyed but 'a real tragedy in human life'. The main problem is if "suffering" is a 'tragic state of affair'; of what value can it be in human life? In Christian theology "suffering" has been variously described as the state of affair which "corrects our sinful character", which is mainly a making of devil power or Satan or corruption in intention. If this be the sense in which "suffering" is used, then certainly "suffering" may be a value indicating notion and the value is clearly teleological. Yet, "suffering" in Christian theology has been never used to describe about something which is either 'a spiritual or a moral goal of human life'. "Suffering" is not a general prescription in Christian theology. Even empathetic suffering aims at alleviation of all suffering. We find that in Augustinian theology, "suffering" has been described as a "original sin", whereas in Irenian theodicy it has been used as "original capacity for goodness yet unrealized". We may not raise questions about the correctness or incorrectness of such use of "suffering" or raise questions about truth and falsity but we cannot overlook the truth that the word has not be used uniformly in Christian theology. This may be true in case of the use of "evil". Generally speaking in theodicy, "evil" is often described as a generic notion subsuming sub-notions of "pain" and "suffering" of all human beings. This reminds us of the fact that "evil" is described as 'state of affairs past, present and future in two fundamental forms, pain and suffering'. We are also reminded of the fact that in Christian theology in particular, evil as such a state of affair may be blankly asserted to exist as, "there is evil in the world", which turns out to be a problem in so far as it contradicts the assumed attributes of God's omnipotence and goodness. But then "evil" has been often described as a state of affair, which is "apparent" or "unreal" or "wrongly so called" because it is we who impute such connotations. Whereas others think that "evil" stands for some such fact that needs management. Different meaning of "evil" in Christian theology comes out of its different uses, particularly with a descriptive force. For instance, "evil" described as "natural processes of birth and death" or human "inability or absence of power to remain unblemished. "Evil" in this sense is "physical evil" or evil portrayed in disease, disasters, death, decay and being preyed. "Evil" as a noun with adjective "physical" is in fact used to describe an "evil suffered" or a limitation. Whereas, with "metaphysical", "evil" describes imperfection, privation and non-being. "Evil" is also described in terms of "deliberate suffering" or "infliction of suffering" by man to man, and to animals. This projects use of "evil" with "moral" to convey the sense of "something done" which is essentially immoral. Very close to it is the use of "evil" with "aesthetic" to convey the sense of "imperfection".

Let us now consider the Marxist use of "suffering". As usual, the Marxists use "suffering" as a broad generic notion conveying "pain" but "suffering" and "pain" are not subsumed under the notion of "evil". "Suffering" has been predominantly used as a noun along with "human" in a special way. It is used to refer to the 'practical socio-political and economic problems faced by human beings in exploitative societies'. Hence, "suffering" has been used in a socio-economic and political context in Marxism in relation to its referents, viz. "those who suffer" and "those who inflict suffering" in an exploitative society. Marxists have names for them the working class or those who suffer or the exploited and the bourgeoise or those who inflict suffering or the exploiter. It is clear that although "suffering" has been used as an abstraction, it is nevertheless, based on empirical observation of social, economic and political factors, which govern the structure of an ever-evolving human society. Once we concentrate more on the suffering class, "suffering" does not refer to "biological" or "accidental" suffering rather, refers to "human miseries" in an exploitative society. "Suffering" as "misery" in a general sense is thus predominant in the Marxist literatures. It is but natural that the concept of "suffering" has been used to describe about a "matter of fact" which conveys "misery and the pangs of the masses" or to be precise, "agony". In fact, "suffering" is best described in Marxism as physical as well as mental agony of those who have been deliberately inflicted pain and misery by others well placed. The natural result is that in the Marxist use, "suffering" appears as "human alienation", this is owing to another descriptive use of the notion.

A unique descriptive use of "suffering" in Marxism is seen when the notion has been used in a depersonalized way, i.e. on the basis of an empirically based equation: 'constant value plus variable value plus surplus value'. This equation is in fact a linguistic expression referring to some such matter of fact which may be best understood on the basis of an socio-economic explanation and not otherwise. There is another peculiar descriptive use of "suffering" to tell us about 'a natural outcome of mass revolution'. But such a suffering is marked by "physical suffering" (produced by strife and counter strife). Hence, "suffering" means a state of affair in human society striving for total change. With this, we come to know about the uses of "suffering" in the sense of "alienation", "self sacrifice for total change", "strife" and "misery". Most remarkable fact is that "suffering" in Marxism refers also to 'an everlasting social reality because class struggle is always on'.

A striking similarity between the Marxian use of "suffering" and the existential use of "suffering" is that they concentrate on "human suffering" and describe it as a problem. But the difference between the two is that the former analyzes this problem objectively, i.e. on the basis of empirical studies of society and man, whereas the latter analyzes it subjectively, i.e. on the basis of revelation from within or on the basis of revelation in our consciousness. The existentialists are very particular about stressing this point because they think, this is "suffering" really so-called. "Suffering" really so-called is in the existentialist terminology, "authentic" *vis-a-vis* "inauthentic". In this sense then "suffering" is used in existentialism to describe "anguish" shown by man (and we know it through immediacy of experience). To make it clearer, existentialists like Sartre say that "suffering" may be used in the sense of "mark of man" in so far as man's whole nature is dipped in suffering (agony so to say). "Suffering" may thus describe as "human existence as such". Such a use of the notion is clearly distinct from the use of "pain" mortally as sub-species of "suffering" and as "feeling of man" or "motive of action". Hence, "suffering" is used to describe "total inward experience of man" or "total frame of mind". Clearly, "suffering" is state of affairs in which I am and which consciousness reveals to me. Hence, in relation to its referent, 'human consciousness', "suffering" is used to mean "the resource of the knowledge of agonizing state of affairs in which an individual is and which is unique to him (not known by others)". "Suffering" in this sense, the sense in which it is a revelation to us through introspection has been precisely metaphorically expressed in many ways. Such metaphors may not make the meaning of "suffering" clear, it may rather contribute to vagueness. In a sense, "suffering" should not be so variously, metaphorically used. Thus metaphorically, "suffering" is "dread", "angst", "boredom", "nausea", "incompleteness", "lack", "desire" and "to choose to be". What we get from such metaphors is that the users of such metaphors in relation to "suffering" wanted to convey that 'it is through our consciousness that we come to know about essential negation, contingence, superfluity and passion of human being as teeming existence'. "Suffering" used in the sense of "superfluousness" is in fact "senselessness", "emptiness" and a "tragedy". To focus the sense of "tragedy" more clearly, some existentialists have related "suffering" with its referent, "underground man" (not overman of Dostoevsky), i.e. "suffering" is such a state of affair which relegate ordinary beings (not supermen) in a dire condition; it has no majesty and no beauty. It is thus non-teleological; it has a negative value because it crushes man to ignominy.

As "pain" has not been clearly mentioned as sub-species of "suffering", generally speaking, existentialists do not speak of "suffering" as sub-species of "evil" either. But if we elaborate the meaning of "human suffering" in existential context, it is often described as a "mystery". To be clearer, "mystery" in this context is "a mechanical dysfunction in nature" or "a living unsolved puzzle" and in this sense, some existentialists hold that "suffering" is an evil or a species of evil. "Suffering" used, as a state of affair is thus essentially an evil state. Now, if "suffering" is used to describe about a state of affair in terms of evil then the basic tone is, 'how could such a thing fit in this world'? And it is not a generic question but a matter of subjective inquiry. Further, both in Marxism and existentialism "suffering" has been viewed as a problem (for man) but in existentialism, it is particularly pictured as catastrophic by relating the notion with "anxiety". "Suffering", used as "anxiety" pictures life both 'meaningless' and 'empty' and in its gravest form, it is as 'sick' as 'death'. What is interesting is to notice that "suffering" used in this way is thoroughly evocative because the inner sense is to move out of such anxiety and sickness. The same evocative use of the notion could be seen when "suffering" is used to describe a "despair of despair" in man's life in so far as human beings are caught in the riddle of the finite and the infinite, and the riddle of the temporal and the eternal. The despair evokes a sense of urgency in us to resolve it. In the above sense then "suffering" in existentialism has a positive tone as well, i.e. it evokes us to 'transmute existence itself, which is not an evil'.

We can now move on to consider the uses of "suffering" and "evil" in Buddhism. First, "suffering", which is expressed in terms of "dukkḥa" is a broad generic notion which is used to mean that it is "existence as such", an existence, which is real. According to its unique existential standpoint, Buddhism speaking of not merely suffering but an "awareness of suffering" to remind us that what we are aware of is not an object but we are aware of something real, the existence as such, which is "an ever living gloom" (dukkḥa). 'Dukkḥa' is used in Buddhism as an abstraction having perhaps wider connotation than "suffering" because "dukkḥa" refers to "grief" as well as "pain" or "misery", and, therefore, covers the con-feeling in its broad connotation. This con-feeling (of pain) is thus contrary to "contentment", which conveys the sense that "suffering" used in a broad way is "discontentment", a basic corrosion in human mentality and morality. "Suffering" in relation to "human existence" thus conveys the sense that it is essentially "imperfect" and "lack in wholeness or integration". More than that, "dukkḥa" may be used to describe a state of affair at three basic levels; at the corporeal level or at he psycho-physical level, it has to be understood as "birth", "growth", "decay" and "death"; at the experiential level or at the level of cognition, it should be understood as "impermanence" and at the ethical level or at the desire non-fulfilment level, it is "imperfection". If we put together the cognitive and the ethical levels of understanding the notion, what we get is that "dukkḥa" refers to those "rāgas" or desires due to which are the aggregates of existence (five skandhas). This also takes us to the not of such desires, viz. "ignorance". If "suffering" conveys the sense that it is "impermanence" as well as "imperfection" then it takes the shape of a 'great judge' because it lulls us to the "kārmic cycle". "Suffering" described in such metaphysical terms carries with it the sense that human existence may turn out to be a great "evil" (only if we realize). But we must be careful about the fact that "evil" is not a broader notion covering "suffering" rather, "evilness" is a property of a state called "suffering".

But the use of "suffering" in Jaina philosophy is different. We have the word "vedanā" for 'suffering", which has been clearly used as a broad abstraction covering 'dukḥa' or psycho-physical pain. In fact, more than that, it covers the feeling of pleasure as well. Now, if both "pleasure" and "pain" are notions subsumable under the notion of "vedanā" or "suffering" then the Jaina intention to make a distinction between uses of "feeling terms" and a "non-feeling term" is clear. Really speaking, the Jaina is very particular about clarifying that human beings are constantly under the grip of feelings like pleasure and pain. This is such a state that the Jiva or individual soul gets engrossed and bonded causing far-reaching agonies for them. To be precise, "vedanā" is not merely "dukḥa", it is "sukḥa-dukḥa phala", that is, it is used to describe a state in which individual souls are owing to wrong intentions (saṁkleśas) like distress and/or aggression. Hence, the description is both in ethical and psychological terms. The Jaina also makes it clear that the notion "vedanā" need not be used along with feeling-terms like "unpleasantness" (amanojña) because "unpleasantness" is not the synonym of "pain". Hence, it is "dukḥa" or "pain" which may be subsumed under "suffering" or "vedanā' but not "unpleasantness". One may wonder whether or not "dukkḥa" in Buddhism and both "dukḥa" and "vedanā" in Jainism have evocative use. Clearly they have such use if we only take care of the fact that both these systems are basically interested in not mental gymnastics but pragmatics. They aim at human liberation and for that matter they lay great importance in managing both pain and suffering at the corporeal, the ethical and the metaphysical levels. Hence, it is not out of the way to think that using "dukkḥa" (in Buddhism) in relation to "kārmic cycle" and using "vedanā" in relation to "sukḥa-dukḥa phala" does have an emotive impact on the user and the hearer so that effective management may ensue. Another point is that the more and more we delve into the Indian philosophic literature, the more and more do we come to know about the varied uses and meaning of "suffering", "pain" playing a second fiddle to it.

We may start with Vedas, Upaniṣadas and the Gitā as we come to consider the orthodox systems in Indian philosophy. As usual, Vedas use "suffering" as a noun with adjective "human" and refers to those 'immoral activities of people for which they are punished by Gods at different proportions'. In this sense then "suffering" is misery inflicted on man by Gods. This is the deterrent sense of the term, uniquely presented in the Vedas. "Suffering" is thus a word used in Vedas to refer to 'moral disharmony' and for that reason has been projected as a 'personalized evil', which, nevertheless may fizzle out. In relation to "worldly" or "corporeal", "suffering" has been used to convey the sense of 'human misery in perspective'. In relation to "ethical", "suffering" has been used to mean 'corruption in intentions and deeds' and in relation to "metaphysical" the notion conveys the sense that 'the Divine system has been disturbed'. The evocative sense lurks within these uses. What we get is that "misery ought to be managed". However, in Upaniṣadas the notion has been meaningfully used to refer to the duality of principle of good and evil and our understanding of such duality. In fact, "suffering" has been used to refer to 'our mental projections of this duality in Reality' and with it, 'wrong intentions and misdeeds of man'. This may be said to be the use bearing metaphysical and ethical connotation of the notion. The use of "suffering" according to Upaniṣadas is highly relative as how and when it should be used, depends on the user's mind's eye. It may be used as a feeling-term (bodily pain) as well as 'lack of true knowledge'. In so far our mind's eye or our intuitive disposition is concerned, the "evilness" of a state called "suffering" is reflected in it. Hence, the meaning of "suffering" is not "evil" rather; it is a property of "suffering". The evocative use of "suffering" is much clear in Upaniṣadas. "Suffering" has been often descriptively used to tell us about a "problem" which is essentially "intellectual", because theologically speaking, "suffering" is 'lack of the true knowledge of reality'. This Upaniṣadic sense has thoroughly pervaded many philosophical schools, particularly the Vedānta.

The Upaniṣadic use of the notion is clear in the Gitā as well, particularly in the context of Arjuna's suffering at the battlefield. The word has been especially used in this context to tell us about the 'grief' and 'misery' of people (like Arjuna) owing to the lack of true knowledge of reality. On the other hand the word has been used as 'infliction of misery' by people (like Arjuna) on the wrongdoers. Hence, Arjuna's suffering protects two uses of the notion; one, 'metaphysical suffering' and the other, 'physical suffering'. But says, the Gitā, that in the context of psycho-physical suffering of man, when we speak of the "suffering self", "self" need not be taken as something "damaged" rather, 'damage is to the body'. Hence, no suffering could ever blemish the eternal Self, only body suffers. "Suffering" has thus no referential relation with "Self". The Gitā thus clarifies four basic senses conveyed through "suffering" (of man)—"despondence", "infatuation", "harm" and "lack of true knowledge". And to be precise, the word evokes us to dispel such things from our life.

In the Sāṁkhya and the Yoga systems, "pain" (dukḥa) and "suffering" (kleśa) has been used differently. The Sāṁkhya uses the notion of "pain" in such a manner that it becomes meaningful particularly when we describe about a state of human beings under the 'principle of dynamics'. Thus internal and external dynamics of human beings gives rise to a state called "pain". Such a state (owing to dynamics) may be further described as those affecting the body and mind, which may be called, "ādhyātmika dukḥa"; as those elicited from several noxious sources, which are essentially outside our own being, viz. other people, animals and static things, called, "ādhibhautika dukḥa" and as those emanating from supernatural entities, called "ādhidaivika dukḥa". Hence, the notion of "pain" may be meaningfully used to cover some such states, which are due to several internal and external sources, essentially averse to us. "Pain" may be then used with "the consciousness of a aversion" (pratikulatā) to convey the sense that "pain" is a feeling, of which we are conscious (and this is very important), which affects man internally and which should be managed. "Pain" in this sense goes with the conception of 'determined self', who has senses and feelings. Further, it is in this sense that the force of the feeling term ("pain") motivates us to do something for its avoidance. Not only this, "pain" may be used along with an adjective "endured" to convey the sense that a more dire state may be imagined when the 'bondage of human intellect' could be conceived. This comes closer to "suffering" or "kleśa". Now, as the locus of pain feeling is the human ego not the pure Self, "I feel pain" refers to the feelings of ego. But "kleśa" or "suffering" has not been used as a feeling term in the Sāṁkhya, it has been used as a generic notion covering "pain" or to be clearer, "endured pain" that pervades the whole personality of man. Yet, "suffering" may be 'great' not through endured feeling of pain but through the "ignorance of the pure nature of Self". Hence, "suffering" may be descriptively used to tell us about the state of a person in deep rooted ignorance. It we delve deep into the "suffering" owing to ignorance of the Pure nature of self, we come to know that it refers to the lack of knowledge of an essential "bheda" or "difference" between the principles of Purūṣa and Prakṛti. Hence "suffering" may be used to describe the state of a determined self when thoroughly under the intellectual corruption of the non-difference of Purūṣa and Prakṛti.

The Yoga philosophy may be commended for its clear distinction between the uses and meaning of "keleśa" and "dukḥa". The Yoga use of "pain" or "dukḥa" is quite akin to psycho-physics. First, Yoga uses "pain" to refer to those feeling which we have owing to our association with some external noxious substances. Second, "pain" refers to those projections of our internal-organs, which, when influenced by noxious substances, permeate the whole personality of a man. Hence, "dukḥa" has been used both in relation to physical and mental referent. Further, "dukḥa" used with "pariṇāma", "tāpa" and "saṁskāra" elaborates the all pervading nature of a feeling called "dukḥa". "Pariṇāma dukḥa" refers to those pains feeling which we owe to our hopeless enjoyment of sense pleasures. Whereas "tāpa-dukḥa" means "noxious feelings owing to comparison of pleasures" and "saṁskāra dukha" means those feeling which is owing to infatuation in our memory. On the other hand, the Yoga has been emphatic in using the notion of "suffering" to refer to 'state of affairs', namely, avidyā, asmitā, rāga, dvesa and abhiniveśa. The first of it, 'avidyā' reminds us of the fact that "suffering" is a state in which human being are owing to ignorance of truth, which is nothing but intellectual pollution. Further, the Yoga uses "suffering" to describe a state of human being, which is due to the sensuous desires of corporeal objects or corporeal cravings or desiring the undesirable things. Thus, "suffering" describes ethical corruption and its natural consequence. To move into the realm of mind, we find that "suffering" describes consequences of mental corruption like, nourishing anger, hatred and infatuation. Interestingly, the Yoga also uses "suffering" in relation to metaphysical entity like God to convey a negative sense. i.e. "something of which God is deprived but not man". This may be determination of the nature of God through negation.

"Pain" or "dukḥa" has been used in the Nyāya system to refer to an unique connotation of individual self or liṅga, which may be known through different valid sources of knowledge. But the Nyāya use of "pain" with self or ātma reminds us of the fact that it is not a property of mind or internal organs. More interesting is to notice that individual soul is the locus of "pleasure" or sukḥa as well, and, therefore, pleasure and pain need not be antagonized to each other as contrary feelings. In fact, both are used in the sense of "vādhanas" or "elements of human bondage". In this sense then, both "pain" and "pleasure" may be subsumed under "suffering", which refers to state of affairs in which all bonded human souls are. However, "pain" has been also used to refer to those "sensations" (saṁvedanas) which we get from the physical world and which lull human beings into bondage. In this sense, "pain" has a physiological reference, meaning thereby "inciters which are essentially noxious". Thus, "pain" should be understood both in the sense of "sensations obtained from harmful agents" and "human bondage". In the former sense, we may speak of different pain feeling like severe pain and moderate pain of not merely human beings but also animals. In the latter sense, which is more important, it is "cycle of birth and rebirth". Another interesting use of "pain" in the Nyāya is to evoke our emotion favourably to free from such a vicious cycle. In this sense, "shunning all pain" means, "stopping the kārmic cycle for ever. But the Vaiśeṣika does not use "pleasure" and "pain" as non-corollaries, rather, "pain" has been clearly used as "unpleasant" and "pleasure" as "not-painful". "Pain" in this sense is an "unfavourable feeling", which may be used to mean "aversion", "paleness" and so on.

Vedānta is the backbone of contemporary trends in Indian philosophy and takes some interest in pain and suffering. Its chief exponent, Saṅkara uses "pain" or "dukḥa" and "suffering" or "kleśa" as clear instances of "evil" or "aśubha". Hence, "evil" is the broad notion under which "pain" and "suffering" may be conceived. "Evil" on the other hand being used to describe a state of affair in which human beings are if they are ignorant of the true knowledge, i.e. the knowledge of non-difference or abheda. Hence, all pain and suffering as forms of evil are due to the ignorance that "I" and "Thou" are not different. To tell us more about the use of "pain" and "suffering", Saṅkara brings in the conception of individual self or Jivātma as an agent of the 'superimposition' of 'I' over and above 'Thou'. Hence, "pain" and "suffering" are notions used to refer to those beings that falsely impose self over Brahman. But Saṅkara makes it very clear that "pain" need not be used in relation to "death" meaning, "a state has ended", rather 'the state has renewed'. Saṅkara uses "suffering" in relation to three referents, the 'hiraṇyagarbha' the 'virātapuruṣa' and the 'taijasa' to convey the meaning that "suffering" is a 'state of affair owing to the affects of subtle elements on self'; to mean that "suffering" is a "state of affair in which a phenomenally determined self is, and "suffering" is a state of affair in which human soul is entrapped in the cycle of birth and death". But "suffering" should not be used in relation to "Brahmatva" rather, it may be used in relation to "Iśvaratva", i.e. "suffering" has no referential meaning if we use it in the context of the supreme Reality but it does have a meanings when we use it in the context of God because the latter may be in 'metaphysical suffering', in some sense different from 'human suffering'. But human beings may be said to be 'suffering metaphysically' as well, in a very special since. In this context, "suffering" describes the state of a person under the influence of the principles of māya and avidyā to nurture a misconception that 'I am different from the supreme self or Brahman'. Hence, in Sankara too, we may find "suffering" used both in relation to the physical as well as the metaphysical. However, Rāmānuja does not agree. He uses "suffering" in relation to "body" in the sense that it is real suffering of the individual, not to be so played down because the individual self is as real as Brahman Himself, and thus suffers. But Brahman does not suffer because he being one and supreme remain qualitatively separate from His manifestation, the individual self. Thus "suffering" may have no sensible referential use in relation to Brahman but does have a clear sense to convey in relation to human beings that their state of affair of misery and ignorance are real and ought to be cared. Hence, "suffering" does not find any sensible relation with "māya" but does find a relation with "avidyā" or ignorance (that God is Supreme and One and our aim in life ought to attain this abode). Rāmānuja thinks that the notion of "suffering" used most sensible with "self" should be taken as 'a natural consequence in evolution' as well as 'a test of God on man'. Thus, "suffering" may be used to describe a state, which is a natural outcome of evolution, as well as a test that God imposes on man.

We shall now skip Krishṇamūrthi's use of these notions for much has been covered elsewhere. What is a great interest at this juncture is to notice that we are at the brink of evaluating "pain", "suffering" and "evil" for we have obtained criteria for making such evaluation. I shall argue why. First, we were not concerned with making a clear distinction between pain-sensation, a state of suffering and something evil because that may be undertaken by anyone except philosophers. But we were concerned with making a distinction between the conceptions "pain", "suffering" and "evil", which both scientists and philosophers have. Second, making-distinctions or evaluation of these concepts take us to perform a linguistic task, uniquely undertaken by philosophers (not by grammarians and lexicographers), i.e. to see the basic distinction between the words "pain", "suffering" and "evil". This is very important as in science and philosophy, a great deal of ambiguity, synonimity and vagueness clouds the meanings of these words in different literatures and in different contexts. But no doubt we use these concepts unhesitatingly and widely without caring for how they should be used and how they should not be used. When we care for such things, we are performing a philosophical task but for all that we have to depend on how these concepts have been used and what sense and reference do they convey. Thus, evaluation of these concepts depends heavily on how they have been used in different contexts and in different technical languages. But use alone is not sufficient, we have to care for what meanings are conveyed to us and what are their referents. Hence, we may conclude that the bases of evaluation or criteria of evaluation of these notions are the uses, meanings and references of these notions in the scientific and non-scientific writings. Let us now move to frame the criteria clearly and propose an evaluation in the conclusive chapter.

5

An Evaluation of "Pain", "Suffering" and "Evil"

CRITERIA OF EVALUATION

If we look back now, we shall find that an inquiry into the cases of "pain" and "suffering" (also "evil") has revealed that, (a) when scientists and philosophers are said to have these concepts (not things), they are said to use them in many ways for all practical purpose; (b) when they do so, they are not confined in using these concepts in a non-linguistic symbolic manner, rather, they need some verbal signs or well articulated words to do what they want to do with the concepts 'they have' and for that reason, words like "pain", "suffering" and "evil" have been chosen from vast repository of English language (in case of other languages, we have different words to do the same); (c) these words are not used in isolation but in association with other words in sentences which constitute meaningful discourses within technical contexts (in this case, sciences and philosophy). However these words are themselves not technical but can be used for that purpose because they may have numerous uses allowing a large number of meanings within technical as well as non-technical contexts; (d) apart from being used differently in these technical contexts and apart from having a large number of meanings, these words may have some references as well, either in the sense of referring to extralinguistic entities or in relation to what they denote or refer to; and (e) yet, these words are not synonymous and not to be synonymously used or meant. But there is a considerable confusion regarding this matter.

Let us start from the last point mentioned just now. I have been maintaining throughout this book that owing to ambiguity and vagueness arising out of using these words differently in different technical languages and owing to our effort to 'give them a meaning', more often than not it becomes difficult to understand the basic difference if any between these words and to understand that despite a strong family resemblance, how should we make a clear distinction among these words in force. One attempt is to provide definitions of these words, the purpose of which is to make such a distinction and to enable us to know about what they exactly mean. But we have seen that at both fronts the definitions of "pain", "suffering" and "evil" failed. Neither did they clarify distinction among these words in use, nor did they enable us to know their exact meanings. The reason of such failure is that we often fail to realize that making a clear distinction among words bearing strong family resemblance to clearly understand their meaning (not exact meanings or synonyms), depends on the 'activity of the user of such words in technical contexts'. Thus, we come to the conclusion that for evaluation and clarity of meaning, we ought to concentrate on the purpose of the language-user's use of language.

The moment we focus our attention to the activity of the language-users, we are naturally drawn to what they do (behaviourally) or what their ideas are (ideationally) or what things shall they show us (extralinguistically). We have to be careful about these things because to focus on language-user's use of a language, we have to take care of what they do with words (in this case, "pain", "suffering" and "evil") in practical linguistic situations or what are their practical linguistic concern. To be precise, the practical linguistic concern of the language users in technical subjects like the sciences and philosophy is to use clearly, effectively and distinctively the concepts they have. This is not wholly a psychological purpose or a mental need rather a practical need to express what language user thinks best about using a word or words in relation to other words in meaningful sentences in the vast body of a technical matter involving those words and sentences. The language users therefore, cannot play their whims to give meaning in technical contexts and leave the rest for others to follow; they have to consider the real context of language use and their motto should be, clarity, effectiveness and distinctiveness in language use. We must remember that when one is deeply engrossed in technical matters in technical subjects, one cannot overlook careful use of language to do what he or she intends to do and for that reason, it is not the same as uttering words and sentences of writing them according to one's convenience because he or she has a great mental urge to express any way. Hence we must remember that proper language use is not what we often do or what language users usually do, i.e. what language usage is. It is a question of not what people's usage of "pain", "suffering" and "evil" is because usage have created a lot of problems, one is a total confusion about how these words should be clearly distinguished and thus effectively used to do practical things in practical contexts.

If one practical urge in philosophy of language is to make clear distinction among "pain", "suffering" and "evil", one has to clearly spell out the criteria of such distinction making or evaluation. We are at the brink of understanding now that a search for criteria cannot be extralinguistic but should be located in the activity of the user of the concepts of "pain", "suffering" and "evil". We ought to cover the meaning of these words and their references as well. Thus, the criteria of evaluation should be discovered within the uses, meanings and references of these concepts in sciences and philosophy. A few eyebrows may be raised for one may ask, 'when you have not considered all the sciences and all other subjects using these concepts, how can you be so sure about the discovery of criteria'? I have made it very clear that I shall restrict my effort in this regard to the sciences (which I have considered) and philosophy (the way I have considered), which may be enough ground for discovery of criteria of evaluation. It may not be necessary and sufficient nevertheless. One may find interesting things in English literature in particular but when I have made my point, they may have a second thought whether or not something more is needed. If there is such a need, further discovery shall reveal clearer grounds for evaluation, and even then, what I have said may be justified and not defeated.

Let us perform the task of discovery now. We are well placed at this juncture to further simplify the findings in chapter 4 that the concept "pain", "suffering" and "evil" have been used in three major ways in sciences and philosophy to acquire three distinct meanings. First, these abstractions have been *descriptively used* and there have been corresponding *descriptive meaning* emerging out of such uses. Second, these words have been *referentially used* having *referential meaning*. Finally, these notions have been *evocatively used* covering *evocative meaning*. The descriptive use of these words (and sentences bearing these words in force) are those which describe a real or imagined situation or real or imagined property or real or imagined state of affairs distinct from other situations, properties and state of affairs. The descriptive meaning of these words are those meanings, which convey the sense that 'some such situation, property and state of affairs are conceivable and distinct from others owing to some specific mark'. To be more precise the 'descriptive use' is "to describe x, y, etc., when, x, y, etc., are state of affairs" and 'descriptive meaning' is to convey the sense that some such Xs and Ys (state of affairs) are owing to p, q, etc., when 'p', 'q', are marks of distinction. But we shall see in a short while that the descriptive uses and meanings of "pain", "suffering" and "evil" are *not stable*, rather they are highly unstable, i.e. their descriptive uses and meanings vary greatly or are not uniform (depending on technical information obtained till date, which are only probable).

The 'referential uses' of "pain", "suffering" and "evil" are those uses which either attempt at pointing out extralinguistic entities to be called by those names or pointing out the relation between any of these words with their referents or what they denote. To be precise, 'referential use' of these abstractions is to refer to x, y, etc., when, x, y, etc. are things in the outer world or to refer to p, q, etc. when p, q are referents of these words, which the language user relates with these words to serve a practical purpose. Subsequently, "pain", "suffering" and "evil" have 'referential meanings', i.e. to convey the sense that 'something is there in the world as distinct from others which may be referred to as 'pain', 'suffering' and 'evil' or "there are things or properties with which these terms may be related because these things and properties are denoted by these terms". However, the referential uses and meanings of "pain", "suffering" and "evil" are moderately *stable*, not unstable in so far as we shall see that the technical language users either refer to things or relate these words with referents which are 'intrinsically undesirable' for man as a whole (also for animals and the whole nature).

The 'evocative uses' of "pain", "suffering" and "evil" are those uses which 'aim at evoking the feelings, emotions and attitudes of hearers of these words in force in different contexts so that something is definitely expected at the behavioural level of the hearer'. Whereas, the 'evocative meaning' of these words in force is, 'some such states having psycho-physical affects on living and non-living beings demanding some managing-reactions towards them'. The evocative uses and meanings of "pain", "suffering" and "evil" are *extremely stable* in so far as they establish a hearer-user relation at the emotive level, which transcends language itself.

Let us go back to the descriptive uses and meanings of "pain", "suffering" and "evil". We have seen (in Chap 1to 4) that the language users in sciences and philosophy are concerned with, describing some such 'state of affairs' affecting human beings, animals and the nature as a whole which are quite different from many other states affecting them favourably or not so disturbingly (at the psycho-physical levels). But which 'mark' or 'marks' clearly distinguish that state of affairs from others is crucial to notice with respect to language users in science and philosophy. To call those 'marks' 'unfavourable or disturbing to....' is trite, it needs further clarification. The moment the language users in science and philosophy enter knowingly to point out clearly these 'marks', they invite a risk because in doing so they are so heavily determined by their previous knowledge of a subject and the probable nature of such knowledge that whatever they say, although free from subjectivism (with greatest care possible), still leaves the door open to disagreement and dissatisfaction among other language users. It is due this relativity of knowledge and at times limitation of the knower (who is language user) that 'mark' to describe some state as "pain" and others as "suffering" and "evil" vary greatly. With this, the words "pain", "suffering" and "evil" acquire different descriptive meanings in sciences and philosophy. It is not that the language users give these words different meanings, rather, the language user's use of such words in technical languages conveys different senses to hearers. It is not that the difference among these words depends on us or how we understand them, rather, in what ways the user's descriptive use for a practical purpose has established a relation with the hearer who is a party to language use (another party may be the user himself when he or she make themselves understand what they are doing when they are doing something with these words). The language users in sciences and philosophy are thus in search of those 'marks' which distinguishes not only those states which ought to be called "pain" and "suffering" and "evil" from those which ought not to be so-called but also to distinguish the abstraction, "pain", "suffering" and "evil" while they are in force in science and philosophy. Hence, it is on the basis of the highly 'unstable' descriptive uses and meanings of "pain", "suffering" and "evil" that their evaluation is possible and not in any other way.

This claim may be fortified by saying that both the referential and the evocative uses and meanings of "pain", "suffering" and "evil" being either moderately stable and highly stable, are not the proper basis or criteria for evaluation. In fact both the descriptive and the referential uses and meanings are factual because they allude to real or imaginary state of affairs as distinct from others but the thin line of difference between the two is that in the former case, these abstractions are 'used factually', whereas in the latter case, they are factually translated and/or related. Interesting is to notice that when these abstractions are factually translated, the meanings conveyed to us may be peculiar because they are used to mean that 'there is one x in nature which is pain/suffering/evil', which it cannot be because these abstractions are not objects in the world. Thus, we may conveniently avoid such referential uses and meanings of these notions because they involve category mistake. However, when "pain", "suffering" and "evil" is referentially used in the sense of a factual relation with some things or properties which they denote, the basic sense conveyed to us is that the user clarifies that these abstractions need to be related to those referents which are "intrinsically undesirable" (not noxious or unpleasant etc) and, therefore, the sense is stable, which hardly provides a strong basis for evaluation.

Our claim is justified further by the fact that the evocative use and meaning of these abstractions although strong enough, are nevertheless, very stable because in technical situations, when these terms describe some state of affairs as distinct from others owing to such and such marks, the parallel use and meaning more often than not is, "allude with this meaning and react accordingly" or "allude with this meaning and do accordingly". Similarly, when these abstractions are referentially used (extralinguistically or otherwise) the parallel use and meaning more often than not is, "allude with this meaning and do accordingly". The close relation which the descriptive and the referential uses and meanings hold with the evocative use and meaning is clear, as it is clear that such evocative meaning is fairly stable. Thus, this cannot be the proper basis of evaluation of "pain", "suffering" and "evil".

But we have to remember that to pay attention to uses and meanings of these words may not be enough, we have to look for references of these words as well, for which there is no way but to go through the referential uses of these abstractions. But we have seen just now that the logical grammar of 'referential use.' is not 'referential use is translation of an abstraction'. Hence, we may avoid such referential uses and thus avoid so-called translated referents of "pain", "suffering" and "evil" as real, because there is none. Although in popular usage such translations are common. We have to rely on the relation of these notions with their referents in the actual context of language use. Again, we have seen, in so far as evaluation is concerned, it bears little value. We thus come to conclude that the proper basis or criteria of evaluation of "pain", "suffering" and "evil" as abstractions are their descriptive uses and meanings. Such uses and meanings are wide ranging in sciences and philosophy, which has to be carefully considered before evaluation.

Without going into further elaboration we may now say that if one carefully goes through the different descriptive uses and meanings of "pain", "suffering" and "evil", one gets an idea that these abstractions may be clearly evaluated in so far as there are distinguishable stretching in the descriptive uses and meanings of these abstractions. "Pain" having the narrowest stretch, "suffering" the greater and "evil" the greatest. In fact, in the sciences and philosophy, we may 'stretch' "suffering" and "evil" differently and widely than "pain" to use them to describe different state of affairs clearly distinct from others on the basis of numerous 'marks' that they have. Whether or not we should allow such use, is pointless because we allow it or not, such descriptive stretchings are there in scientific and philosophic conventions, and interestingly that has become the basis for evaluation. These notions have other stretchings, the referential and the evocative respectively, but they are not satisfactory for evaluation.

CONCLUSION

We have raised an interesting question early on in this book. In what sense do we say that we have the concepts of "pain", "suffering" and "evil"? Having these concepts is not having an idea or a behaviour pattern or an extra linguistic object, rather, knowing how to evaluate these vaguely, ambiguously and clumsily used abstractions. It is very important according to me to have a clear idea of distinction or evaluation of these abstractions otherwise we are not in a position to use them clearly, distinctly and efficiently, which ought to be the aim of language users in sciences and philosophy. Once we concentrate merely on the overall activity of the language users, it may be of some value in knowing about the different uses, meanings and references of these concepts. But it is of great value when we focus our attention on not merely knowing when these concepts should be used and when not to use them, rather, how to use them as distinct from other concepts in a particular technical context when situation so demands. This is of great importance when we are at hand some such concepts which come together to form a clumsy cluster of concepts. They come together for they bear a family resemblance, in this case, the resembling features are drawn from their referential and evocative uses and meanings. But their distinction (as abstractions) is draw from their descriptive uses and meanings, which is as important as noticing their resemblance. When we do this, we are performing a linguistic task, which contributes greatly in 'having clear concept of any one, two or many of those members of a clumsy set of concepts bearing a family resemblance'. Among many such clusters we have "pleasure", "happiness", "eudaemonia" and "bliss", which is very important to evaluate. One may wonder how 'having a concept' may be so artificially related to 'evaluation of concepts' because in real language-use, users never do such things. What I have said is not that language users make or frame a concept (through an arduous mental process) after evaluating it from other concepts, which are already given to us. Rather, language-users are involved in intricate linguistic activities within technical contexts and one important activity called 'evaluation' comes naturally to the user because it is in-built in such linguistic activities, it is not like an artificial 'building up' process. There is no doubt that involving in linguistic activity like this one, presupposes (a) user's previous knowledge of a subject, (b) user's previous knowledge of a language and ability to use the language, and (c) user's aim to clearly, distinctly and effectively use the concepts he or she have to perform the technical task he or she has undertaken. First two among the three presuppositions are non-technical in nature, whereas the latter one is technical in nature. It holds that 'having a concept' clearly so that it may be 'used clearly', demands 'making a clear distinction among clumsy cluster of concepts'. Interestingly even if we have not so clumsy cluster of concepts or a fairly simple concept to be used to perform a specific task, still we ought to involve in the task of evaluation so that use of the concept may not jumble up with other concepts to form a clumsy cluster or that the use of the concept does not become either vague or ambiguous. I think, the vast body of sciences and philosophy is a mesh of language-use (proper of course) and in such a context, evaluation needs to be seriously considered as a useful linguistic activity.

Bibliography

Aiken, H.D. *Reason and Conduct*, Alfred A Knopf, New York, 1962.

Apte, K.V. and Apte, V.M (translated), *Brahma Sūtra: Saṅkara Bhasya*, Popular Book Depot, 1960.

Baier, K. *The moral point of view*, Cornell University Press, N.Y.,1964.

Bentham, J. *The Principles of morals and legislation*, Clarendon Press, Oxford, 1789.

Bhāttachārya, Ramśaṅkar "*Saṁkhyatattvakaumūdi*", Motilal Banarasidass, New Delhi, 1989.

Biro, J.L. (Ed.), *Mind, Brain and Function*, Harvester Press, Brighton, Sussex, 1982.

Block, N. (Ed), *Readings in the Philosophy of Psychology (Vol. I)*, Methuen, London, 1980.

Bottomore, T. B., and Rubel, M. (Ed), *Karl Marx*, Watts, C.A. London, 1963.

Bousefield P. *Pleasure and Pain*, Routledge & Kegan Paul, London 1962.

Bowker, J. *The Problem of Suffering in the Religion of the World*, Cambridge University Press, Cambridge, 1970.

Brandt, R.B. *Ethical Theory*, Prentice Hall, Englewood Cliffs, N.J., 1959.

Brown, S.C. (Ed.), *Reason and Religion*, Cornell University Press, Ithaca, 1977.

Cell, R.E. *Divine Impassability*, Cambridge University Press, Cambridge, 1986.

Chattopadhyaya, D. *Lokāyata Darśana*, People's Publishing House, New Delhi, 1959.

Cowan, J. L. *Pleasure and Pain: A Study in Philosophical Psychology*, St. Martin's Press, Macmillan, N. Y., 1968.

Dennett, D.C. *Brainstorms*, Harvester Press, Hassocks, Sussex, 1979.

Deussen, P. *The Philosophy of Upaniṣadas* Translated by, A.S. Geden, T & T Clark, Edinburgh, 1906.

Dore, C. *God, Suffering and Solipsism*, Macmillan, London, 1989.

Dougal, J.D. and Johnson, J.M. (Eds.), *Epistemological Sociology,* Cambridge University Press, Cambridge, 1977.

Edwards, P. (Ed.), *The Encyclopaedia of Philosophy,* Vol. 1-8, The Macmillan Co. & The Free Press, N.Y., 1962.

Eliade, M. *Yoga, Immortality and Freedom*, Routledge Kegan & Paul, London, 1958.

Eliade, M., (Ed.) *The Encyclopedia of Religion, Vol. 5 & 14,* Macmillan, N.Y., 1962.

Fitch, W., *God and Evil*, Gospel Literature Service, Bombay, 1967.

Foot, Philippa, *Theories of Ethics*, Oxford University Press, London, 1968.

Geach, P. *Providence and Evil*, Cambridge University Press, Cambridge, 1977.

Goyandkā, Harikṛisṇadās, *Pātanjalayogadrśṇa*, Gita Press, Gorakhpur, 2025 (Samvad).

Goerman, U. *A Good God*, Verbum, Stockholm, 1977.

Griffith, R.T.H. *The Hymns of Ṛg Veda,* The Chowkhambā Press, Vārāṇasi, 1963.

Hare, R.M. *The Language of Morals,* Clarendon Press, Oxford, 1952.

Harre, R. & Laws, R. (Ed.) *The Encyclopaedic Dictionary of Psychology,* Basil Blackwell, 1983.

Hebbelthwaite, B. *Evil, Suffering and Religion,* Sheldon, London, 1976.

Heidegger, M. *Existence and Being*, Vision Press Ltd., London, 1956.

Herman, A.L. *The Problem of Evil and Indian Thought,* Motilal Banarasidass, New Delhi, 1996.

Hick, J. *Evil and the God of Love,* Macmillan, Basingstoke, Hampshire, 1985.

Hook, S. (Ed.), *Dimensions of Mind,* New York University press, N.Y., 1960.

Hospers, John, *An Introduction to Philosophical Analysis,* Allied Publishers, India, 1998.

Hudson, W. D. *Modern Moral Philosophy,* Macmillan, London, 1970.

Jha, Harimohan, *Bharatiya Darśana Pariçaya, Vol. II,* Pustak Bhandār Lehriyāsarāi.

Jones, E.S. *Christ and Human Suffering*, London, Hodder and Stoughton, 1933.

Keele, C.A. et al. (Eds.), *Samson Wright's Applied Physiology,* O.U.P., London, 1989.

Kikegaard, S., *The Concept of Dread,* O.U.P., London, 1946.

Kerner, G.C., *The Revolution in Ethical Theory,* Clarendon, Oxford, 1966.

Krishnamurthy, J. *Truth and Actuality*, Krishnamurthy Foundation India, Pondichery, 1995.

Lee, J.Y. *God Suffers for Us,* Martinus Nijhoff, The Hague, 1974.

Lee, J.Y. *Christian Concept of Man*, Philosophical Library, N.Y., 1971.

Ling, T.O. *Buddhism and the Mythology of Evil,* George Allen & Unwin Ltd., London, 1962.

Mādhvācārya, *Sarvadarśanasṅgraha,* Hindi Translation & Commentary by Umāśaṅkara Śarmā, Chowkhamba, Vārāṇasi, 1994.

Mahādevan, T.M.P. *The Philosophy of Advaita,* Luzac & Co., London, 1938.

Matthews, W.R. *God in Christian Thought and Experiences,* Nisbet & Co, London, 1930.

McCloskey, H. J. *God and Evil,* Martinus Nijhoff, The Hague, 1974.

Midgley, M. *Wickedness*, Routledge & Kegan Paul, London 1984.

Mill, J.S. *Utilitarianism*, H.B. Acton (Ed.), Everyman's Library, London, 1992.

Miri, S. *Suffering*, IIAS, Shimla, 1976.

Mitchell, B. *The Justification of Religious Belief,* Macmillan, London, 1973.

Moore, G.E. *Principia Ethica*, Cambridge University Press, Cambridge, 1962.

Nietzche, F.W. *Beyond Good and Evil,* George Allen & Unwin, London, 1967.

Nishida, K. *A Study of Good*, Printing Bureau, Japanese Govt., Tokyo, 1960.

Noordenbos, W. *Pain*, Elsevier Publishing Co., Amsterdam, 1959.

Ofstad, H. *An Inquiry into the Freedom of Decision,* George Allen and Unwin Ltd., London, 1961.

Parkin, D. (Ed.), *The Anthropology of Evil,* Basil Blackwell, Oxford, 1985.

Pike, N. (Ed.), *God and Evil,* Prentice Hall, Englewood Cliffs, N. J., 1964.

Plantinga, A. *God, Freedom and Evil,* George Allen & Unwin, London, 1975.

Rādhākrishnan, S. *Bhāgavada Gitā*, Blackie & Sons India Ltd., New Delhi, 1976.

Rescher, N, *Introduction to Value Theory*, Prentice Hall, Englewood Cliffs, N.J., 1969.

Russell, Bertrand *Human Knowledge: Its Scope and Limits*, Simon and Schuster Inc, London, 1948.

Ryle, G. *The Concept of Mind,* Hutchinson Univ. Library, 1949.

Saddhajiva Bikkhu, *Anguish-the mark of man in three facts of Existence, Vol. III*, Buddhist Publications.

Sartre, *J.P. Existentialism,* Translated by, B. Fretchman, Philosophy Library, N.Y., 1947.

Sathaśstri, Dvārkānātha (Ed.) *Vātsāyana Bhāṣya on Nayāya Sūtra* by Gotama, Buddha Bhārati, Vārāṇasi.

Sauerbach, F & Wenke, H. *Pain: Its Meaning and Significance*, George Allen and Unwin, London, 1963.

Scarry, E. *The Body in Pain,* O.U.P., N.Y., 1985.

Schlick, M. *Problem in Ethics*, Dover Publication, N. Y., 1962.

Seminar Proceedings, *The Problem of Evil,* Poona, 1962.

Shearman, M. *The Purpose of Tragedy,* Theosophical Publishing House, Adyar, Madras, 1954.

Sillis, D.L. (Ed.), *The Encyclopedia of Social Sciences, Vol. II,* The Macmillan Co. & The Free Press, N.Y., 1968.

Singer, M.G. *Generalization in Ethics*, Eyre & Spottiswood, London, 1963.

Siwek, P. *The Philosophy of Evil,* Ronald Press, N.Y. 1951.

Smith-Nowell, P. H. *Ethics*, Pelican, London, 1961.

Sternbach, R.A. *Pain Patients: Traits and Treatment,* Academic Press, N.Y., 1974.

Surin, K., *Theology and the Problem of Evil,* Basil Blackwell, Oxford, 1986.

Taylor, D.M. *Explanation and Meaning,* Cambridge, 1970.

Trigg, R. *Pain and Emotion,* Clarendon, Oxford, 1970.

Warner, R. *Freedom, Enjoyment and Happiness,* Cornell University Press, Ithaca, 1987.

Webb, C.C.J. *Problem in the Relation of God and Man,* Nisbet & Co. Ltd., London, 1915.

Weber, M. *The Sociology of Religion,* Methuen, London, 1965.

Wilson, B.R. *Rationality*, Basil Blackwell, Oxford, 1974.

Woolf, Virginia *Collected Works, Vol. 4,* Hartcourt, NY, 1967.

Index